M.A.Buth

3D Printer: Patents & Innovations

M.A.Buth

3D Printer: Patents & Innovations

1. English edition

Stand: 1/10/14

All rights reserved
by
adrenalinemedia © 2013

Publisher

adrenalinemedia
Marcel A. Buth
Neue Strasse 32b
61250 Usingen
adrenalinemedia@web.de

Table of content

Preface..6
Patents and copyrights..7
   Patent terms and their meaning...8
      Definition of "patent"..8
      Prior art..8
      Public participation in patent examination..................................9
      The Blackboard patent case...10
      US patent law..10
      Effects...11
      Enforcement...12
      Governing laws..12
      Application and prosecution..13
      Alternatives to applying for a patent...14
      Criticism...14
      Is it legal to use patents for private purpose?...........................17
      Patent lawsuits in 3D printing...18
         The 925 patent 20
         The 058 patent..20
         The 124 patent..21
         The 239 patent..22
   Patent Research..25
      Systematic patent research...26
Selected patents...31
   3D Printer...32
      Inkjet/Sand printing/Powder printing..33
         Ingredients of a binder composition...................................34
         Selective powder printer with consumables management.........35
      Stereolithography...44
         Support structure using recycled resin...............................45
         Photocurable resin composition for producing three dimensional articles having high clarity 47
         Photocurable compositions for preparing ABS-like articles......50
         Multicolored STL Prints..52
      FDM Printer...68
         Multiextruder with only one drive.....................................69
         Filament Kassette..77
         Grayscale rendering in 3D printing....................................85
         Smothing method for layered deposition modeling..................89

    A digitally active 3-D object creation system............................93
    Printable support structure from silicone + polymer..................99
    Volumetric feed control for flexible filaments........................107
    Auto tip calibration in an extrusion apparatus........................115
    Rapid prototype injection molding 117
    Melt flow compensation for filaments.......................................123
    Water soluble rapid prototyping support and mold material...129
  Dispenser..135
    3D print under water..136
  Other methods..140
    3D print, multicolor, with multiple materials 141
    Three dimensional printing using imaged layers....................167
Hexapod...171
3D Scanner..173
  Scanner system and method for scanning 174
More relevant patents..192
Links and faires...201
  Links..201
  Fairs...201
Index..203

Preface

The first true 3D patents came up in the early 1970s. But also earlier in the 1950s and 60s, there were first technologies, that later were being used for 3D printing, such as how to feed a filament, the composition of resins and so on.

Since the 1990s the number of 3D related patents exploded and there seems to be no end in this trend for the foreseeable future.

Patent research remains hard manual labor. Patent databases are rather old fashioned IT systems, that do not make it easy to search for relevant documents. Not all 3D printer patents even carry the word "3D printing" in their description or claims. That makes it very hard to identify them. In this book you will find a concept for a systematic patent research that is based on referrers from the patent text itself. If you follow this procedure, you are very likely to find all relevant data in a shortest possible time.

In order to determine the value of an invention, a reader not only has to process the data but also to understand the meaning and the context. Today no machine, no artificial intelligence and no search engine can do this job. Only humans are able to see the value of these information and rank them in the overall context.

Many patents have expired or will expire in the near future, due to their age or because the holder could not afford the annual fees. The innovations becomes freely available and can be used, even in commercial products. Therefore it makes sense to know them, study them and prepare for the times when they can be freely used, by anyone.

Patents are no "secret files" that remain behind closed doors. They are intended for the public and their information can be of great value for the interested reader. So make use of it!

Marcel A. Buth   Bad Homburg, 12th of December 2013

Patents and copyrights

8 Patents and copyrights

Patent terms and their meaning

Here are some basic facts and definitions of patent related terms summarized, with special regards to the US legislation.

Definition of "patent"

*A **patent** is a set of exclusive rights granted by a sovereign state to an inventor or their assignee for a limited period of time, in exchange for the public disclosure of the invention. An invention is a solution to a specific technological problem, and may be a product or a process. Patents are a form of intellectual property. (wikipedia)*

Prior art

Prior art (also known as **state of the art**, which also has other meanings, or **background art**), in most systems of patent law, constitutes all information that has been made available to the public in any form before a given date that might be relevant to a patent's claims of originality. If an invention has been described in the prior art, a patent on that invention is not valid.

Information kept secret, for instance, as a trade secret, is not usually prior art, provided that employees and others with access to the information are under a non-disclosure obligation. With such an obligation, the information is typically not regarded as prior art. Therefore, a patent may be granted on an invention, although someone else already knew of the invention. A person who used an invention in secret may in some jurisdictions be able to claim "prior user rights" and thereby gain the right to continue using the invention. As a special exception, earlier-filed and unpublished patent applications do qualify as prior art as of their filing date in certain circumstances.

In order to anticipate a claim, prior art is generally expected to provide a description sufficient to inform an average worker in the field (or the *person skilled in the art*) of some subject matter falling within the scope of the claim. Prior art must be available in some way to the public, and in many countries, the information needs to be recorded in a fixed form somehow. Prior art generally does not include unpublished work or mere conversations (though **according to the European Patent Convention, oral disclosures also form prior art**—see Article 54(2) EPC).

Patents disclose to society how an invention is practiced, in return for the right (during a limited term) to exclude others from manufacturing, selling, offering for sale or using the patented invention without the patentee's permission. Patent offices deal with prior art searches in the context of the patent granting procedure.

More on how to fight unfair patents in the following section:

Public participation in patent examination

The involvement of the public in patent examination is used in some forms to help identifying relevant prior art and, more generally, to help assessing whether patent applications and inventions meet the requirements of patent law, such as novelty, inventive step or non-obviousness, and sufficiency of disclosure.

The rationale for public participation in patent application review is that knowledgeable persons in fields relevant to a particular patent application will provide useful information to patent examiners if the proper forum is provided. One model for such a forum is a wiki model where the public may submit prior art and commentary relevant to a given patent application and patent examiners can consult that forum. The hoped-for effect is that patent examination will be more efficient and thorough thus patents that do issue will be of higher quality than is currently possible.

Legal constraints

United States

In the United States, the third parties may not provide commentary or opinions directly to a patent examiner during the prosecution of a patent unless the patent applicant gives the examiner written permission to do so. Rule 99, which previously allowed a member of the public to submit prior art to an examiner within two months of application publication, has been repealed by the AIA.

10 Patents and copyrights

The Blackboard patent case

Wikipedia has also been used to collect early references related to controversial patents. History of virtual learning environments, for example, is an article that was created primarily to list prior art that would potentially invalidate U.S. Patent 6,988,138, "Internet-based education support system and methods". This patent issued to Blackboard Inc. in June 2000. The Moodle wiki has a similar page. Once the patent was issued, Blackboard Inc. sued its competitor Desire2Learn to stop them from infringing the patent. In July 2009, the Court of Appeals for the Federal Circuit held that all of the claims of the Blackboard patent were invalid either for being too vague or for being already in practice before Blackboard filed their application. Blackboard, however, has four continuation applications pending where it can correct the deficiencies in its claims and get new patents to issue.

While the lawsuit was moving forward, the Software Freedom Law Center filed for a reexamination citing that new prior art had been discovered that raised a substantial new question of validity. The USPTO agreed and the patent is currently undergoing reexamination.

US patent law

United States patent law is authorized by Article One, Section 8(8) of the U.S. Constitution which states:

The Congress shall have power ... To promote the progress of science and useful arts, by securing for limited times to authors and inventors the exclusive right to their respective writings and discoveries;

In the U.S., a patent is a right to exclude others from making, using, selling, offering for sale, exporting components to be assembled into an infringing device outside the U.S., importing the product of a patented process practiced outside the U.S., inducing others to infringe, offering a product specially adapted for practice of the patent, and a few other very carefully defined categories. The distinctions between what patent rights include are complex. For example, merely thinking about an invention or drawing a diagram is not an infringement. **Likewise, research for "purely philosophical"**

Patents and copyrights 11

inquiry is not an infringement. Sometimes, this analysis can be much more sophisticated and difficult: i.e., research directed to commercial purposes may be an infringement—but may not be when the research is directed toward obtaining approval of the Food and Drug Administration for introduction of a generic version of a patented drug.

Under current U.S. law, the term of patent is 20 years from the earliest claimed filing date (which can be extended via Patent Term Adjustment[*clarification needed*] and Patent Term Extension[*clarification needed*]). **For applications filed before June 8, 1995, the term is either 17 years from the issue date or 20 years from the earliest claimed domestic priority date, whichever is longer.**

Effects

A patent does not give a right to make or use or sell an invention. Rather, a patent provides the right to *exclude others* from making, using, selling, offering for sale, or importing the patented invention for the term of the patent, which is usually 20 years from the filing date subject to the payment of maintenance fees. A patent is a limited property right the government gives inventors in exchange for their agreement to share details of their inventions with the public. Like any other property right, it may be sold, licensed, mortgaged, assigned or transferred, given away, or simply abandoned.

A patent, being an exclusionary right, does not necessarily give the patent owner the right to exploit the patent. For example, many inventions are improvements of prior inventions that may still be covered by someone else's patent. If an inventor obtains a patent on improvements to an existing invention which is still under patent, they can only legally use the improved invention if the patent holder of the original invention gives permission, which they may refuse.

Some countries have "working provisions" that require the invention be exploited in the jurisdiction it covers. Consequences of not working an invention vary from one country to another, ranging from revocation of the patent rights to the awarding of a compulsory license awarded by the courts to a party wishing to exploit a patented invention. The patentee has the opportunity to challenge the revocation or license, but is usually required to provide evidence that the reasonable requirements of the

12 Patents and copyrights

public have been met by the working of invention.

Enforcement

Patents can generally only be enforced through civil lawsuits (for example, for a U.S. patent, by an action for patent infringement in a United States federal court), although some countries (such as France and Austria) have criminal penalties for wanton infringement. Typically, the patent owner seeks monetary compensation for past infringement, and seeks an injunction that prohibits the defendant from engaging in future acts of infringement. To prove infringement, the patent owner must establish that the accused infringer practises all the requirements of at least one of the claims of the patent. (In many jurisdictions the scope of the patent may not be limited to what is literally stated in the claims, for example due to the doctrine of equivalents).

An accused infringer has the right to challenge the validity of the patent allegedly being infringed in a countersuit. A patent can be found invalid on grounds described in the relevant patent laws, which vary between countries. Often, the grounds are a subset of requirements for patentability in the relevant country. Although an infringer is generally free to rely on any available ground of invalidity (such as a prior publication, for example), some countries have sanctions to prevent the same validity questions being relitigated. An example is the UK Certificate of contested validity.

Patent licensing agreements are contracts in which the patent owner (the licensor) agrees to grant the licensee the right to make, use, sell, and/or import the claimed invention, usually in return for a royalty or other compensation. It is common for companies engaged in complex technical fields to enter into multiple license agreements associated with the production of a single product. Moreover, it is equally common for competitors in such fields to license patents to each other under cross-licensing agreements in order to share the benefits of using each other's patented inventions.

Governing laws

The grant and enforcement of patents are governed by national laws, and also by international treaties, where those treaties have been given effect in national laws. Patents are granted by national or regional patent

Patents and copyrights 13

offices. A given patent is therefore only useful for protecting an invention in the country in which that patent is granted. In other words, patent law is territorial in nature. When a patent application is published, the invention disclosed in the application becomes prior art and enters the public domain (if not protected by other patents) in countries where a patent applicant does not seek protection, the application thus generally becoming prior art against anyone (including the applicant) who might seek patent protection for the invention in those countries.

Application and prosecution

A patent is requested by filing a written application at the relevant patent office. The person or company filing the application is referred to as "the applicant". The applicant may be the inventor or its assignee. The application contains a description of how to make and use the invention that must provide sufficient detail for a person skilled in the art (i.e., the relevant area of technology) to make and use the invention. In some countries there are requirements for providing specific information such as the usefulness of the invention, the best mode of performing the invention known to the inventor, or the technical problem or problems solved by the invention. Drawings illustrating the invention may also be provided.

The application also includes one or more claims that define what a patent covers or the "scope of protection".

After filing, an application is often referred to as "patent pending". While this term does not confer legal protection, and a patent cannot be enforced until granted, it serves to provide warning to potential infringers that if the patent is issued, they may be liable for damages.

Once filed, a patent application is "prosecuted". A patent examiner reviews the patent application to determine if it meets the patentability requirements of that country. If the application does not comply, objections are communicated to the applicant or their patent agent or attorney through an Office action, to which the applicant may respond. The number of Office actions and responses that may occur vary from country to country, but eventually a final rejection is sent by the patent office, or the patent application is granted, which after the payment of additional fees, leads to an issued, enforceable patent. In some jurisdictions, there are opportunities for third parties to bring an

14 Patents and copyrights

opposition proceeding between grant and issuance, or post-issuance.

Once granted the patent is subject in most countries to renewal fees to keep the patent in force. These fees are generally payable on a yearly basis. Some countries or regional patent offices (e.g. the European Patent Office) also require annual renewal fees to be paid for a patent application before it is granted.

Alternatives to applying for a patent

> **A defensive publication is the act of publishing a detailed description of a new invention without patenting it, so as to establish prior art and public identification as the creator/originator of an invention, although a defensive publication can also be anonymous. A defensive publication prevents others from later being able to patent the invention.**

This kind of protest against the big market leaders to accumulate patents, that are obvious and only intend to scare any competitor off, is very popular in public internet platforms that deal with Open Source like the reprap.org forums.

It is one way to ensure, that an invention a user has made, cannot be covered by a patent (A patent can be filed but the fact that someone else has published the method makes it invalid). Still there has to be someone who notices that an invention has bee published before! And in case a applicant files a patent it takes a lawsuit to bring it down again – so publishing new ideas on the internet has no automatic function. Moreover we should not trust the internet alone to archive important data. Today websites come and go, admins may delete postings, many thing can happen that will make it impossible to prove the prior art.

Criticism

As state-granted monopolies, patents have been criticized as inconsistent with free trade. On that basis, in 1869 the Netherlands abolished patents, and did not reintroduce them until 1912.

Patents have also been criticized for being granted on already-known inventions, with some complaining in the United States that the USPTO

Patents and copyrights 15

fails "to do a serious job of examining patents, thus allowing bad patents to slip through the system. On the other hand, some argue that because of low number of patents going into litigation, increasing quality of patents at patent prosecution stage increases overall legal costs associated with patents, and that current USPTO policy is a reasonable compromise between full trial on examination stage on one hand, and pure registration without examination, on the other hand.

Enforcement of patents – especially patents perceived as being overly broad – by patent trolls, has brought criticism of the patent system,though some commentators suggest that patent trolls are not bad for the patent system at all but instead realign market participant incentives, make patents more liquid, and clear the patent market.

The 3D printing community has very strong feelings about this matter. 3D printing is regarded as a "game changer", allowing private persons and small enterprises to become more independent of large companies, maker revolution etc. – we have read this all before.

Now some wish, the centuries old patent laws will be changed in favour to a better world that only consists of happy, honest and unselfish makers. We know the world is not like that. More and more commercial projects and company will enter the market. Like it or not, also this business will one day be part of the old fashioned economy. Maybe many the guys in those companies will be lovely nerds and enthusiasts, just like it the IT business. But there will always be some who abuse the system, seeking only their own favor, without giving anything back. We cannot change the laws for the nice guys and let the not-so-nice guys deny the same rights.

On the other hand many of the hundreds of patents that I had to go through to research for this book, appear to be beyond their time. Just like in the IT business, the 3D printing complex is very innovative, fast and 20 years is a very long time in terms of product evolution.

By the time the technology gets free for all to use the then state-of-the-art is far ahead. It is a difference, whether a product generation has a live span of up to 100 years, as some machines have, or if product improvements or new products could be offered to the market within 6 to 12 months.

16 Patents and copyrights

It is therefore true, that the current US patent system leads to lower progress in the field of 3D printing.

If the 3D printing is really regarded as a technological revolution, and a national effort was made, like with the landing on the moon, in times of war, or under very special conditions, the government may change the rules in order to come faster forward.

If not, then other areas in the world might not be so reluctant, pushing the development ahead and surpassing the US producers....

Part of this chapter contains extracts of texts supplied by wikipedia, the free encyclopedia. The author regularly donates to the wikipedia project, since it does help to reduce the time-to-market for literature, because known facts don't have to be researched again. Consider making your own contribution, next time you use wikipedia!

Patents and copyrights 17

Is it legal to use patents for private purpose?

This question can not be answered in one short sentence. The patent laws are quite complicated and it is always a question of a certain case. Furthermore the US patent laws are more restrict than those in Europe or other regions of the world.

In any case it is allowed to read and study them. Patents texts are public files, everyone can see them trough.

We have learned from a previous chapter (US patent law, page 10), that research on a patented technology in the sense of **"purely philosophical" inquiry is not an infringement.** Now where does a philosophical inquiry start and where doe sit end? Surely the term does not cover any real commercial activity, the law says, **not even only the intention** to probably use the technology in a commercial product.

Looking through patents can be interesting if the invention was only protected in some areas of the world. International patents are costly and require expensive translations as well as market research in that region.

So a patent that was filed in Europe may not be in effect in the US and vice versa.

Patent infringement filings are usually a question of economical interests and value. A company will not waste resources and efforts in suing small scale patent infringers. But that is no guarantee! They still may if they like to.

To ensure your legal position, it is absolutely necessary to consult a patent attorney before using known patent protected technology in a commercial product.

18 Patents and copyrights

Patent lawsuits in 3D printing

In the recent past market leader Stratasys Inc. has started to claim its patent rights against competitors, mainly those who derived their products from the Open Source Hardware project RepRap.

In 2012 3S Systems Inc. sued Formlabs- a crowd funded project – and the crowd funding platform **Kickstarter** for patent infringement.

Formlabs sells a 3D printer that works with the DLP technology. A "beamer" in the bottom of the device produces sliced layers of an object onto a bath of UV light curing resin. The projection platform is lifted with each layer, so that the object is produced down-facing.

1: Formlabs Form1 printer. Photo © M.A.Buth 2014

The invention that 3D Systems Inc. claimed as their very own, is based on patent US 5597520 A with the title: "Simultaneous multiple layer curing in stereolithography" and describes a process which is summed up as:

"*A method and apparatus for making high resolution objects by stereolithography utilizing low resolution materials which are limited by their inability to form unsupported structures of desired thinness and/or their inability to form coatings of desired thinness. Data manipulation techniques, based on layer comparisons, are used to control exposure in order to delay solidification of the material on at least portions of at least some cross-sections until higher layers of material are deposited so as to allow down-facing features of the object to be located at a depth in the building material which is equal to or exceeds a minimum cure depth that can effectively be used for solidifying these features. Similar data manipulations are used to ensure minimum reliable coating thicknesses exist, above previously solidified material, before attempting solidification of a next layer. In addition, horizontal comparison techniques are used to provide enhanced cross-sectional data for use in forming the object.*"

The patent description leads to the conclusion, that this is a pure optimizing process- one may dare to say, it describes some kind of algorithm- that does not directly include any claims concerning a specific hardware. So from that point of view, 3D Systems does not sue Formlabs over the way there printer looks or what parts it is made of, but because of the way **how it works** to achieve a higher-than-standard resolution.

At the first claim, the patent holder claims that:

"*We claim:*

1. An improved method of stereolithographically forming a three-dimensional object by forming cross-sectional layers of said object from a material capable of physical transformation upon exposure to synergistic stimulation comprising the steps of receiving data descriptive of said cross-sectional layers, forming said cross-sectional layers by selectively exposing said material to said synergistic stimulation according to said data descriptive of said cross-sectional layers to build up the three-dimensional object layer-by-layer, the improvement comprising the steps of:

modifying data descriptive of at least a portion of at least one cross-sectional layer by copying said data from a first cross-section to a second cross-section; and using said modified data in forming said three-dimensional object.(..)"

20 Patents and copyrights

A small technical detail one might say. If it is enough to convince experts and judges remains to be seen.

Another popular case is the patent infringement law suit Stratasys vs **Afinia** or better, Microboards Technology, LLC, the company behind the Afinia H-Series 3D printer. The printer is a FDM type device and therefore uses molten plastic to form objects layer wise.

Stratasys brings forward four technologies, they claim to hold exclusive patents on:

The 925 patent

Title: **"Method for controlled porosity three-dimensional modeling"**

This patent describes the infill procedure, where solid areas of a layer of an object are fabricated with honeycomb or other geometrical forms that reduce the material needed to produce an object.

Metadata:

Publication number	US5653925 A
Publication type	Grant
Application number	US 08/533,793
Publication date	Aug 5, 1997
Filing date	Sep 26, 1995
Priority date	Sep 26, 1995
Fee status	Paid
Also published as	DE69625222D1, 6 More »
Inventors	John S. Batchelder
Original Assignee	Stratasys, Inc.
Export Citation	BiBTeX, EndNote, RefMan

Patent Citations (6), Referenced by (61), Classifications (9), Legal Events (6)

External Links: USPTO, USPTO Assignment, Espacenet

The 058 patent

Title: "**Method for rapid prototyping of solid models**"

Patents and copyrights 21

This patent refers to the heated chamber of a 3D printer and an enclosure for a 3D printer to control the production process in general.

Metadata:

Publication number	US5866058 A
Publication type	Grant
Application number	US 08/862,933
Publication date	Feb 2, 1999
Filing date	May 29, 1997
Priority date	May 29, 1997
Fee status	Paid
Also published as	DE69839217D1, 5 More »
Inventors	John Samuel Batchelder, Steven Scott Crump
Original Assignee	Stratasys Inc.
Export Citation	BiBTeX, EndNote, RefMan

Patent Citations (4), Referenced by (94), Classifications (7), Legal Events (4)

External Links: USPTO, USPTO Assignment, Espacenet

The 124 patent

Title: "**Thin-wall tube liquifier**"

This patent describes a special FDM extruder design.

Metadata:

Publication number	US6004124 A
Publication type	Grant
Application number	US 09/013,388
Publication date	Dec 21, 1999
Filing date	Jan 26, 1998
Priority date	Jan 26, 1998
Fee status	Paid
Also published as	WO1999037453A1
Inventors	Paul E. Hopkins, William J. Swanson
Original Assignee	Stratasys, Inc.

22 Patents and copyrights

Export Citation　　　　　BiBTeX, EndNote, RefMan

Patent Citations (17), Referenced by (47), Classifications (19), Legal Events (5)

External Links: USPTO, USPTO Assignment, Espacenet

The 239 patent

Title: "**Seam concealment for three-dimensional models**"

The seam concealment method describes a method to make the start and the end of a fabrication more or less "seamless".

Metadata:

Publication number	US8349239 B2
Publication type	Grant
Application number	US 12/565,397
Publication date	Jan 8, 2013
Filing date	Sep 23, 2009
Priority date	Sep 23, 2009
Also published as	US20110070394, US20130095303
Inventors	Paul E. Hopkins, Donald J. Holzwarth
Original Assignee	Stratasys, Inc.
Export Citation	BiBTeX, EndNote, RefMan

Patent Citations (32), Non-Patent Citations (1), Classifications (18), Legal Events (1)

External Links: USPTO, USPTO Assignment, Espacenet

A long discussion on how to fight these patent claims has been held at the Reprap.org forums (http://forums.reprap.org/read.php?1,271908,page=1). Users tried to help by contributing links and patents that would prove, that the inventions had been made before the patents where filed. They searched for arguments and flaws in the patent text, that would render the claims invalid. Maybe this will help the sued company and many others that fear being sued, maybe not. The court will decide on the legitimacy of the patent infringement case, if not those two parties agree to settle the case and find an arrangement. This arrangement

Patents and copyrights 23

could be a one-time compensation payment or a license fee for each printer being produced. That would end the scenario but not help the hundreds of small 3D printer manufactures out there and it would not clarify the situation of the non-commercial hobbyists.

Anyhow- if you expect to see the full patents listed here -all these four patents are rather trivial than groundbreaking inventions. They are not even worth to be featured in full in this book. However what they do teach the observer is that, there are a lot of patent protected technologies which many take for granted, that may cause harm to a potential start up or even frighten the average user and hobbyist. As long as he or the company stays "below the radar" of the big 3D printer companies there is not much to worry. But once a product is displayed in the market- and any company needs marketing to promote their products- or a private user puts his works on sale at ebay, there is a chance of getting into a deep and costly conflict.

But at the end of the day, law is law and companies like 3D Systems or Stratasys offers jobs for many and have a granted right to protect themselves from unfair competition. Even some crowd funded projects have applied for patents on their inventions and strive to seek protection of their investments and innovations. This is where the Open Source idea ends for many of them.

Here is an example and an explanation of the head of a project called the PiMaker, initiated by a maker called Bill Steele:

I've received numerous questions and concerns about my comments on the PiMaker not being Open Source and the patent application I filed. I can't discuss the details of the patent application at this time... but I can talk about open source.

First off... let me state that I have always been and always be an open hardware supporter. I would be nowhere without the work of others and I will continue to honor that going forward. The PiMaker represents a major shift in the way 3D printers are done and I know a lot of people want to utilize it's unique aspects in their own designs.

A lot of people confuse copyright with patents. One is for the design files... the other is for the design/implemenation. We will publish the design files of the PiMaker on Thingiverse in a non-commercial license so that hackers/hobbyists will be able to use the design, modify it and adapt it to their own use... as long as no commercial interest is involved.

24 Patents and copyrights

The patent is to protect our IP and to prevent other commercial companies from utilizing our designs in their own printers. There is a clear separation between commercial interests and hobbyists here. Hobbyists will be able to hack, modify, understand, improve... what ever they want too with their printer or derivative, including making their own from our published design files. Commercial companies that produce 3D printers will need to license our technology in order to utilize our designs.

The PiMaker wouldn't exist if it wasn't for folks like Adrian Bowyer, Bre Pettis, Josef Prusa, Erik Zalm... this list goes on and on and I fully intend to give as much back as possible... but I also have to eat... and my true target market is not the home hobbyist... it's the home that has kids in it... the small business that needs to prototype something... it's the person who doesn't want to put together their own machine... but just wants to buy one and not have to worry about all the details about how it was made... that's my true target audience.

I hope that clears it up a bit. As we complete the shipment of these first PiMakers we'll get back to opening up 100% of what we can under a license model that supports this vision.

Bill

(Extracted from: http://www.kickstarter.com/projects/wjsteele/ultra-bot-3d-printer/posts/362886 *)*

As we can see, hobby and commerce are not so far from each other. A private maker can easily get into a commercial situation, if his products turn out to be a great success and could offer him to pay his bills.

It is therefore a thin red line between what is good for the public and what is good for some individuals.

Patent Research

The following databases can be used for own research through the internet:

USA:

http://www.uspto.gov/patents/process/search/index.jsp

Europe and Germany:

http://www.dpma.de/patent/recherche

Another informative source is Google. Using the search string Patent number + the term "patent" will return patent information, both meta data and the patent text for many patents, even in several languages.

Another rich source of patent information is:

http://www.patentbuddy.com

After a quick registration the user can find valuable information on, how many patents a company holds, how many have been filed recently, which individual of a company has supplied how many patents and much more.

The annual cost (fee) of each single patent is calculated and shown as well.

26 Patents and copyrights

Systematic patent research

Google alone will not help in finding

The patent databases are a vast ocean of information. Finding a specific patent on a subject is time consuming, sometimes even frustrating experience.

A better systematic way to identify potentially relevant patents is a hierarchic search. At first the market leader in a specific segment is selected. The results are compiled in a list. Next a relevant patent is selected and the patent citations are again compiled to a second level list. Large companies hire lots of patent attorneys and other specialist, who will research the current state of the art and name those sources in the patent text. These referrers will help the user to find relevant information in a very short time, because he benefits from the work of those who spend an enormous amount of time and energy to find theses works. In addition, the editors also will scan all relevant literature and name them as non-patent citations. An average user usually does not have access to all these information, books, magazines. So again he benefits from the research someone else has done.

So at the end of the first round, we have gathered patent citations, which will lead us to more relevant patents and non-patent citations which will give us valuable information of the starte of the art of the industry or science and where to source more information on the matter besides researching patents.

Once citations appear which have been named in previous patents, it can be assumed that the research has most likely covered the majority of the field of interest.

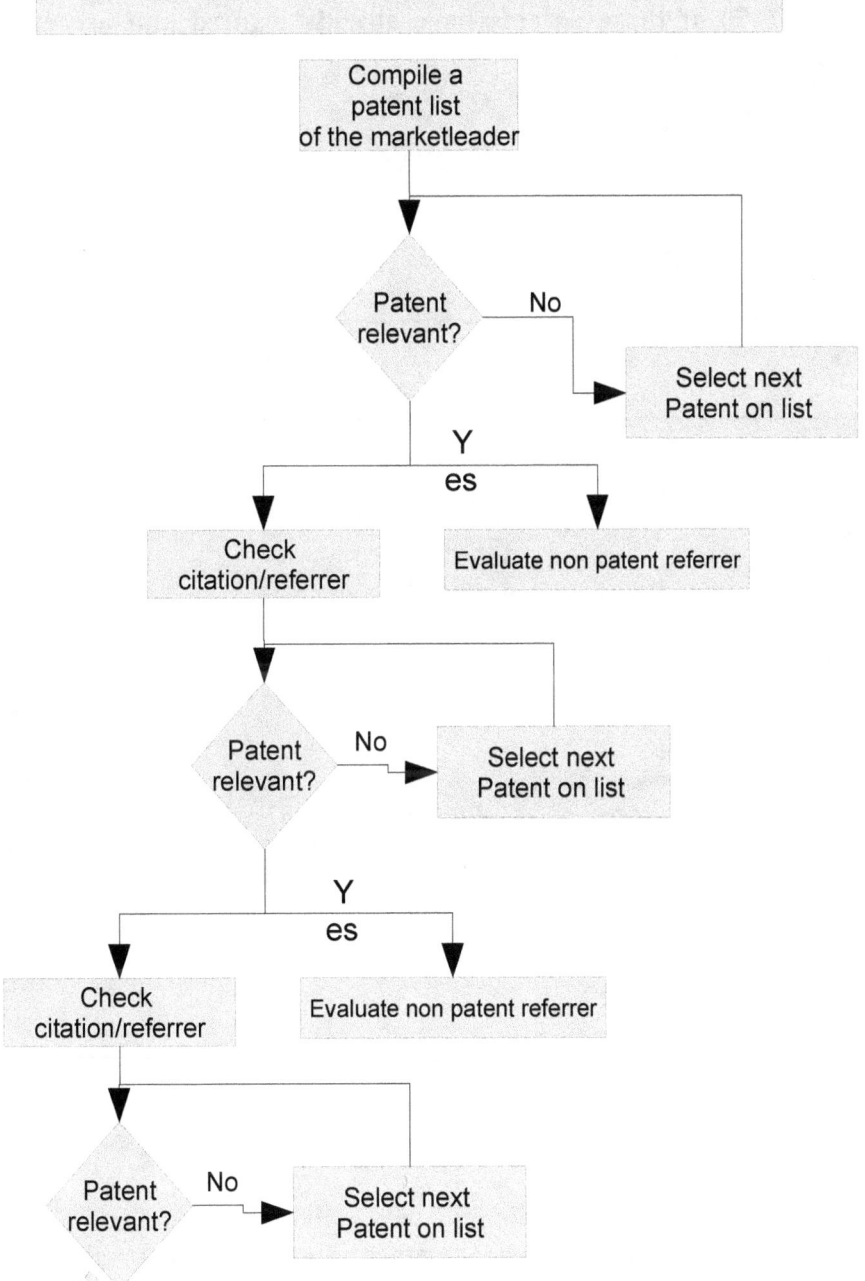

28 Patents and copyrights

Pionier, market leader and also #1 patent is the company 3D System. It accounts for the most numbers of patents in the 3D printing field – more than 450. **70 of those patents have already expired and are worth taking a closer look at.**

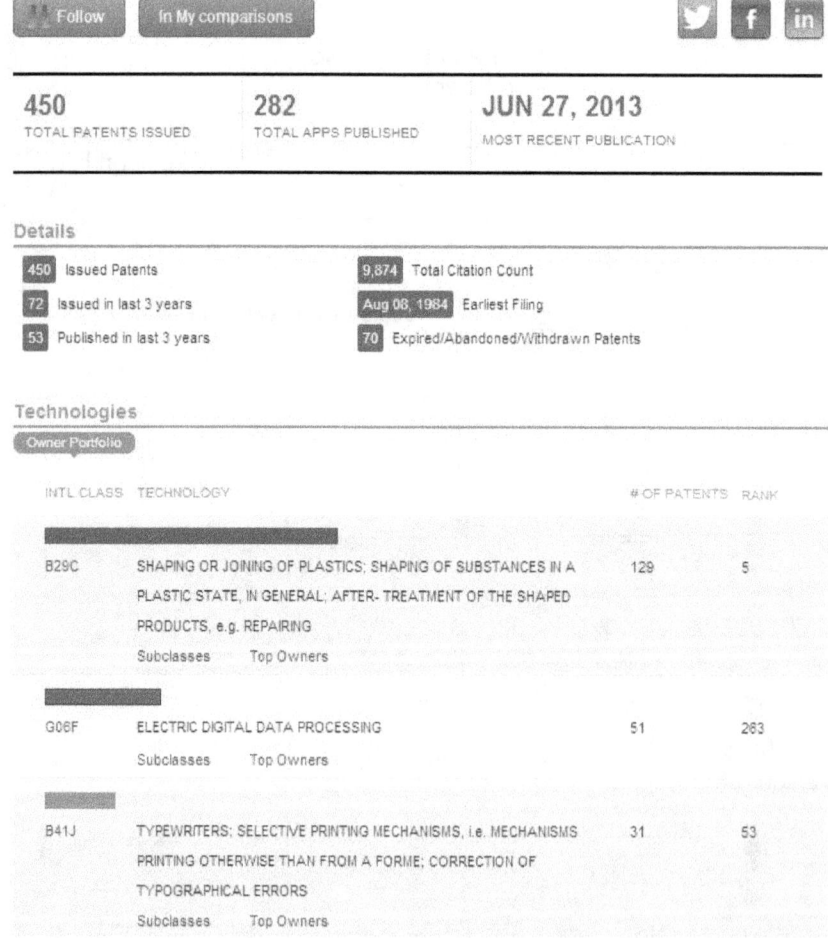

Intellectual property has become a very important asset for high-tech companies. It is valuable when them, or estimating the value of a company. Large companies therefor are eager to enforce their patents not only to keep competitors away from their turf, but also to increase their company value.

Patents and copyrights 29

Stratasys Inc. is another big player in the 3D printing field but with approximately 114 patents far away from 3D systems pole position.

The research of patents and their annual fees to maintain them is a big

30 Patents and copyrights

cost factor for any company and therefore the number of patents also reflects the economical strength of the holder.Makerbot, founded in 2006 out of the Open Hardware Source Project RepRap, holds 6 patents and has applied for another 17 so far.

Some other well known global companies without any 3D printer products in the market such as IBM or Sony also hold several patents referring to 3D printing. It is unclear what their intention with the ongoing of these inventions is - if there is any.

Selected patents

Table of content

Selected patents..31
   3D Printer..32
      Inkjet/Sand printing/Powder printing...33
         Ingredients of a binder composition...34
         Selective powder printer with consumables management.........35
      Stereolithography..44
         Support structure using recycled resin.....................................45
         Photocurable resin composition for producing three dimensional articles having high clarity 47
         Photocurable compositions for preparing ABS-like articles......50
         Multicolored STL Prints..52
      FDM Printer..68
         Multiextruder with only one drive..69
         Filament Kassette..77
         Grayscale rendering in 3D printing...85
         Smothing method for layered deposition modeling...................89
         A digitally active 3-D object creation system...........................93
         Printable support structure from silicone + polymer.................99
         Volumetric feed control for flexible filaments.........................107
         Auto tip calibration in an extrusion apparatus.........................115
         Rapid prototype injection molding 117
         Melt flow compensation for filaments.....................................123
         Water soluble rapid prototyping support and mold material...129
   Dispenser...135
      3D print under water...136
   Other methods..140
      3D print, multicolor, with multiple materials 141
      Three dimensional printing using imaged layers....................167
   Hexapod...171
   3D Scanner...173
      Scanner system and method for scanning 174

32 Selected patents

3D Printer

The following patents are mostly extracts from the full patent text. In case further research is needed, please refer to the Patent number and perform a search using this index.

Selected patents 33

Inkjet/Sand printing/Powder printing

34 Selected patents

Ingredients of a binder composition

Patent number	US5660621 A
Publication type	Grant
Application number	US 08/581,319
Published	26. Aug. 1997
Application	29. Dez. 1995
Priority	29. Dez. 1995
Fee status	Expired
Also published as	US5851465, WO1997026302A1
Inventors	James F. Bredt
Original Assignee	Massachusetts Institute Of Technology

Patent citations (64), Non patent citations (10), Referenced by (29), Classifications (20), Legal Events (7)

External links: USPTO, USPTO assignment, Espacenet

This patent describes a chemical composition for a binder for powder printer (inkjet technology). **The patent has expired.**

DETAILED DESCRIPTION OF THE INVENTION

To make the binder composition according to the preferred embodiment, the following components are combined and mixed thoroughly to dissolve the solids:

distilled water 385.9 cc (385.9 g)propylene glycol 58.4 cc (65.1 g)triethanolamine 21.7 cc (24.4 g)diethylene glycol monobutyl ether 12.6 cc (12.2 g)polyethylene glycol 1.0 gthymol blue 0.5g

To this mixture, 525.0 cc (735.0 g) of Nyacol 9950 are added. The silica appears to flocculate upon mixing. According, this mixture should be allowed to stand for a time or should be filtered by pumping in a closed circuit through a 5 μm filter for a time to redisperse the flocs.

The specific gravity of this mixture is 1.21 for 17.5 vol. % silica. The pH is between 9 and 9.5. The viscosity is approximately 2 to 3 cP (0.002 to 0.003 Pa-s). The surface tension is 54 dyn/cm (0.054 Pa-m).

Other methods to reduce the pH of the binder composition to cause gelation are possible. For example, gaseous CO_2 can be applied to each layer of the powder after printing of the binder.

The invention is not to be limited by what has been particularly shown and described except as indicated by the appended claims.

Selective powder printer with consumables management

Patent number	US8523554 B2
Publication type	Grant
Application number	US 13/150,913
Published	3. Sept. 2013
Application	1. June 2011
Priority	2. June 2010
Inventors	Ya Ching Tung, Kwo Yuan Shi
Original Assignee	Microjet Technology Co., Ltd.

Classifications (10), Legal Events (1)

External links: USPTO, USPTO assignment, Espacenet
Comment:

A rather complicated, yet still interesting way of creating 3D objects. A major advantage is claimed concerning the reduction of dust that is usually a side effect of powder printing. The printer f. i. features a closed loop system for the powder. Moreover, a specially designed valve mechanism will only supply the amount of powder needed for each pass.

36 Selected patents

Drawings:

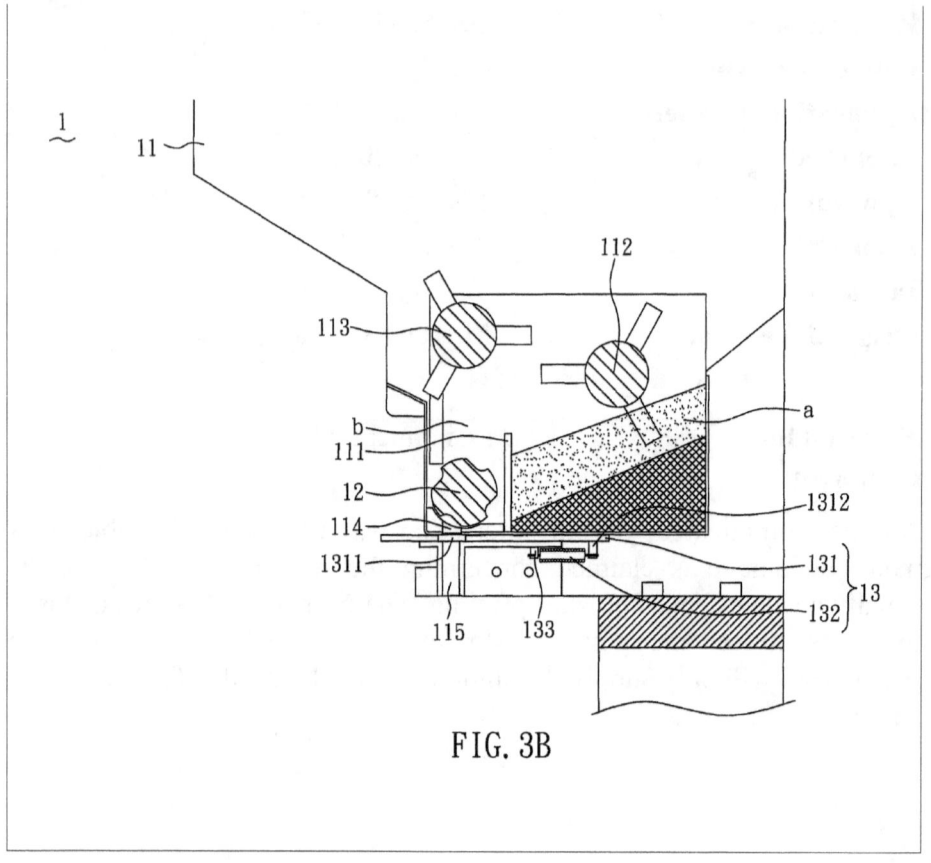

FIG. 3B

Selected patents 37

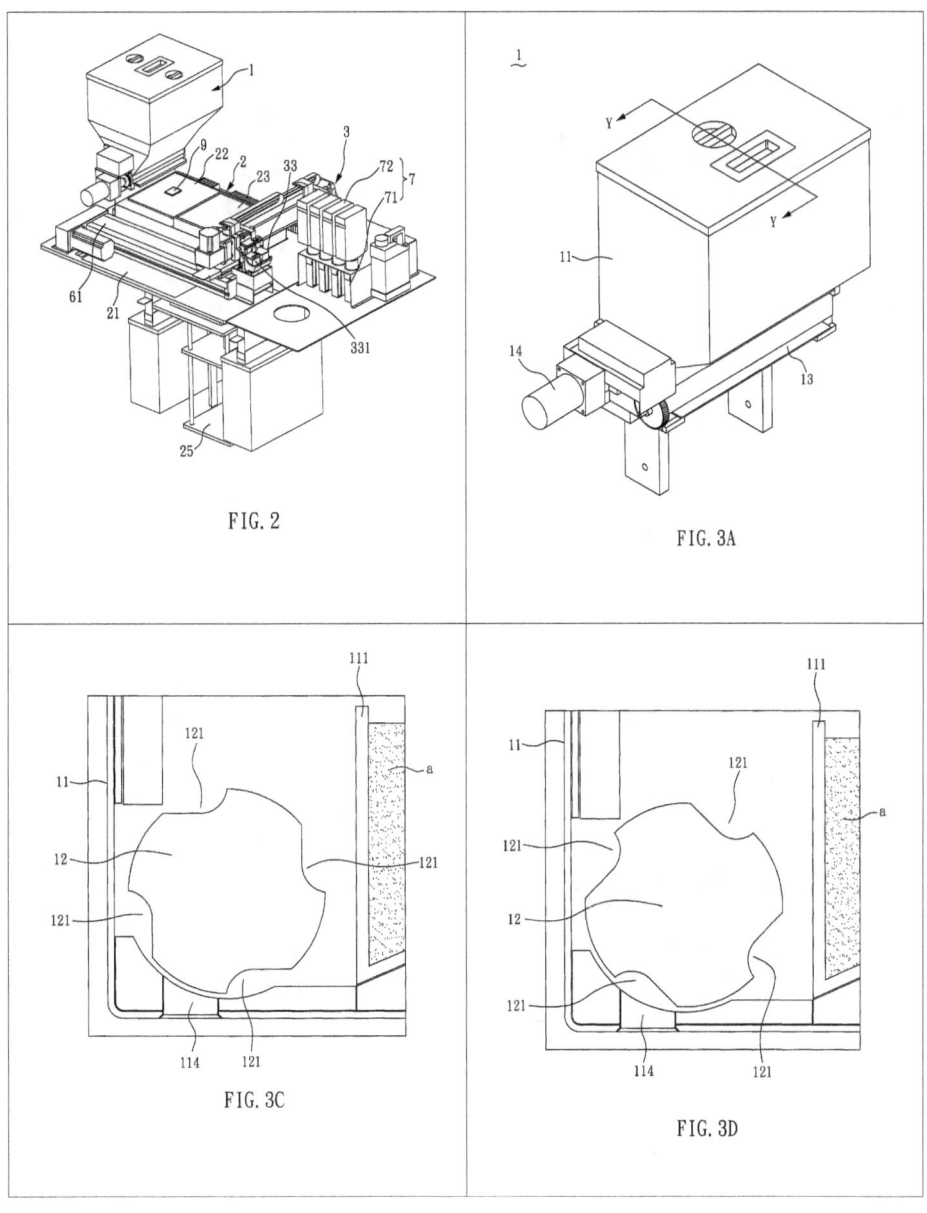

FIG. 2

FIG. 3A

FIG. 3C

FIG. 3D

38 Selected patents

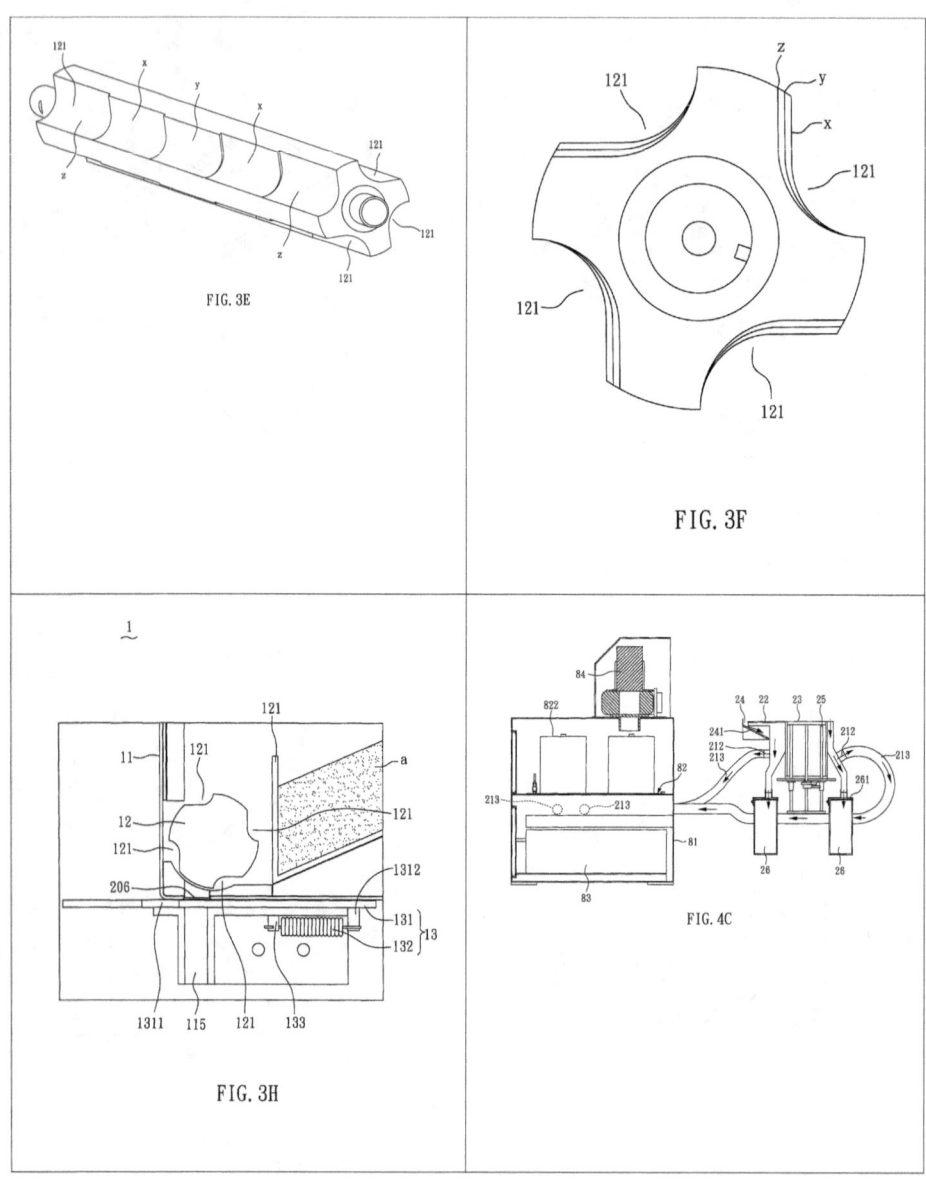

SUMMARY OF THE INVENTION

The object of the present invention is to provide a three-dimensional object-forming apparatus, which has a quantitative powder-supplying tank system to regulate the corresponding times between the cavities of the in-batches rationing roller under rolling and the dropping-powder opening according to requirements of different powder-application thicknesses so as to control the output amount of the construction powder. Therefore, redundant construction powder drawn in the powder collection tank can be reduced to avoid the waste of the construction powder and decrease the production costs. In addition, each cavity of the in-batches rationing roller has a plurality of compartments, and the capacity of the compartments increases from the center of the cavities to the both sides thereof so as to achieve even powder application and improve the drawback of powder deficiency at the both sides.

Besides, the three-dimensional object-forming apparatus of the present invention further comprises a heating device used to heat during the printing of the printing module to accelerate the combination between the adhesive and the construction powder and reduce one-third to half time of forming a three-dimensional object. The three-dimensional object-forming apparatus of the present invention further comprises a successive liquid-supplying device which can successively supply an adhesive into the printing cartridge to make the printing module inkjet-print on the construction powder for a long term of time.

Furthermore, the three-dimensional object-forming apparatus of the present invention has a dust-proof device for a driving component to prevent the contamination of the disturbed powder during the powder application and inkjet printing so that the apparatus and components of the three-dimensional object-forming apparatus all can be kept anytime in a normal operation and achieve absolute dust-proofing overall.

Meanwhile, the three-dimensional object-forming apparatus of the present invention is provided with an inkjet-print head maintenance device which comprises a cleaning unit and a sealing unit. After the inkjet-printing operation is completed by the inkjet-print head, the inkjet-print head can be completely cleaned by the scrapers of the cleaning unit and sealed in the sealing part of the sealing unit to achieve thorough anti-contamination and anti-drying of the inkjet-print head.

Moreover, the three-dimensional object-forming apparatus of the present invention has the design of the print quality detection, in which ground glass is used as a print quality detection member to real-timely observe whether the pattern inkjet-printed by the inkjet-print head is normal and determine whether the inkjet-print head is blocked so as to clean the inkjet-print head in time and keep the print quality.

In order to achieve the abovementioned objects, a generalized aspect of the present invention provides a three-dimensional object-forming apparatus comprising an in-batches powder-rationing tank system, a construction tank system, a printing powder-applying system, a rapid drying heating system, a printing maintenance device, a dust-proof device, a successive liquid-supplying device, a powder auto-filtrating and recycling device, and a print quality detection device.

40 Selected patents

BRIEF DESCRIPTION OF THE DRAWINGS

FIG. 1 shows an exterior view of the three-dimensional object-forming apparatus in the preferred example of the present invention;

FIG. 2 shows an interior view of the three-dimensional object-forming apparatus in the preferred example of the present invention;

FIG. 3A shows a structural view of the quantitative powder-supplying tank system;

FIG. 3B shows a Y-Y cross-sectional view of FIG. 3A;

FIG. 3C shows a structural view of the partial powder-supplying tank and in-batches rationing roller in FIG. 3B;

FIG. 3D shows a structural view of supplying powder in FIG. 3B;

FIG. 3E shows a structural view of the in-batches rationing roller in FIG. 3B;

FIG. 3F shows a front view of the in-batches rationing roller in FIG. 3B;

FIG. 3G is a structural view of the closing device and dropping-powder channel shown in FIG. 3B;

FIG. 3H shows a structural view of the opening of the closing device unconnected to the dropping-powder opening shown in FIG. 3G;

FIG. 4A shows a structural view of the construction tank system;

FIG. 4B shows a structural view of the partial remaining powder auto-collection area of the construction tank system;

FIG. 4C shows a view of recycling the remaining powder in the construction tank system;

FIG. 5A shows a structural view of the printing powder-applying system;

FIG. 5B shows a structural view of the printing module of the printing powder-applying system;

FIG. 5C shows a cross-sectional view of FIG. 5B;

FIG. 6 shows a view of the dust-proof device;

FIG. 7A shows a view of the printing maintenance device;

FIG. 7B shows a structural view of the cleaning unit;

FIG. 7C shows a cross-sectional view of FIG. 7B;

FIG. 7D shows a structural view of the sealing unit;

FIG. 8 shows a view of the liquid supplying in the successive liquid-supplying device;

FIG. 9 shows a view of the connection between the powder auto-filtrating and recycling device and the three-dimensional object-forming apparatus; and

FIG. 10 shows a cross-sectional view of the powder auto-filtrating and recycling device.

DETAILED DESCRIPTION OF THE PREFERRED EMBODIMENT

Several typical embodiments showing the features and advantages of the present invention are explained in relation in the following paragraphs, and it is to be understood that many other possible modifications and variations can be made without departing from the spirit and scope of the invention as hereinafter claimed.

With reference to FIGS. 1 and 2, they are

exterior and interior views of the three-dimensional object-forming apparatus in a preferred example of the present invention. As shown in FIGS. 1 and 2, the three-dimensional object-forming apparatus of the present invention mainly includes an in-batches powder-rationing tank system 1, a construction tank system 2, a printing powder-applying system 3, a rapid drying heating system 4 (shown in FIG. 5C), a printing maintenance device 5 (shown in FIG. 7A), a dust-proof device 6 (shown in FIG. 6), a successive liquid-supplying device 7 (shown in FIG. 8), a powder auto-filtrating and recycling device 8 (shown in FIG. 9), and a print quality detection device 9.

The in-batches powder-rationing tank system 1 and the construction tank system 2 of the present invention are provided in view of that there is no in-batches powder-rationing device in the conventional rapid-forming apparatus and it causes the uneven density and redundant powder drawn in the trihedral auto-recycling tub resulting in uneven powder application. Therefore, an in-batches rationing roller and a trihedral auto-recycling tub are installed in the powder-supplying system to overcome the abovementioned drawbacks. How to overcome the drawbacks is the main topic of developing the in batches powder-rationing tank system 1 and the construction tank system 2 of the present invention. The following are illustrations of the related components.

With reference FIGS. 3A and 3B, FIG. 3A shows a structural view of the in-batches powder-rationing tank system in a preferred example of the present invention, and FIG. 3B shows a Y-Y cross-sectional view of FIG. 3A. As shown in FIGS. 3A and 3B, the in-batches powder-rationing tank system 1 includes at least one powder-supplying tank 11, an in-batches rationing roller 12, and a closing device 13. The powder-supplying tank 11 is a hollow tank structure and used for storage of the construction powder "a". Within the powder-supplying tank 11, a baffle plate 111, a first roller 112, and a second roller 113 are installed. Additionally, a dropping-powder opening 114 and a dropping-powder channel 115 are disposed on the bottom of the powder-supplying tank 11. A lateral of the baffle plate 111 and the dropping-powder opening 114 are separated by a dropping-powder zone "b". The construction powder "a" accumulated outside the dropping-powder zone "b" of the baffle plate 111 can be disturbed by the first roller 112 and then drop within the dropping-powder zone "b" of the baffle plate 111 by the rotation of the second roller 113.

With reference to FIGS. 3C and 3D, they are partially structural views of the powder-supplying tank and the in-batches rationing roller in FIG. 3B. As shown in FIGS. 3C and 3D, the in-batches rationing roller 12 is installed in the dropping-powder zone "b" of the powder-supplying tank 11, close to the dropping-powder opening 114, used to supply the construction powder "a" in batches required for total application of a construction-forming area, and has a plurality of cavities 121. Each cavity 121 is mainly used to receive the construction powder "a". When the cavities 121 of the in-batches rationing roller 12 do not correspond to the dropping-powder opening 114, the construction powder "a" can not be output (as shown in FIG. 3C). On the contrary, when one of the cavities 121 corresponds to the dropping-powder opening 114, the construction powder "a" contained in the powder-supplying tank 11 are output via the dropping-powder opening 114 (as shown in FIG. 3D).

42 Selected patents

Besides, in the in-batches powder-rationing tank system 1 of the present invention, the corresponding times between the cavities 121 of the in-batches rationing roller 12 under rolling and the dropping-powder opening 114 can be regulated by a motor 14 according to the requirements of different powder application thicknesses so as to control the output amount of the construction powder "a" to avoid the waste of the construction powder "a". For example, if the powder application thickness of the construction-forming area has the maximum of 0.12 mm and the minimum of 0.08 mm. The amount of the construction powder "a" received in a cavity 121 of the in-batches rationing roller 12 approximately forms a thickness of 0.04 mm. Therefore, when the construction powder "a" is formed in a thickness of 0.08 mm, the motor 14 has to rotate twice to make two cavities 121 of the in-batches rationing roller 12 connect to the dropping-powder opening 114 and thus the construction powder "a" received in the cavities 121 can be output via the dropping-powder opening 114. When the construction powder "a" is formed in a thickness of 0.12 mm, the motor 14 has to rotate three times to make three cavities 121 of the in rationing roller 12 cannot to the dropping-powder opening 114 and thus the construction powder "a" received in the cavities 121 can be output via the dropping-powder opening 114. Accordingly, the redundant construction powder "a" drawn into a powder collection tank can be reduced.

With reference to FIGS. 3E and 3F, they are structural and front views of the in-batches rationing roller shown in FIG. 3B. As shown in FIGS. 3E and 3F, each cavity 121 of the in-batches rationing roller 12 of the present invention has a plurality of compartments "x", "y", and "z". In the present example, one compartment "x", two compartments "y", and two compartments "z" are contained in each cavity 121, but not limited thereto. The compartment "x" is set in the center of the cavities 121 and both sides of the compartment "x" are provided respectively with the compartments "y". The compartments "z" are set at the other side of the compartments "y". The cavities of the compartment "x" are shallowest and have the least amount of the received powder. The cavities of the compartments "y" are deeper and have more amount of the received powder than those of the compartment "x". The cavities of the compartments "z" are deeper than those of the compartment "x" and the compartments "y" and thus have the largest amount of the received powder. In other words, the amount of the received powder in one compartment "x" and plural compartments "y" and "z" increase from the center to the both sides of the cavities 121, i.e. compartment "x"<compartments "y"<compartments "z". Based on the structural designs that each cavity 121 has one compartment "x" and plural compartments "y" and "z" and the capacity of one compartment "x" and plural compartments "y" and "z" increases from the center of the cavities 121 to the both sides thereof, the construction powder "a" can be applied evenly on the construction-forming area so as to overwhelm the drawbacks of more and more differences of the construction powder amounts between the center and the both sides in the conventional technique as the times of the powder application increase.

With reference to FIG. 3G, it is a structural view of the closing device and dropping-powder channel shown in FIG. 3B. As shown in FIG. 3G, the closing device 13 included in the in-batches powder-rationing tank system 1 of the present invention has a board 131, an elastic member 132, and a retention member 133. The board 131 is movable and has an opening 1311 and a fixing member 1312. An end of the elastic member 132 is connected to the fixing member 1312, and the other end thereof is connected to the retention member 133 mounted on the bottom of the powder-supplying tank 11. During the powder supply of the powder-supplying tank 11, the board 131 of the closing device 13 is moved by a thrust towards the direction "f" and thus the opening 1311 thereof is connected to the dropping-powder opening 114. At this instance, the construction powder "a" received in one cavity 121 of the in-batches rationing roller 12 is output via the dropping-powder opening 114, the opening 1311, and the dropping-powder channel 115 (as shown in FIG. 3G).

44 Selected patents

Stereolithography

Selected patents 45

Support structure using recycled resin

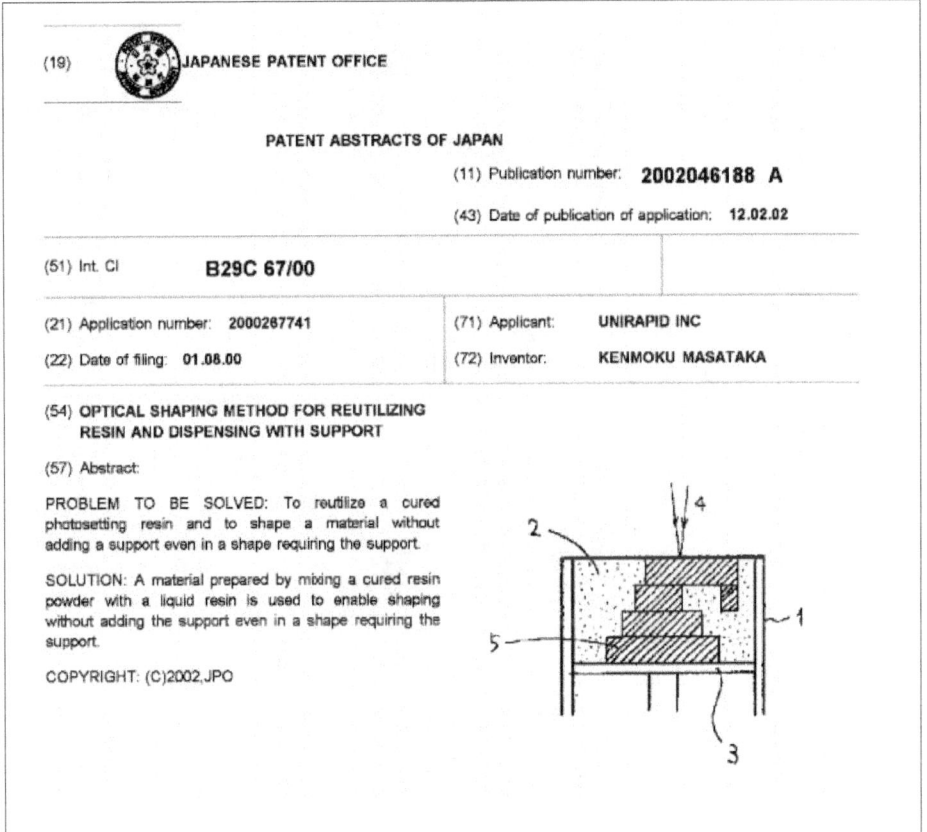

Comment:

The inventor presents an intriguing and clever way on how to save printing material and recycle used and hardened resin.

By fine grinding the cured material and mixing it with fresh resin, a paste is created that serves as support layer.

The patent text was only found in Japanese, but with this short explanation and the drawings the process should be understandable.

46 Selected patents

Drawings:

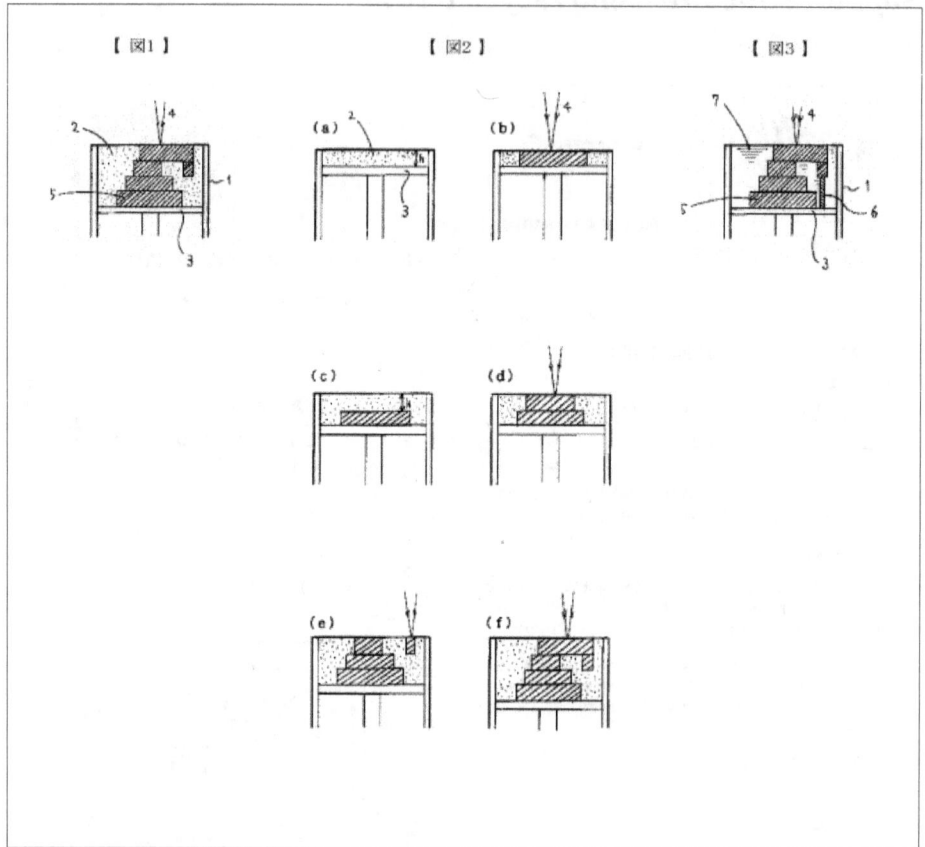

Selected patents 47

Photocurable resin composition for producing three dimensional articles having high clarity

Patent number	US8377623 B2
Publication type	Grant
Application number	US 12/745,036
Published	19. Febr. 2013
Application	21. Nov. 2008
Priority	27. Nov. 2007
Also published as	EP2215525A1, EP2215525A4, US20100 304100, WO2009070500A1
Inventors	John Wai Fong
Original Assignee	3D Systems, Inc.

Patent citations (25), Non patent citations (1), Classifications (13), Legal Events (3)

Comment:

The following patent description feautures the composition of a highly transparent resin.

Claims

What is claimed is:

1. A photocurable composition comprising: (a) 35-80% by weight of a cationically curable component comprising a polyglycidyl epoxy compound; (b) 5-60% by weight of a free radically active component comprising an ethoxylated and/or propoxylated poly(melh)acrylate; (c) 0.1-10% by weight of a antimony-free cationic photoinitiator; (d) 0.01-10% by weight of a free radical photoinitiator; and (e) 0-40% by weight of one or more optional components wherein the percent by weight is based on the total weight of the photocurable composition and wherein the photocurable composition, after cure, is clear and has a yellowness index/inch thickness of less than 70 and a flexπral modulus of at least 1000 MPa. 2. The photocurable composition of claim 1 wherein the cationically curable component and free radically active component produce a C:H:O ratio of at least 3.0:3.75:1

3. The photocurable composition of claim 2 wherein the C:H:O ratio is at least 3.5:5.0:1.

4. The photocurable composition of claim 2 wherein the poly(meth)acrylate further comprises a non-aromatic poly(meth)acrylate. 5. The photocurable

48 Selected patents

composition of claim 4 wherein the poly (meth)acrylate is an alicyclic poly(meth)acrylale.

6. The photocurable composition of claim 1 wherein the antimony-free cationic photoinitiator is of the formula (1):

where

R1, R2 and R3 are each independently of one another Cβ-is aryl that is unsubstituted or substituted by radicals selected from the group consisting of C1-6 alkyl; C\.6 alkoxy; Ci .6 alkylthio; halogen; amino groups; cyano groups; nitro groups, and arylthio;

Q is boron or phosphorus;

X is a halogen atom; and m is an integer corresponding to the valence of Q plus 1.

7. The photocurable composition of claim 1 wherein the polyglycidyl epoxy compound comprises a hydrogenated bisphenol epoxy-containing compound.

8. The photocurable composition of claim 7 wherein the cationically curable component further comprises an oxetane compound.

9. The photocurable composition of claim 1 wherein the cationic photoinitiator is a triarylsulfonium hexafluorophosphate salt.

10. A photocurable composition comprising: (a) 40-70% by weight of a cationically curable component comprising one or more epoxy-containing compounds and one or more oxetane compounds;

(b) 15-60% by weight of a free radically active component comprising

(i) at least one ethoxylated or propoxylated poly(meth)acrylate or mixture thereof and

(ii) a non-aromatic poly(meth)acrylate;

(c) 0, 1-10% by weight of an antimony-free cationic photoiniliator;

(d) 0.1-10% by weight of a free radical photoiiiitiator;

(e) 0-40% by weight of one or more optional components wherein the amount of the ethoxylated or propoxylated poly(meth)acrylate or mixture thereof is greater than 40% by weight of the total amount of free radically active component and wherein the photocurable composition, after cure by exposure to actinic radiation and optionally heat, has a yellowness index/inch thickness of less than 70.

11. The photocurable composition of claim 10 wherein the cationically curable component and free radically active component produce a C:II:O ratio of at least 3.0:3.75:1.

12. The photocurable composition of claim 1 1 wherein the C:H:O ratio is at least 3.5:5.0:1.

13. The photocurable composition of claim 10 wherein the cationically curable component comprises a hydrogenated bisphenol epoxy-containing compound.

14. Λ process for producing a colorless three dimensional article comprising: (a) forming a first layer of the photocurable composition of claim 1 on a surface; (b) exposing the layer imagewise to actinic radiation to form an imaged cross- section, wherein the radiation is of sufficient intensity to cause substantial curing of the layer in the exposed areas;

(c) forming a second layer of the composition of claim 1 on the previously exposed imaged cross-section;(d) exposing the second layer from step (c) imagewise to actinic radiation to form an additional imaged cross-section, wherein the radiation is of sufficient intensity to cause substantial curing of the second layer in the exposed areas and to cause adhesion to the previously exposed imaged cross-section; and (e) repeating steps (c) and (d) a sufficient number of times in order to build up the three-dimensional article.

15. A three-dimensional medical article produced according to the process of claim 14.

16. The three-dimensional article of claim 15 wherein the article is a container, headlight, shade or decorative object. 17. A process for producing a three dimensional article by jet printing comprising the steps of:

(a) applying successive droplets of the photocorable composition of claim 1 at targeted locations on a substrate in accordance with a desired shape stored on a computer file; (b) exposing the droplets to electromagnetic radiation to cure the droplets in the exposed areas; (c) repeating steps (a) and (b) a sufficient number of times in order to build up the three dimensional article.

18. The process of claim 17 wherein the substrate comprises paper, textiles, tiles, printing plates, wallpaper, plastic, powder or paste. 19. The process of claim 18 wherein the photociirable composition is exposed to electromagnetic radiation pixel by pixel, line by line, layer by layer, after several layers have been formed, and/or after all layers have been formed.

20. The process of claim 19 wherein the electromagnetic radiation employed is UV light, microwave radiation, visible light, or laser beams. 21. A photociirable composition comprising:

(a) 30-55% by weight of a cationically curable component comprising a hydrogenated aromatic polyglycidyl epoxy compound;

(b) 5-60% by weight of a free radically active component comprising an ethoxylated and/or propoxylated poly(meth)acrylate; (c) 0.1-10% by weight of a antimony-free cationic photoinitiator;

(d) 0.01-10% by weight of a free radical photoinitiator; and

(e) 0-40% by weight of one or more optional components

(f) 5-25% of an oxetane compound having one oxetane ring wherein the percent by weight is based on the total weight of the photocurable composition and wherein the photocurable composition has a C:II:O ratio of at least 3.0:3.75:1 and after cure, is clear and has a yellowness index/inch thickness of less than 70 and a flexural modulus of at least 1000 MPa.

22. The photocuiable composition of claim 21 wherein the C;II:O ratio is at least 3.5:5.0:1.

50 Selected patents

Photocurable compositions for preparing ABS-like articles

Publication number	CA2620714 A1
Publication type	Application
Application number	CA 2620714
PCT number	PCT/EP2006/066264
Publication date	22 Mar 2007
Filing date	12 Sep 2006
Priority date	13 Sep 2005
Also published as	CN101263428A, EP1924887A1, US8227048, US201102 93891, WO2007031505A1
Inventors	Carole Chapelat, 6 More »
Applicant	3D Systems, Inc., 8 More »

Classifications (6), Legal Events (2)

External Links: CIPO, Espacenet

Comment:

A short patent text, that features a photocureable resin, that has ABS-like properties

ABSTRACT

The present invention provides a clear, low viscosity photocurable composition including (i) a cationically curable compound (ii) an acrylate-containing compound (iii) a polyol-conyaining mixture (iv) a cationic photoinitiator and (v) a free radical photoinitiator. The photocurable composition can be cured using rapid prototyping techniques to form opaque-white three-dimensional articles having ABS-like properties.

CLAIMS

1) A photocurable composition comprising:

a. 30-80% by weight of an epoxy-containing compound;

b. 5-40% by weight of a polyfunctional (meth)acrylate;

c. 5-40% by weight of a polyol-containing mixture comprising (1) at least one component of low to medium molecular weight which component contains at least one epoxy or alcohol functionality and (2) at least one polyol, which is different from compound (1) and has a higher molecular weight than compound (1) d. a cationic photoinitiator;

e. a free radical photoinitiator; and optionally f. one or more stabilizers wherein the percent by weight is based on the total weight of the photocurable composition.

2) The photocurable composition of claim 1 wherein component (1) is a polyol chosen amongst the following types: poly(oxytetramethylene) polyol, poly(oxypropylene) polyol, poly(oxyethylene) polyol, hydroxy-terminated polybutadiene or hydroxy-terminated polysiloxane.

3) The photocurable composition of claim 2 wherein the molar ratio of the poly(oxytetramethylene)polyol over the at least one other polyol is equal to or less than 25.

4) The photocurable composition of any preceding claim wherein the polyol of component (2) is a polyether polyol.

5) The photocurable composition of any preceding claim wherein the photocurable composition is a clear liquid.

6) The photocurable composition of any preceding claim which, after cure by exposure to actinic radiation is opaque.

7) The photocurable composition of any preceding claim which, after cure by exposure to actinic radiation is opaque-white that simulates ABS.

52 Selected patents

Multicolored STL Prints

Title: "Colored stereolithographic resins"

Publication number	WO2004077157 A1
Publication type	Application
Application number	PCT/US2004/000354
Publication date	10 Sep 2004
Filing date	8 Jan 2004
Priority date	27 Feb 2003
Also published as	EP1597628A1, US20040170923
Inventors	Manfred Hofmann, Alfred Steinmann, Bettina Steinmann
Applicant	3D Systems Inc
Export Citation	BiBTeX, EndNote, RefMan

Patent Citations (3), Non-Patent Citations (2), Classifications (9), Legal Events (6)

External Links: Patentscope, Espacenet

Comment:

A detailed description of a chemical composition for multicolored STL resins. A huge source of information on chemicals, procedures, trade names, supplier companies and more.

ABSTRACT

A liquid colored radiation-curable composition that comprises: (A) at least one cationically polymerizing organic substance; (B) at least one free-radical polymerizing organic substance; (C) at least one cationic polymerization initiator; (D) at least cone free-radical polymerization initiator; and (E) an effective color-imparting amount of at least one soluble dye compound selected from the group consisting of diarylmethane and triarylmethane dyes, rhodamine dyes, azo dyes, thiazole dyes, anthraquinone dyes and safranine dyes; said liquid colored radiation-curable composition having substantially the same photospeed as the composition without dye component (E) and the liquid dye compound does not bleach out during radiation exposure.

Selected patents 53

BACKGROUND OF THE INVENTION

1. Field of the Invention

The present invention relates to selected liquid, colored radiation-curable compositions which are particularly suitable for the production of colored three-dimensional articles by stereolithography as well as a process for the production of colored cured articles and the cured three-dimensional shaped colored article themselves. In particular, this invention relates to a liquid, radiation-curable resin compositions from which cured three-dimensional shaped articles having excellent color properties.

2. Brief Description of Art

The production of three-dimensional articles of complex shape by means of stereolithography has been known for a relatively long time. In this technique the desired shaped article is built up from a liquid, radiation-curable composition with the aid of a recurring, alternating sequence of two steps (a) and (b); in step (a), a layer of the liquid, radiation-curable composition, one boundary of which is the surface of the composition, is cured with the aid of appropriate radiation, generally radiation produced by a preferably computer-controlled laser source, within a surface region which corresponds to the desired cross-sectional area of the shaped article to be formed, at the height of this layer, and in step (b) the cured layer is covered with a new layer of the liquid, radiation-curable composition, and the sequence of steps (a) and (b) is repeated until a so-called green model of the desired three- dimensional shape is finished. This green model is, in general, not yet fully cured and must therefore, normally, be subjected to post-curing.

The mechanical strength of the green model (modulus of elasticity, fracture strength), also referred to as green strength, constitutes an important property of the green model and is determined essentially by the nature of the stereolithographic resin (SL) composition employed. Other important properties of a stereolithographic resin composition include a high sensitivity for the radiation employed in the course of curing and a minimum curl factor, permitting high shape definition of the green model. In addition, for example, the precured material layers should be readily wettable by the liquid stereolithographic resin composition, and of course not only the green model but also the ultimately cured shaped article should have optimum mechanical properties.

In order to achieve the desired balance of properties, different types of stereolithographic resin systems have been proposed. For example, radical-curable stereolithographic resin systems have been proposed. These systems generally consist of one or more (meth)acrylate compounds (or other free-radical polymerizable organic compounds) along with a free-radical photoinitiator for radical generation. U.S. Patent No. 5,418,112 describes one such radical-curable system. Another type of resin composition suitable for this purpose is a dual-type stereolithographic resin system that comprises (i) epoxy resins or other types of cationic polymerizable compounds; (ii) cationic polymerization initiator; (iii) acrylate resins or other types of free radical polymerizable compounds; and (iv) a free radical polymerization initiator. Examples of such dual or hybrid systems are described in U.S. Patent Nos. 5,434,196, 5,972,563; 6,100,007 and 6,287,748.

Separately, there have been four (4) general ways to produce a colored stereolithographic resin product. The first way was to disperse color pigments into the uncured resin formulation and then cure that pigment-laden formulation. There are several disadvantages associated with the use of pigment materials in stereolithographic resin production. A relatively high concentration of pigment is needed in the uncured resin formulation for a strong coloration and special blending equipment and/or additives are required to produce uniform and stable pigment dispersions. Undesirable absorption and light scattering may occur during the SL laser exposure because of the pigment particles. Also, unwanted sedimentation of the pigment particles can occur in the SL vat before or during the laser exposure causing a color differential in the layers of the cured product. Accordingly, because of these reasons, colored pigment use in stereolithographic resins has not been favored for widespread commercial applications.

The second prior art method of coloring an SL resin has been to apply a dye solution to the surface of cured SL resin after laser exposure. See European Patent Application No. 0250121 A2 (e.g. column 22, lines 16-41) as an example of this technique. This dyeing technique requires an additional processing step and may lead to undesirable swelling of the cured part by absorption of the liquid colorant into the part. Also, the color is only at the surface of the cured part. Wear or scratching of the cured part may remove the color. Accordingly, this coloring method is also not commercially acceptable. The third prior method of coloring an SL resin product entailed surface coloring the cured part with a colored lacquer. Again, this surface coating with a lacquer requires an additional processing step that raises the cost of each part and the color is only at the surface of the cured part. Furthermore, the lacquer may undesirably fill small or fine holes or textures in the part, thus making them unuseful or unattractive. The fourth prior art method of coloring SL resins is to add to the uncured SL resin formulation a material that changes color upon irradiation. One such material is SOMOS 7620, an epoxy based stereolithography resin available from DSM Desotech, that becomes dark gray upon laser irradiation. Such color change materials are not acceptable for certain applications. Also, the color change reaction of these materials depends on the irradiation dose and consumes protons that are normally needed for the polymerization of the SL base resins (these protons are formed by the cationic photoinitiator upon irradiation). This makes curing much slower and the physical properties of the cured resin may be adversely affected.

Again, this method like the other three, has not gained widespread acceptance for making cured colored SL products because of these problems.

Accordingly, there is a need for an improved liquid, colored stereolithographic resin that does not have these prior art problems. The present invention offers an answer to that need.

BRIEF SUMMARY OF THE INVENTION

Therefore, one aspect of the present invention is directed to a liquid colored radiation- curable composition useful for the production of three dimensional articles by stereolithography comprising a substantially homogeneous admixture of (1) liquid radical- curable or dual-type stereolithographic resin system and (2) an effective color-imparting amount of at least one soluble dye compound selected from the group consisting of di- and triarylmethane dyes, rhodamine dyes, azo dyes, thiazole dyes, anthraquinone dyes and safranine dyes, said colored radiation-curable composition having substantially the same photospeed as the uncolored resin system and the liquid dye compound does not bleach out during radiation exposure. Another aspect of the present invention is directed to a liquid radiation-curable composition useful for the production of three dimensional articles by stereolithography that comprises a substantially homogeneous admixture of:

(A) at least one cationically polymerizing organic substance;

(B) at least one free-radical polymerizing organic substance; (C) at least one cationic polymerization initiator;

(D) at least one free-radical polymerization initiator; and

(E) an effective color-imparting amount of at least one soluble dye compound selected from the group consisting of di- and triarylmethane dyes, rhodamine dyes, azo dyes, thiazole dyes, anthraquinone dyes and safranine dyes, said colored radiation-curable composition having substantially the same photospeed as the uncolored resin system and the soluble dye compound does not bleach out during radiation exposure.. Another aspect of the present invention is directed to a process for forming a three- dimensional article, said process comprising the steps:

(1) coating a thin layer of a radiation-curable composition as described above onto a surface;

(2) exposing said thin layer imagewise to actinic radiation to form an imaged cross-section, wherein the radiation is of sufficient intensity to cause substantial curing of the thin layer in the exposed areas;

(3) coating a thin layer of the composition onto the previously exposed imaged cross-section;

(4) exposing said thin layer from step (3) imagewise to actinic radiation to form an additional imaged cross-section, wherein the radiation is of sufficient intensity to cause substantial curing of the thin layer in the exposed areas and to cause adhesion to the previously exposed imaged cross-section;

(5) repeating steps (3) and (4) a sufficient number of times in order to build up the three-dimensional article; wherein the radiation-curable composition is that which is described above. Still another aspect of the present invention is directed to three-dimensional articles made by the above process using the above-noted radiation-curable compositions.

The colored stereolithographic resin compositions of the present invention have several advantages over the prior art methods for achieving colored stereolithographic resin products.

The colored parts may have excellent lightfastness that make the cured resins particularly visible. This is especially important for stereolithographic resin products in the jewelry industry, which require good color contrast in thin layers and with the transparent silicone molds from which the SL resin must be removed along a parting line, or in the electronic or watch industries which work with very small parts that need strong colorations to improve magnified viewing of the parts. Another advantage of the present invention is that the inclusion of these selected soluble dye compounds does not result in undesirable viscosity changes in the uncured resin.

Furthermore, the liquid, colored radiation-curable compositions of the present

56 Selected patents

invention do not experience a dropoff in photospeed properties because of the inclusion of these specific dyes.

Since the dyes are soluble in the liquid SL resins, there is no unwanted light scattering, sedimentation or line broadening caused by their inclusion. Those dyes with amino groups in their molecules may also act as stabilizers to extend the shelf life of the liquid dual-type SL resins having cationically and free-radical polymerizing substances. Dyes that have primary or secondary amino groups, hydroxyl groups, carboxyl groups or (meth)acrylate groups in the molecule react with the functional groups of the resin composition and are covalently bound to the resulting network upon irradiation. These selected dyes are not extracted by solvents after curing and do not bleach out upon irradiation. Also they are effective at relatively low concentrations, and do not require a second dying step after curing and have very good long term stability in air and exposure to UV light.

DETAILED DESCRIPTION OF THE INVENTION

The term "(meth)acrylate" as used in the present specification and claims refers to both acrylates and methacrylates.

The term "liquid" as used in the present specification and claims is to be equated with "liquid at room temperature" which is, in general, a temperature range between 5°C and 30°C. The novel compositions herein contain, in the broadest sense, a mixture of at least one liquid radical-curable or dual-type stereolithographic resin system with an effective amount of one or more of the above-noted soluble dye compounds. Preferably, the resin system is a dual-type SL system that is a mixture of at least one cationically polymerizable organic substance; at least one selected free-radical polymerizing organic substance; at least one cationic polymerization initiator and at least one free-radical polymerization initiator; and at least one hydiOxyl-functional compound. These SL compositions may further optionally contain other additives. If the SL resin system is a dual-type resin system, the preferred components are as follows: (A) Cationically Polymerizable Organic Substances

The cationically polymerizable compound may expeditiously be an aliphatic, alicyclic or aromatic polyglycidyl compound or cycloaliphatic polyepoxide or epoxy cresol novolac or epoxy phenol novolac compound and which on average possess more than one epoxide group (oxirane ring) in the molecule. Such resins may have an aliphatic, aromatic, cycloaliphatic, araliphatic or heterocyclic structure; they contain epoxide groups as side groups or these groups form part of an alicyclic or heterocyclic ring system. Epoxy resins of these types are known in general terms and some are commercially available.

Examples of such suitable epoxy resins are disclosed in U.S. Patent No. 6,100,007. Also conceivable is the use of liquid prereacted adducts of epoxy resins, such as those mentioned above, with hardeners for epoxy resins.

It is of course also possible to use liquid mixtures of liquid or solid epoxy resins in the novel compositions. Examples of cationically polymerizable organic substances other than epoxy resin compounds include oxetane compounds, such as trimethylene oxide; 3,3-dimethyloxetane and 3,3-dichloromethyloxetane; 3-ethyl-3-phenoxymethyloxetane; oxolane compounds, such as tetrahydrofuran and

2,3-dimethyl-tetrahydrofuran; cyclic acetal compounds, such as trioxane, 1,3-dioxolane and 1,3,6-trioxan cyclooctane; cyclic lactone compounds, such as β-propiolactone and e-caprolactone; cyclic carbonates, such as propylene carbonate and l,3,dioxolane-2-carbonate; thiirane compounds, such as ethylene sulfide, 1,2-propylene sulfide and thioepichlorohydrin; and thiotane compounds, such as 1,3-propylene sulfide and 3,3- dimethylthiothane.

Examples of such other cationically polymerizable compounds are also disclosed in U.S. Patent No. 6,100,007.

Preferably, the cationically polymerizable compounds of the present invention constitute about 30% to 80% by weight of the radiation-curable composition.

One particularly preferred embodiment of the present invention contains two types of cationically polymerizing organic substances. One type is an alicylic epoxide having at least one to two epoxy groups. The other type is at least one difunctional or higher functional-glycidylether of a polyhydric compound.

(1) Alicyclic Epoxides Having at Least Two Epoxy Groups The cationically polymerizing alicyclic epoxides having at least two epoxy groups include any cationically curable liquid or solid compound that may be an alicyclic polyglycidyl compound or cycloaliphatic polyepoxide which on average possesses two or more epoxide groups (oxirane rings) in the molecule. Such resins may have a cycloaliphatic ring structure that contain the epoxide groups as side groups or the epoxide groups form part of the alicyclic ring structure. Such resins of these types are known in general terms and some are commercially available. Examples of compounds in which the epoxide groups form part of an alicyclic ring system include bis(2,3-epoxycyclopentyl) ether; 2,3 -epoxy cyclopentyl glycidyl ether; 1,2- bis(2,3-epoxycyclopentyloxy)ethane; 3,4-epoxycyclohexylmethyl-3',4'-epoxycyclohexanecarboxylate; 3 ,4-epoxy-6-methyl-cyclohexylmethyl 3 ,4-epoxy-6- methylcyclohexanecarboxylate; di(3,4-epoxycyclohexylmethyl) hexanedioate; di(3,4-epoxy-6-methylcyclohexylmethyl) hexanedioate; ethylenebis(3 ,4-epoxycyclohexane-carboxylate; ethanediol di(3,4-epoxycyclohexylmethyl) ether; vinylcyclohexene dioxide; dicyclopentadiene diepoxide; and 2-(3,4-epoxycyclohexyl-5, 5-spiro-3,4-epoxy)cyclohexane-l,3-dioxane. The preferred alicyclic epoxide is 3,4-epoxycyclohexylmethyl-3',4'-epoxy-cyclohexanecarboxylate which is available as Cyracure UVR 6110.

For this particularly preferred embodiment, these alicyclic epoxides preferably constitute from about 50%) to about 90% by weight, more preferably from about 60% to 85% by weight of the total cationic polymerizing organic substances.

(2) Difunctional or Higher Functional Glycidylethers of a Polyhydric Compound The cationically polymerizing difunctional or higher functionality glycidylethers of a polyhydric compound are obtainable by reacting a compound having at least two free alcoholic hydroxyl groups with a suitably substituted epichlorohydrin under alkaline conditions or in the presence of an acidic catalyst followed by alkali treatment. Ethers of this type may be derived from primary or secondary alcohols, such as ethylene glycol; propane- 1,2-diol or poly (oxy propylene) glycols; propane- 1, 3 -diol; butane- 1,4-diol; poly (oxytetramethylene) glycols; pentane-l,5-diols; hexane-l,6-diol; hexane-

58 Selected patents

2,4-,6-triol; glycerol; 1,1,1-trimethylol propane; bistrimethylol propane; pentaerythritol; sorbitol and the like when reacted with polyepichlorohydrins. Such resins of these types are known in general terms and are commercially available. The most preferred difunctional or higher functional glycidylether is trimethylol propane triglycidylether which is available as Araldite DY-T.

For this particular preferred embodiment, these difunctional or higher functional glycidylether preferably constitute from about 10% to about 50% by weight, more preferably about 15%) to about 40% by weight of the total cationic polymerizing organic substances. (B) Free-Radical Polymerizing Organic Substance

The free radically curable component preferably comprises at least one solid or liquid poly(meth)acrylate, for example, di-, tri-, tetra- or pentafunctional monomeric or oligomeric aliphatic, cycloaliphatic or aromatic acrylates or methacrylates. The compounds preferably have a molecular weight of from 200 to 500. Examples of suitable aliphatic poly(meth)acrylates having more than two

(meth)acrylate groups in, their molecules are the triacrylates and trimethacrylates of hexane- 2,4,6-triol; glycerol or 1,1,1-trimethylolpropane; ethoxylated or propoxylated glycerol or 1,1,1 - trimethylolpropane; and the hydroxyl-containing tri(meth)acrylates which are obtained by reacting triepoxide compounds, for example the triglycidyl ethers of said triols, with (meth)acrylic acid. It is also possible to use, for example, pentaerythritol tetraacrylate, bistrimethylolpropane tetraacrylate, pentaerytliritol monohydroxytriacrylate or -methacrylate, or dipentaerythritol monohydroxypentaacrylate or -methacrylate.

It is additionally possible, for example, to use polyfunctional urethane acrylates or urethane methacrylates. These urethane (meth)acrylates are known to the person skilled in the art and can be prepared in a known manner by, for example, reacting a hydroxyl-terminated polyurethane with acrylic acid or methacrylic acid, or by reacting an isocyanate-terminated prepolymer with hydroxyalkyl (meth)acrylates to give the urethane (meth)acrylate.

Preferably, these free radical polymerizable compounds constitute about 1%> to about 20% of the radiation-curable composition.

One particularly preferred class of free radical polymerizable compounds are aromatic di(meth) acrylate compounds. Optionally, this particular preferred embodiment also contains a trifunctional or higher functionality (meth) acrylate compound.

(1) Aromatic Di(meth)acrylate Compounds The aromatic di(meth)acrylate compounds include difunctional aromatic acrylates or difunctional aromatic methacrylates. Suitable examples of these di(meth)acrylate compounds include di(meth)acrylates of aromatic diols such as hydroquinone; 4,45-dihydroxybis-phenyl; bisphenol A; bisphenol F; bisphenol S; ethoxylated or propoxylated bisphenol A; ethoxylated or propoxylated bisphenol F or ethoxylated or propoxylated bisphenol S. Di(meth)acrylates of this kind are known and some are commercially available.

The most preferred aromatic difunctional (meth)acrylate is bisphenol A diglycidylether diacrylate which is available as Ebecryl 3700.

These aromatic difunctional

(meth)acrylates preferably constitute from 0 to about 20% by weight, more preferably, from about 3% to about 10% by weight of the total liquid radiation-curable composition.

(2) Optional Trifunctional or Higher Functionality (Meth) acrylate Compounds
The optional trifunctional or higher functionality meth(acrylates) are preferably tri-, tetra- or pentafunctional monomeric or oligomeric aliphatic, cycloaliphatic or aromatic acrylates or methacrylates. Such compounds preferably have a molecular weight of from about 200 to about 500.

Examples of suitable aliphatic tri-, tetra- and pentafunctional (meth)acrylates are the triacrylates and trimethacrylates of hexane-2,4,6-triol; glycerol or 1,1,1-trimethylolpropane; ethoxylated or propoxylated glycerol or 1,1,1-trimethylolpropane; and the hydroxyl-containing tri(meth)acrylates which are obtained by reacting triepoxide compounds, for example the triglycidyl ethers of said triols, with (meth)acrylic acid. It is also possible to use, for example, pentaerythritol tetraacrylate, bistrimethylolpropane tetraacrylate, pentaerythritol monohydroxytriacrylate or -methacrylate, or dipentaerythritol monohydroxypentaacrylate or -methacrylate. Examples of suitable aromatic tri(meth)acrylates are the reaction products of triglycidyl ethers of trihydroxy benzene and phenol or cresol novolaks containing three hydroxyl groups, with (meth)acrylic acid.

These higher functional (meth) acrylates are known compounds and some are commercially available, for example from the SARTOMER Company under product designations such as SR295, SR350, SR351, SR367, SR399, SR444, SR454 or SR9041.

The most preferred higher functional (meth)acrylate compound is SARTOMER SR399, which is dipentaerythritol monohydroxy-pentaacrylate.

These optional higher functional (meth)acrylates, if used, preferably constitute about 1% to about 20% by weight, more preferably, from about 5%> to about 15%> by weight of the total liquid radiation-curable composition. (C) Cationic Polymerization Initiators

In the compositions according to the invention, any type of photoinitiator that, upon exposure to actinic radiation, forms cations that initiate the polymerization reaction of the epoxy material(s) can be used. There are a large number of known and technically proven cationic photoinitiators for epoxy resins that are suitable. They include, for example, onium salts with anions of weak nucleophilicity. Examples are halonium salts, iodosyl salts or sulfonium salts, such as described in published European patent application EP 153904, sulfoxonium salts, such as described, for example, in published European patent applications EP 35969, 44274, 54509, and 164314, or diazonium salts, such as described, for example, in U.S. Patent Nos. 3,708,296 and 5,002,856. Other cationic photoinitiators are metallocene salts, such as described, for example, in published European applications EP 94914 and 94915. Other preferred cationic photoinitiators are mentioned in U.S. Patent Nos. 5,972,563 (Steinmann et al); 6,100,007 (Pang et al.) and 6,136,497 (Melisaris et al).

More preferred commercial cationic photoinitiators are UVI-6974, UVI-6976, UVI- 6990 (available commercially from Union Carbide Corp.), CD-1010, CD-1011, CD-1012

(available commercially from Sartomer

60 Selected patents

Corp.), Adekaoptomer SP-150, SP-151, SP-170, SP- 171 (available commercially from Asahi Denka Kogyo Co., Ltd.), Irgacure 261 (available commercially from Ciba Specialty Chemicals Corp.), CI-2481, CI-2624, CI-2639, CI-2064 (available commercially from Nippon Soda Co., Ltd.), and DTS-102, DTS-103, NAT-103, NDS-103, TPS-103, MDS-103, MPI-103, BBI-103 (available commercially from Midori Chemical Co., Ltd.). Most preferred are UVI-6974, UVI 6976, CD-1010, UVI-6970, Adekaoptomer SP-170, SP-171, CD-1012, and MPI-103. The above mentioned cationic photoinitiators can be used either individually or in combination of two or more. The most preferred cationic photoinitiator is a triarylsulfonium hexafluoroantemonate such as UVI-6974 (from Union Carbide).

The cationic photoinitiators may constitute from about 0.01) to about 10 % by weight, more preferably, from about 0.02%> to about 5 by weight, of the total radiation-curable composition. (D) Free Radical Polymerization Initiators

In the compositions according to the invention, any type of photoinitiator that forms free radicals when the appropriate irradiation takes place can be used. Typical compounds of known photoinitiators are benzoins, such as benzoin, benzoin ethers, such as benzoin methyl ether, benzoin ethyl ether, and benzoin isopropyl ether, benzoin phenyl ether, and benzoin acetate, acetophenones, such as acetophenone, 2,2-dimethoxyacetophenone,

4-(phenylthio)acetophenone, and 1,1-dichloroacetophenone, benzil, benzil ketals, such as benzil dimethyl ketal, and benzil diethyl ketal, antbraquinones, such as 2-methylanthraquinone, 2-ethylantlτraquinone, 2-tert-butylanthraquinone, 1-chloroanthraquinone, and 2-amylanthraquinone, also triphenylphosphine, benzoylphosphine oxides, such as, for example, 2,4,6-trimethylbenzoyldiphenylphosphine oxide (Lucirin® TPO), benzophenones, such as benzophenone, and 4,4'-bis(N,N'-dimethylamino)benzophenone,
thioxanthones and xanthones, acridine derivatives, phenazene derivatives, quinoxaline derivatives or 1-phenyl- 1,2-propanedione-2-O-benzoyloxime, 1-aminophenyl ketones or 1-hydroxyphenyl ketones, such as 1-hydroxycyclohexyl phenyl ketone, phenyl (l-hydroxyisopropyl)ketone and 4-isopropylphenyl(l-hydroxyisopropyl)ketone, or triazine compounds, for example, 4'methyl thiophenyl- 1 -di(trichloromethyl)-3 ,5 S-triazine, S-triazine-2-(stylbene)-4,6-bis-trichloromethyl, and paramethoxy stiryl triazine, all of which are known compounds.

Especially suitable free-radical photoinitiators, which are normally used in combination with a He/Cd laser, operating at for example 325 nm, an Argon-ion laser, operating for example at 351 mn, or 351 and 364 mn, or 333, 351, and 364 nm, or a frequency tripled Nd based solid state laser, having an output of 355 mn, as the radiation source, are acetophenones, such as 2,2-dialkoxybenzophenones and 1-hydroxyphenyl ketones, for example 1-hydroxycyclohexyl phenyl ketone, 2-hydroxy-l-{4-(2-hydroxyethoxy)phenyl}-2-methyl-l- propane, or 2-hydroxyisopropyl phenyl ketone (also called 2-hydroxy-2,2-dimethylacetophenone), but especially 1-hydroxycyclohexyl phenyl ketone. Another class of free-radical photoinitiators comprises the benzil ketals, such as, for example, benzil dimethyl ketal. Especially an alpha-hydroxyphenyl ketone, benzil dimethyl ketal, or 2,4,6-trimethylbenzoyldiphenylphosphine oxide is used as photo-initiator. Another class of suitable free radical photoinitiators comprises the ionic dye-counter ion compounds, wliich are capable of absorbing actinic rays and producing free radicals, which can initiate the polymerization of the acrylates. The compositions according to the invention that comprise ionic dye-counter ion compounds can thus be cured in a more variable manner using visible light in an adjustable wavelength range of 400 to 700 nanometers. Ionic dye- counter ion compounds and their mode of action are known, for example from published European-patent application EP 223587 and U.S. Patent Nos. 4,751,102; 4,772,530 and 4,772,541.

Especially preferred is the free-radical photoinitiator 1-hydroxycyclohexylphenyl ketone, which is commercially available as Irgacure 184. The free-radical initiators constitute from about 0.01% to about 6% by weight, most preferably, from about 0.01% to about 3% by weight, of the total radiation curable composition. (E) Optional Additives

If necessary, the resin composition for stereolithography applications according to the present invention may contain other materials in suitable amounts, as far as the effect of the present invention is not adversely affected. Examples of such materials include radical- polymerizable organic substances other than the aforementioned cationically polymerizable organic substances; heat-sensitive polymerization initiators, antifoaming agents, leveling agents, thickening agents, flame retardants and antioxidants. Optionally, hydroxyl-functional compounds may be added to dual-type SL resins.

The hydroxyl-functional compounds may be any organic material having a hydroxyl functionality of at least 1, and preferably at least 2. The material may be liquid or solid that is soluble or dispersible in the remaining components. The material should be substantially free of any groups which inhibit the curing reactions, or which are thermally or photolytically unstable.

Preferably, the hydroxyl-functional compounds are either aliphatic hydroxyl functional compounds or aromatic hydroxyl functional compounds.

The aliphatic hydroxyl functional compounds that may be useful for the present compositions include any aliphatic-type compounds that contain one or more reactive hydroxyl groups. Preferably these aliphatic hydroxyl functional compounds are multifunctional compounds (preferably with 2-5 hydroxyl functional groups) such as multifunctional alcohols, polyether-alcohols, and polyesters.

Preferably the organic material contains two or more primary or secondary aliphatic hydroxyl groups. The hydroxyl group may be internal in the molecule or terminal. Monomers, oligomers or polymers can be used. The hydroxyl equivalent weight, i.e., the number average molecular weight divided by the number of hydroxyl groups, is preferably in the range of about 31 to 5000.

Representative examples of suitable organic materials having a hydroxyl functionality of 1 include alkanols, monoalkyl ethers of poly oxyalkylenegly cols, monoalkyl ethers of alkylene-glycols, and others.

62 Selected patents

Representative examples of useful monomeric polyhydroxy organic materials include alkylene glycols and polyols, such as 1,2,4-butanetriol; 1,2,6- hexanetriol; 1,2,3-heptanetriol; 2,6-dimethyl-l,2,6-hexanetriol; 1,2,3 -hexanetriol; 1,2,3-butanetriol; 3-methyl-l,3,5- pentanetriol; 3,7,11,15 -tetramethyl- 1 ,2,3 -hexadecanetriol; 2,2,4,4-tetramethyl- 1,3-cyclobutanediol; 1,3-cyclopentanediol; trans- 1,2-cyclooctanediol; 1,16-hexadecanediol; 1,3- propanediol; 1 ,4- butanediol; 1,5-pentanediol; 1,6- hexanediol; 1,7-heptanediol; 1,8- octanediol; 1 ,9-nonanediol; trimethylolpropane; and pentaerythritol.

Representative examples of useful oligomeric and polymeric hydroxyl-containing materials include polyoxyethylene and polyoxypropylene glycols and triols of molecular weights from about 200 to about 10,000; polytetramethylene glycols of varying molecular weight; copolymers containing pendant hydroxyl groups formed by hydrolysis or partial hydrolysis of vinyl acetate homo- and copolymers, polyvinylacetal resins containing pendant hydroxyl groups; hydroxyl-terminated polyesters and hydroxyl-terminated polylactones; hydroxyl-functionalized polyalkadienes, such as polybutadiene; and hydroxyl-terminated polyethers.

Other hydroxyl-containing monomers are 1 ,4-cyclohexanedimethanol and aliphatic and cycloaliphatic monohydroxy alkanols.

Other hydroxyl-containing oligomers and polymers include hydroxyl and hydroxyl/epoxy functionalized polybutadiene, polycaprolactone diols and triols, ethylene/butylene polyols, and combinations thereof. Examples of polyether polyols are also polypropylene glycols of various molecular weights and glycerol propoxylate-block-ethoxylate triol, as well as linear and branched polytetrahydrofuran polyether polyols available in various molecular weights, such as for example 250, 650, 1000, 2000, and 2900 MW. Preferred hydroxyl functional compounds are for instance simple multifunctional alcohols, polyether-alcohols, and/or polyesters. Suitable examples of multifunctional alcohols are, trimethylolpropane; trimethylolethane; pentaeritritol; di-pentaeritritol; glycerol; 1,4- hexanediol; 1,4-hexanedimethanol and the like. Suitable hydroxyfunctional polyetheralcohols are, for example, alkoxylated trimethylolpropane, in particular the ethoxylated or propoxylated compounds, polyethyleneglycol-200 or -600 and the like.

Suitable polyesters include, hydroxyfunctional polyesters from diacids and diols with optionally small amounts of higher functional acids or alcohols. Suitable diols are those described above. Suitable diacids are, for example, adipic acid; dimer acid; hexahydrophthahc acid; 1,4-cyclohexane dicarboxylic acid and the like. Other suitable ester compounds include caprolactone based oligo- and polyesters such as the trimethylolpropane-triester with caprolactone, Tone®301 and Tone®310, both available from Union Carbide Chemical and Plastics Co. (UCCPC). The ester based polyols preferably have a hydroxyl number higher than about 50, in particular higher than about 100. The acid number preferably is lower than about 10, in particular lower than about 5. The most preferred aliphatic hydroxyl functional compound is trimethylolpropane, which is commercially available.

The aromatic hydroxyl functional compounds that may be useful for the present compositions include aromatic-type compounds that contain one or more reactive hydroxyl groups. Preferably these aromatic hydroxyl functional compounds would include phenolic compounds having at least 2 hydroxyl groups as well as phenolic compounds having at least 2 hydroxyl groups which are reacted with ethylene oxide, propylene oxide or a combination of ethylene oxide and propylene oxide.

The most preferred aromatic functional compounds include bisphenol' A, bisphenol S, ethoxylated bisphenol A, ethoxylated bisphenol S.

These hydroxyl functional compounds are preferably present from about 3% to about 20%) by weight, more preferably from about 5% to about 16% by weight, of the total liquid radiation-cured composition.

Two other preferred optional additives are pyrene and benzyldimethylamine. The former acts as a sensitizer and the latter acts as a stabilizer for the cationic polymerization. If used, optional additives such as these preferably constitute from about 0.001 to about 5% by weight of the total liquid radiation-curable compositions. Examples of preferred liquid dual-type SL resins include AccuGen 100 ND, Accura SilO ND and RPCwre 400 ND, all available commercially from 3D Systems, Inc. of Valencia, CA.

An example of a liquid radical-curable SL resin is KPCure 550 ND, also available from 3D Systems, Inc.

Soluble Dye Compounds

The selected soluble dye compounds used in the radiation-curable compositions of the present invention are members of the classes of diarylmethane and triarylmethane dyes, rhodamine dyes, azo dyes, thiazole dyes, anthraquinone dyes and safranine dyes that do not substantially lower the photospeed characteristics of SL resin systems being used and do not bleach out during photoexposure (e.g. during laser exposure). Not all members of these five (5) classes of liquid dyes pass these additional characteristics (see Comparative Examples below). These dyes are added in effective color-imparting amounts, preferably in amounts from about 0.001 to about 0.1 percent by weight of the total radiation-curable composition to impart a sufficient amount of color to the cured composition. Preferred are dyes containing amino,- hydroxyl-carboxyl- or (meth)acrylate groups that are covalently bound to the network prior to or upon irradiation. The preferred dyes are Crystal Violet, Rhodamin B, Coomassie Brilliant Blue R, Basic Red 9, Disperse Orange 11, Disperse Red 19, Thioflavine T, Auramine O and Safranine O. These dyes do not affect the photospeed of the SL composition, as almost identical working curves are obtained before and after the addition of the dye. A viscosity stabilizing effect is observed for dual cure systems with dyes containing amino groups. An effective color-imparting amount is obtained when good color contrasts or sufficient color saturation is present to improve magnified viewing of parts or to impart the desired visual and aesthetic effect.

Formulation Preparation

The novel compositions can be prepared in a known manner by, for example, premixing individual components and then mixing these premixes, or by mixing all of the components using customary devices, such as stirred vessels, in the absence of light and, if desired, at slightly elevated temperature.

One preferred mixing method is to premix ingredients (A), (B), (C), (D) and optionally (E) as forming a regular dual-type stereolithographic resin composition. The previously made mixture of ingredients (A), (B), (C), (D) and optionally (E) are then combined to the liquid dye compound or compounds. These ingredients are thoroughly mixed in a suitable mixer or mixers for a sufficient amount of time.

Process of Making Cured Three-Dimensional Articles The above-noted novel compositions can be polymerized by irradiation with actinic light, for example by means of electron beams, X-rays, UV or VIS light, preferably with radiation in the wavelength range of about 280 to about 650 nm. Particularly suitable are laser beams of HeCd, argon or nitrogen, semiconductor and also metal vapor and d:YAG or other Nd based solid state lasers with frequency multiplication. This invention is extended throughout the various types of lasers existing or under development that are to be used for the stereolithography process, e.g., solid state, argon ion, helium cadmium lasers, and the like. The person skilled in the art is aware that it is necessary, for each chosen light source, to select the appropriate photoinitiator and, if appropriate, to carry out sensitization. It has been recognized that the depth of penetration of the radiation into the composition to be polymerized, and also the operating rate, are inversely proportional to the absorption coefficient and to the concentration of the photoinitiator. In stereolithography it is preferred to employ those photoinitiators which give rise to the highest number of forming free radicals or cationic particles and have a high absorption coefficient at the operating wavelength.

The invention additionally relates to a method of producing a cured product, in which compositions as described above are treated with actinic radiation. For example, it is possible in this context to use the novel compositions as adhesives, as coating compositions, as photoresists, for example as solder resists, or for rapid prototyping, but especially for stereolithography. When the novel mixtures are employed as coating compositions, the resulting coatings on wood, paper, metal, ceramic or other surfaces are clear and hard. The coating thickness may vary greatly and can, for instance, be from 0.01 mm to about 1 mm. Using the novel mixtures it is possible to produce relief images for printed circuits or printing plates directly by irradiation of the mixtures, for example by means of a computer-controlled laser beam of appropriate wavelength or employing a photomask and an appropriate light source. One specific embodiment of the above mentioned method is a process for the stereolithographic production of a three-dimensional shaped article, in which the article is built up from a novel composition with the aid of a repeating, alternating sequence of steps (a) and (b); in step (a), a layer of the composition, one boundary of which is the surface of the composition, is cured with the aid of appropriate radiation within a surface region which corresponds to the desired cross-sectional area of the three-dimensional article to be formed, at the height of this layer, and in step (b) the freshly cured layer is covered with a new layer of the liquid, radiation-curable composition, this sequence of steps (a) and (b) being repeated until an article having the desired shape is formed. In this process, the radiation source used is preferably a laser beam, which with particular preference is computer-controlled.

In general, the above-described initial radiation curing, in the course of which the so-called green models are obtained which do not as yet exhibit adequate strength, is followed then by the final curing of the shaped articles by heating and/or further irradiation.

The present invention is further described in detail by means of the following Examples and Comparisons. All parts and percentages are by weight and all temperatures are degrees Celsius unless explicitly stated otherwise.

EXAMPLES The tradenames of the components as indicated in the Examples below correspond to the chemical substances in the following Table 1 :

TABLE 1

Protocol for Testing

The photosensitivity of the liquid formulations was determined on so-called window panes. In this determination, single-layer test specimens were produced using different laser energies, and the layer thicknesses obtained were measured. The plotting of the resulting layer thickness on a graph against the logarithm of the irradiation energy used gave a "working curve." The slope of this curve is termed Dp (given in mm or mils). The energy value at which the curve passes through the x-axis is termed Ec (and is the energy at which gelling of the material still just takes place; cf. P. Jacobs, Rapid Prototyping and Manufacturing, Soc. of Manufacturing Engineers, 1991, p. 270 ff). Color stability for postcure exposure:

The colored resin formulations noted below were tested for color stability by evaluating their main absorption band in the visible spectrum (400-750 nm range) after a brief exposure (2 min. under a 125 W Hg lamp) and 1 hour in the center of a 3D Systems, Inc. PCA unit with 10 fluorescent UV tubes (or another 15 min. under the 125 W Hg lamp, as mentioned in each example). The spectroscopy samples were prepared as thin films of 0.25 mm sandwiched between 2 microscope slides with appropriate spacers. The absorption maxima were compared before and after UV-curing and color stability was determined sufficient if the decrease of absorption was less than 30%.

Formulation Example 1

100 g AccuGen™ 100 ND resin and 0.01 g Crystal Violet [CAS No. 548-62-9] (dye class: triarylmethane) were heated under stirring to 60° for 2 hours. A homogeneous, dark blue solution was obtained. Photosensitivity measurements (window-panes) give Dp-3.88 and Ec=7.67. The change in absorption before and after curing (bleaching out) was less than about 30%.

Formulation Example 2

100 g AccuGen™ 100 ND resin and 0.025g Rhodamin B [CAS No. 81-88-9] (dye class: rhodamine) were heated under stirring to 60° for 2 hours. A homogeneous, pink, fluorescing solution was obtained. Photosensitivity measurements (window-panes) give Dp=4.1 and Ec=12.1. No color change was detected after UV curing of the composition. Formulation Example 3

100 g Accura® si 10 ND resin and 0.015 g Coomassie Brilliant Blue R 250 [CAS No. 6104-59-2] (dye class: triarylmethane) were heated under stirring to 60° for 2 hours. A homogeneous, dark blue solution was obtained. Photosensitivity measurements (window-panes) give Dp=5.4 and Ec=17.7. Stability: pealc @ 593 nm before exposure to 3D Systems' PCA unit 0.252 absorption units (AU,) after 1 hour exposure to 3D Systems' PCA

unit 0.238 AU (-8%).

Formulation Example 4

99.4 g Accura® si 10 ND resin, 0.6 g pyrene and 0.005 g Crystal Violet [CAS No. 548-62-9] were heated under stirring to 60° for 2 hours. A homogeneous, dark blue solution was obtained. Photosensitivity measurements (window-panes) give Dp=2.3 and Ec=14.2. Stability: peak @ 597 nm before exposure to Hg lamp/25 cm: 0.177 AU, after 15' exposure to Hg lamp/25 cm: 0.123 AU (-30%).

Formulation Example 5

99.8 g RPCure 400 ND resin, 0.2 g pyrene and 0.015 g Basic Red 9 [[CAS no. 569-61-9] (dye class: triarylmethane) were heated under stirring to 60° for 2 hours and then over night at 40° C. A homogeneous, dark purple solution was obtained. Photosensitivity measurements (window-panes) give DP= 3.3 , and Ec= 15.5. The absorption change after curing was less than about 20%>.

Formulation Example 6

99.4g Accura® si 10 ND resin, 0.6 g pyrene and 0.015 g Basic Red 9 [CAS No. 569-61-9] (dye class: triarylmethane) were heated under stirring to 60° for 2 hours and then over night at 40° C. A homogeneous, dark purple solution was obtained. Photosensitivity measurements (windowpanes) give Dp=2.76 and Ec=l 6.34. Stability: peak @ 560 nm before exposure

0.823 AU, after 1 hour exposure to Hg lamp 0.664 AU (-19%) (shifted to higher wavelength). Formulation Example 7

100 g KPCure 400 ND resin, 0.2 g pyrene and 0.01 g Crystal Violet [CAS No. 548-62-9] were heated under stirring to 60° for 2 hours. A homogeneous, dark blue solution was obtained. Photosensitivity measurements (window-panes) give Dp=3 and Ec=l 1.5. The absorption change (bleaching out) after curing was less than about 30%.

Formulation Example 8

100 g RPCure 550 ND resin (an acrylate-based SL resin) and 0.015g Crystal Violet [CAS No. 548-62-9] were heated under stirring to 60° for 2 hours. A homogeneous, dark blue solution was obtained. Photosensitivity measurements (window-panes) give Dp=4.4 and Ec=8.8. The absorption change (bleaching out) after curing was less than about 30%>.

Formulation Example 9

400 g Accura® si 10 resin without Amine-Stabilizer and 0.06 g Basic Red 9 [CAS No. 569-61-9] (dye class: triarylmethane, containing amino groups) were heated under stirring at 60° for 1 hour. A dark purple solution was obtained. The highly stable colored resin did not gel when maintained at 110°C for more than 21 hours.

Formulation Example 10

200 g AccuGen™ 100 ND resin and 0.04 g Disperse Red 19 [CAS No. 2734-52-3] (dye class: Azo) were heated at 60° under stirring for 1 hour. A red solution was obtained. Photosensitivity measurements give Dp=4.3 and Ec=12.7. The absorption change (bleaching out) curing was less than about 20%.

Formulation Example 11

200 g Accura® si 10 resin and 0.03 g Thioflavine T [CAS No. 2390-54-7] (dye class: Thiazole) were heated at 60° under stirring for 1 hour. A clear and brilliant yellow solution was obtained. Photosensitivity was determined to give Dp=5.2 and Ec-12.5. No color change was detected after UV-curing. Formulation Example 12

200 g Accura® si 10 resin and 0.02 g Safranine O [CAS No. 477-73-6 (dye class: Safranine) were heated at 60° under stirring for 1 hour. A bright orange solution was obtained. The absorption change after curing was less than 20%.

Application Example 13

A part was built with the resin from Example 4 on a Viper si2™ SLA® system, using the high resolution mode with 0.05 mm layer thickness. A blue part was obtained with a peak absorption at 597 nm. After post-curing in a PCA unit for 1 hour, there was a slight decrease in color intensity.

Application Example 14

A part was built with the resin from Example 6 on a Viper si2™ SLA® system, using the high resolution mode with 0.05 mm layer thickness. A dark purple part was obtained with a peak absorption at 560 nm. After post-curing in a PCA unit for 1 hour, there was a very slight shift in color toward red. The colored part was immersed in acetone and stirred for 6 hours. No coloration of the acetone solution and no decoloration of the outside of the part was observed.

Application Example 15

A rectangular plate of 10x20x1.5 mm was built with the resin from Example 4 on a Viper si2™ SLA® system, using the high resolution mode with 0.05 mm layer thickness. A blue part was obtained with a peak absorption of 0.91 A.U. at 597 nm. After post-curing in front of a 125 W mercury lamp for 1 hour at a distance of 25 cm, the absorption changed to 0.83 A.U.

Comparative Example 1

200 g Accura® si 10 ND resin and 0.03 g Meldola's Blue [CAS No. 7057-57-0] (dye class: Oxazin) were heated at 60° under stirring for 1 hour. A blue solution was obtained.

After several hours this solution bleached out completely and became colorless. Solidification of this uncolored solution by UV exposure gives colorless parts. Comparative Examples 2-5

Colored solutions were obtained using the same procedures as described in the above examples 1 to 11 with the following dyes:

Eosin Scarlet [CAS No. 548-24-3] (dye class: Fluorone)

Eriochrome Cyanine [CAS No. 3564-18-9] (dye class: Triarylmethane)

Basic Blue 41 [CAS No. 12270-13-2] (dye class: Thiazole)

Acid Alizarin Violet [CAS No. 2092-55-9] (dye class: Azo)

During exposure of these solutions to UV light, the colors disappeared completely and only colorless parts could be obtained. These liquid dye compounds are not useful for the present invention.

While the invention has been described above with reference to specific embodiments thereof, it is apparent that many changes, modifications, and variations can be made without departing from the inventive concept disclosed herein. Accordingly, it is intended to embrace all such changes, modifications and variations that fall within the spirit and broad scope of the appended claims. All patent applications, patents and other publications cited herein are incorporated by reference in their entirety.

68 Selected patents

FDM Printer

Selected patents 69

Multiextruder with only one drive

Patent number	US7604470 B2
Publication type	Grant
Application number	US 11/396,845
Published	20. Oct. 2009
Application	3. Apr. 2006
Priority	3. Apr. 2006
Fee status	Paid
Also published as	CN101460050A, 5 et al»
Inventors	Benjamin N. Dunn, 3 et al»
Original Assignee	Stratasys, Inc.

Comment:

This patent describes a mechanism that can feed the filament to two independent nozzles with only one motor.

BRIEF DESCRIPTION OF THE DRAWINGS

FIG. 1 is a side view of an extrusion-based layered manufacturing system with a portion broken away to show an extrusion head of the present invention.

FIG. 2A is a front perspective view of the extrusion head having a toggle-plate assembly positioned in a build state.

FIG. 2B is a front perspective view of the extrusion head, where the toggle-plate assembly is positioned in a support state.

FIG. 3 is a left side view of the extrusion head 20, where the toggle-plate assembly is positioned in the build state.

FIG. 4A is an expanded view of a left-portion of the toggle-plate assembly shown in FIG. 2A.

FIG. 4B is an expanded view of a right-portion of the toggle-plate assembly shown in FIG. 2B.

FIG. 5 is a sectional view of section 5-5 taken in FIG. 3, showing the toggle-plate assembly.

FIG. 6A is a front exploded view of the extrusion head.

FIG. 6B is a rear exploded view of the extrusion head.

FIGS. 7A-7E are expanded views of a toggle bar of the extrusion head in use for positioning the toggle-plate assembly between the build state and the support state

70 Selected patents

Drawings (8 von 15)

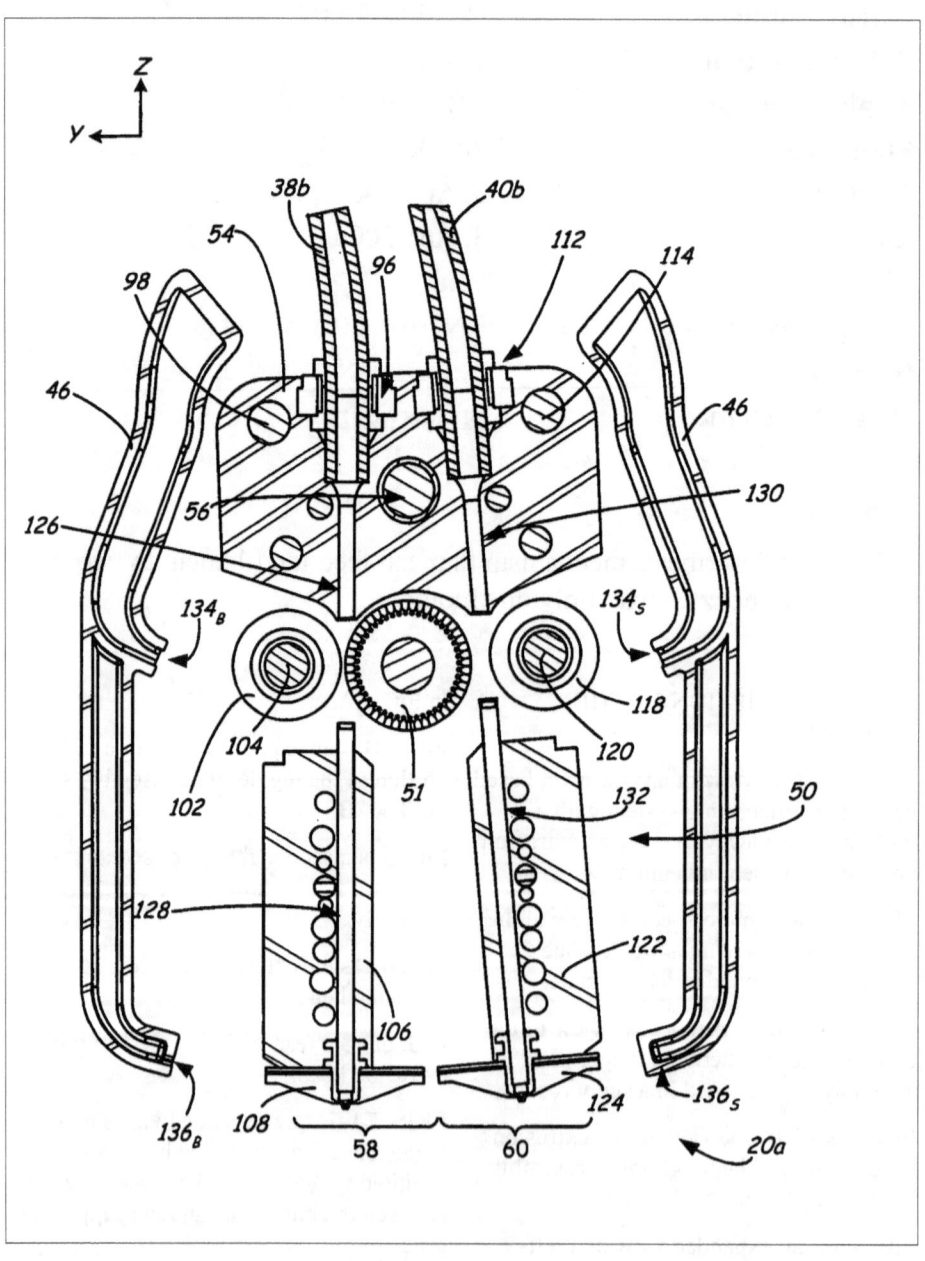

Selected patents 71

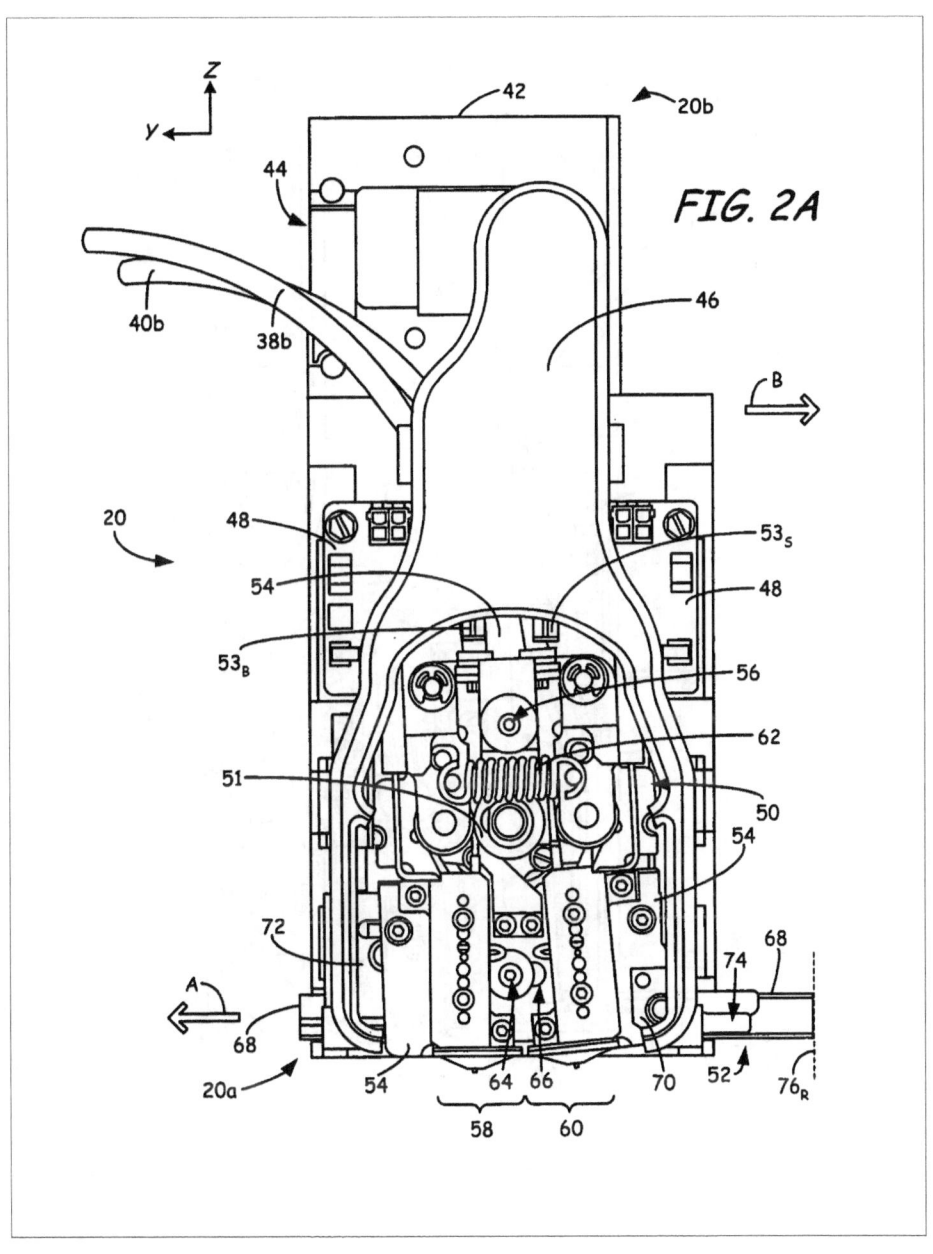

FIG. 2A

72 Selected patents

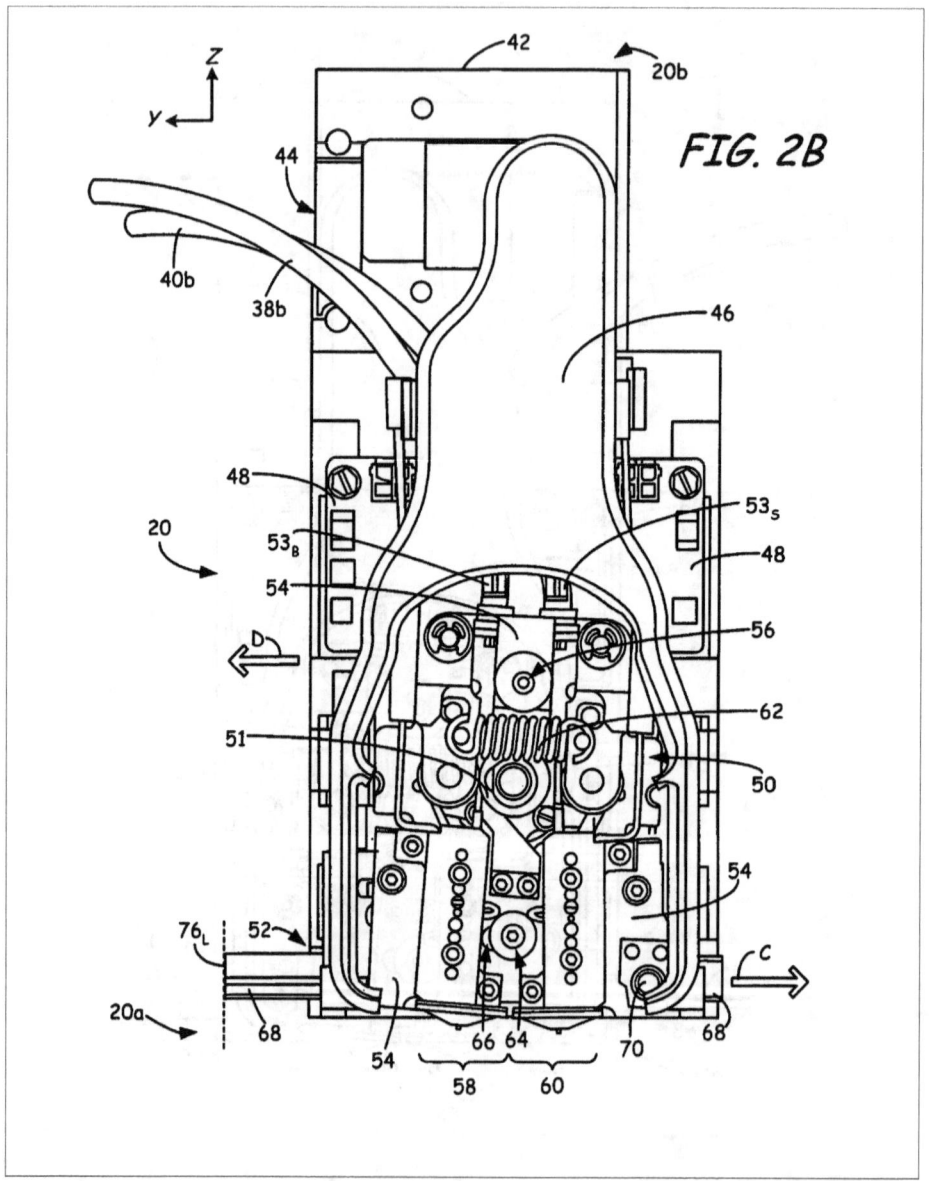

FIG. 2B

Selected patents 73

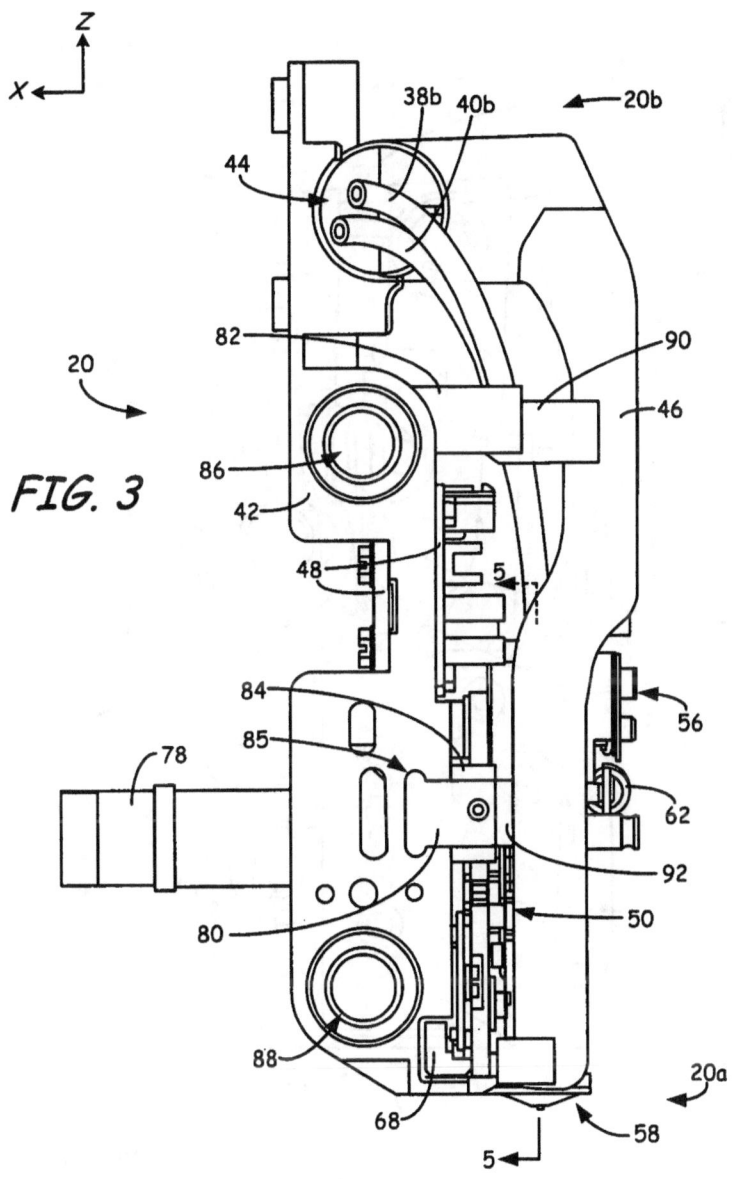

FIG. 3

74 Selected patents

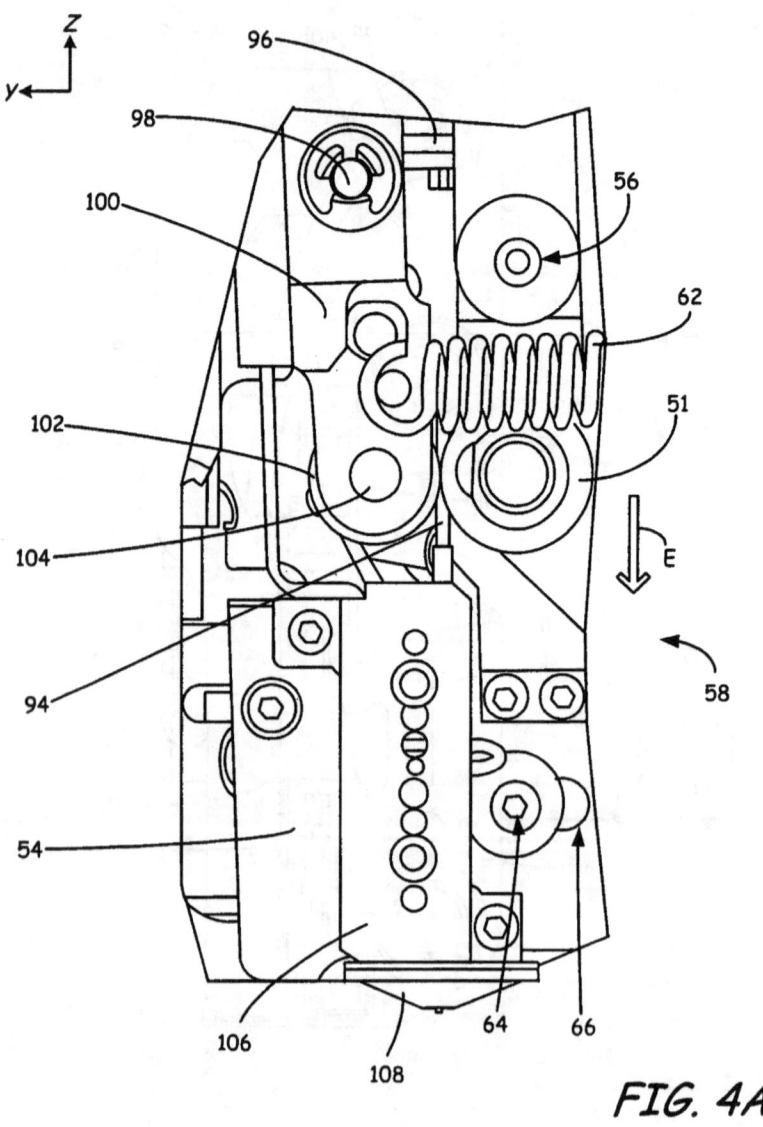

FIG. 4A

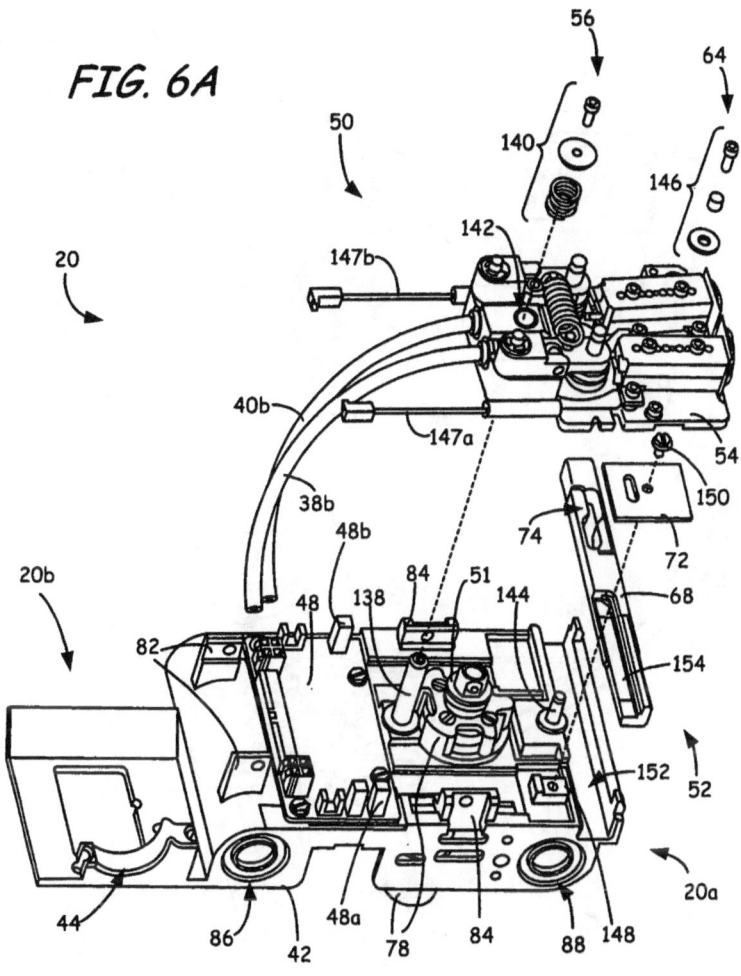

FIG. 6A

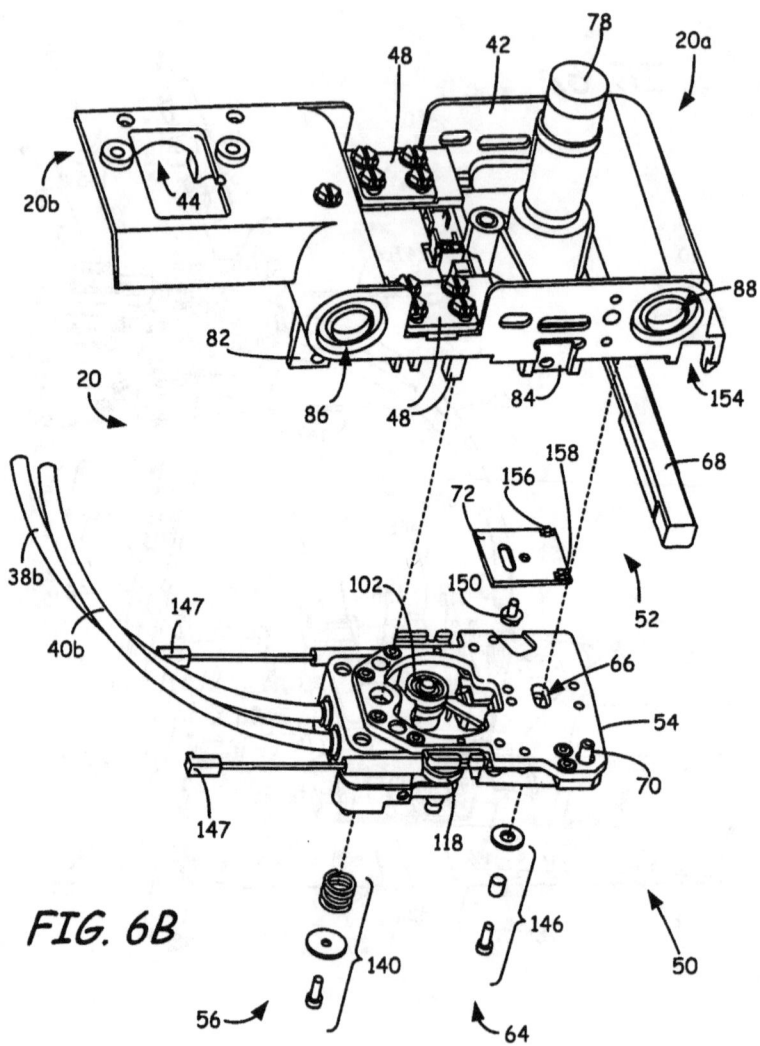

FIG. 6B

Selected patents 77

Filament Kassette

Patent number	EP1299217 B1
Publication type	Grant
Application number	EP20010952987
Published	1. Dez. 2004
Application	12. Juli 2001
Priority	13. Juli 2000
Also published as	CN1216726C, 18 et al»
Inventors	Steve Brose, 8 et al»
Applicant	Stratasys Inc.

BRIEF SUMMARY OF THE INVENTION

[0010]

The present invention is a filament cassette and a filament loading assembly for supplying modeling filament in a three-dimensional deposition modeling machine. The filament cassette has a chamber which contains a rotatable spool of filament, a filament path which leads from the chamber to an exit orifice, and a means for advancing filament from the spool along the filament path and out of the exit orifice. In a first preferred embodiment, the means for advancing comprises a roller which receives a rotational force from an external drive wheel. In a second preferred embodiment, the means for advancing comprises a roller that is manually operated by a user. The filament cassette is airtight to protect moisture sensitive filament from the environment.

[0011]

The filament cassette receiver is on the modeling machine and comprises a conduit and a drive means. The conduit receives a filament strand provided from the exit orifice of the cassette and guides the filament strand along a filament path of the machine. The drive means advances the filament strand through the conduit in response to control signals from a controller. The filament cassette may be unloaded from the machine by controlling the drive means to wind the filament strand back through the conduit and into the cassette. In a preferred embodiment, the latching means engages and disengages the filament cassette in a loading bay of the modeling machine, to both maintain and allow removal of the cassette. One or more filament loading assemblies may be used in a single modeling machine, each receiving a filament cassette.

BRIEF DESCRIPTION OF THE DRAWINGS

[0012]

Figure 1 is a perspective, diagrammatic view of a generic filament-feed used in an extrusion-based three-dimensional modeling machine such as is known in the prior art.

Figure 2 shows a first embodiment of a filament cassette being loaded into a first embodiment of a three-dimensional modeling machine.

Figure 3 is a partially exploded view of the first embodiment of a filament cassette.

Figure 4 is an exploded view of the spool and lower shell of the filament cassette shown in Figure 3.

Figure 5 is a detailed view of the (partially) exploded filament cassette shown in Figure 3, showing a strand of filament in the filament path and a mounted circuit board.

Figure 5A is a detailed view of an alternative configuration of a circuit board mounted onto the first embodiment of a filament cassette.

Figure 6 is a perspective view of the first embodiment of the filament cassette, showing the bottom surface, side and trailing edge of the cassette.

Figure 7 is a front elevation of the first embodiment of the filament cassette.

Figure 8 is top plan view of a first embodiment of a filament cassette receiver of the present invention.

Figure 9 is a front elevation of the first embodiment of the filament cassette receiver.

Figure 10 is a perspective, detailed view of the filament drive shown in Figure 8 as part of the filament cassette receiver.

Figure 11 A is a top plan view of the first embodiment of a filament cassette loaded into the filament cassette receiver of Figure 8, showing the filament drive assembly in a disengaged position.

Figure 11 B is a top plan view of a filament cassette loaded into the cassette receiver of Figure 6, showing the filament drive assembly in an engaged position.

Figure 12 is a perspective detailed view of the filament drive assembly of Figure 11 B engaging a roller on the first embodiment of the filament cassette.

Figure 13 is a perspective view of a filament loading assembly in a second embodiment of the three-dimensional modeling machine.

Figure 14 is a perspective view of a second embodiment of the filament cassette.

Figure 15 is an exploded view of the second embodiment of the filament cassette (guide block not shown).

Figure 16 is a perspective view of the canister base of the second embodiment of the filament cassette.

Figure 17 is a perspective view of the guide block shown in Figure 14, with the access door open.

Figure 18 is an exploded view of the filament cassette receiver shown in Figure 13.

Figure 19 is a sectional view of the filament loading assembly of Figure 13, taken along a line 19-19 thereof.

Drawings (11 von 20)

Selected patents

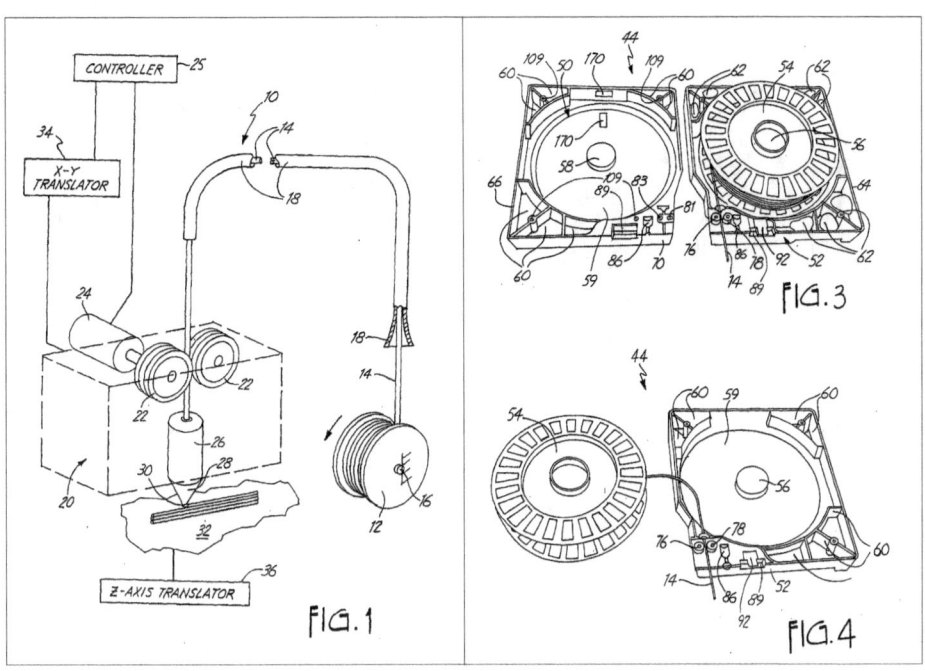

FIG. 1
FIG. 3
FIG. 4

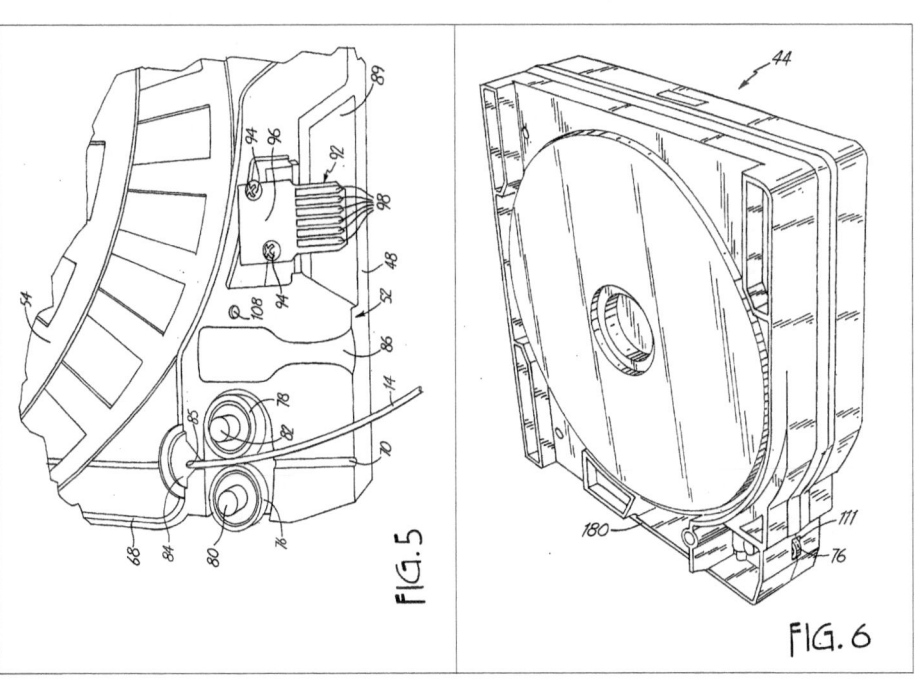

FIG. 5
FIG. 6

80 Selected patents

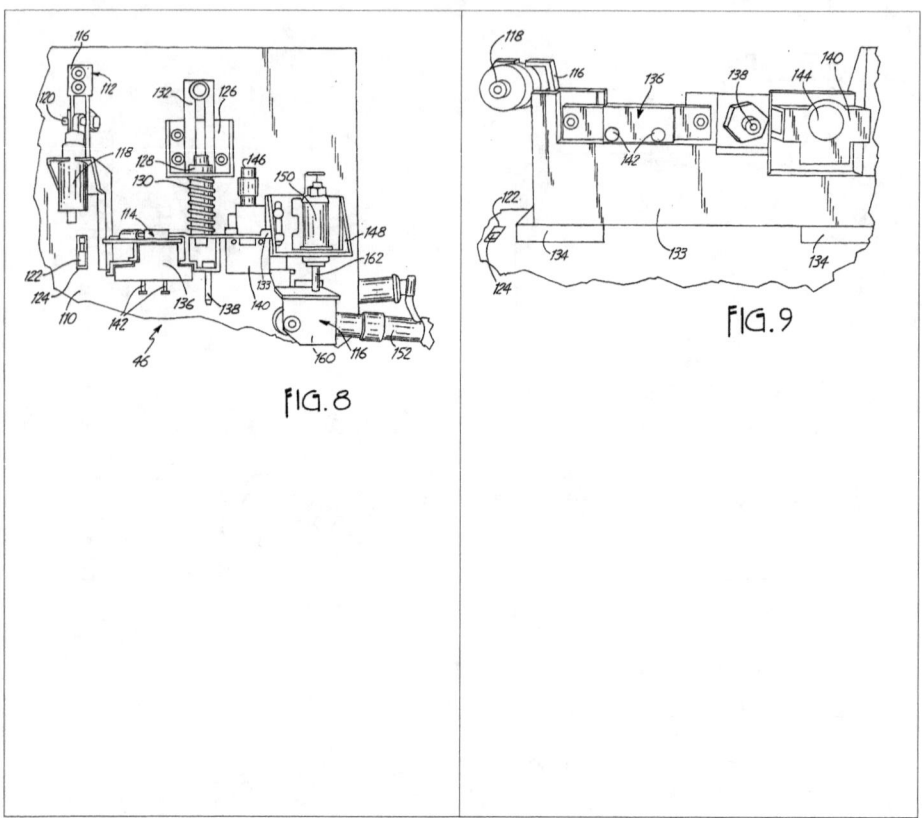

FIG. 8

FIG. 9

Selected patents 81

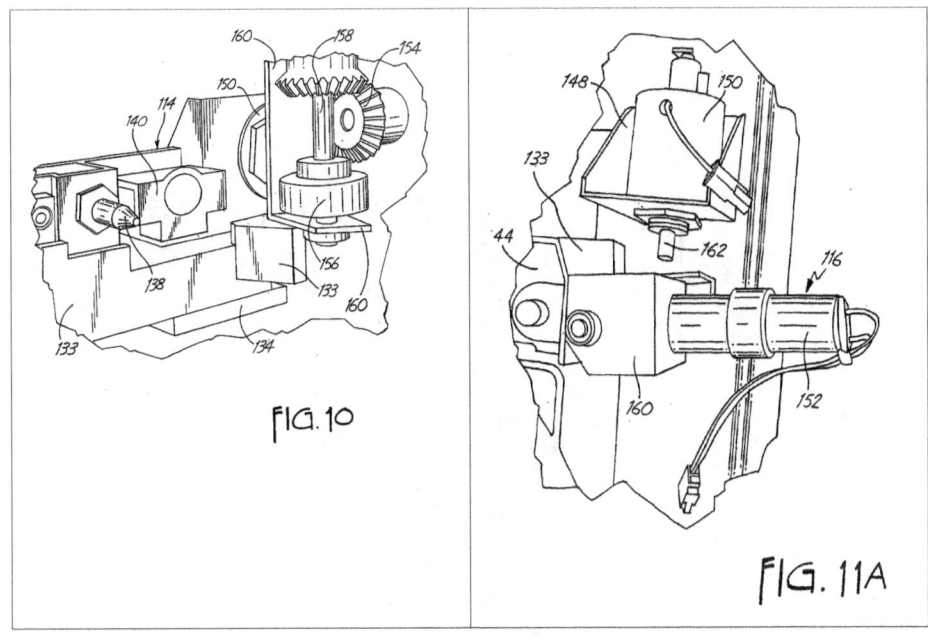

FIG. 10

FIG. 11A

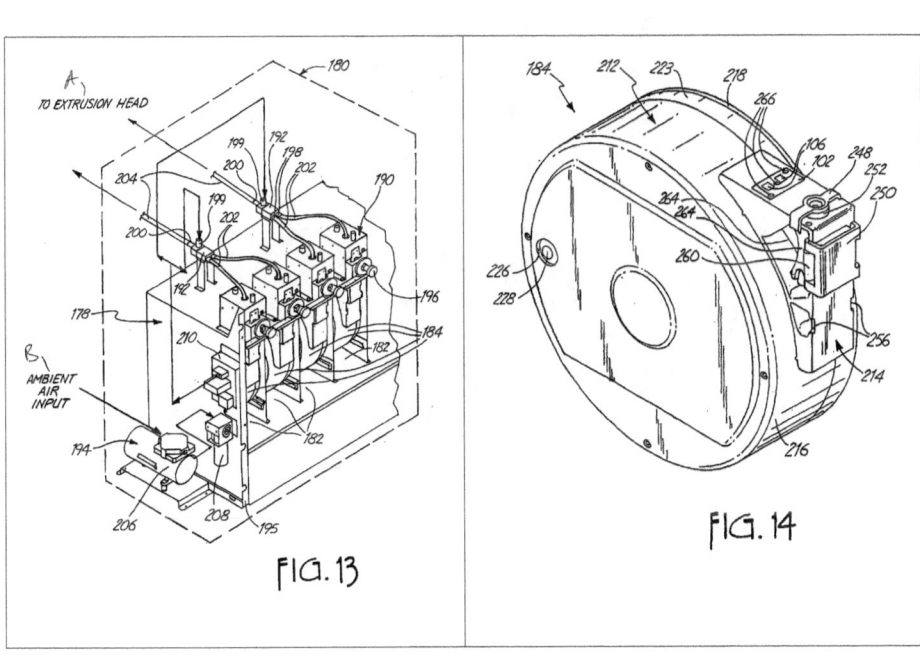

FIG. 13

FIG. 14

82 Selected patents

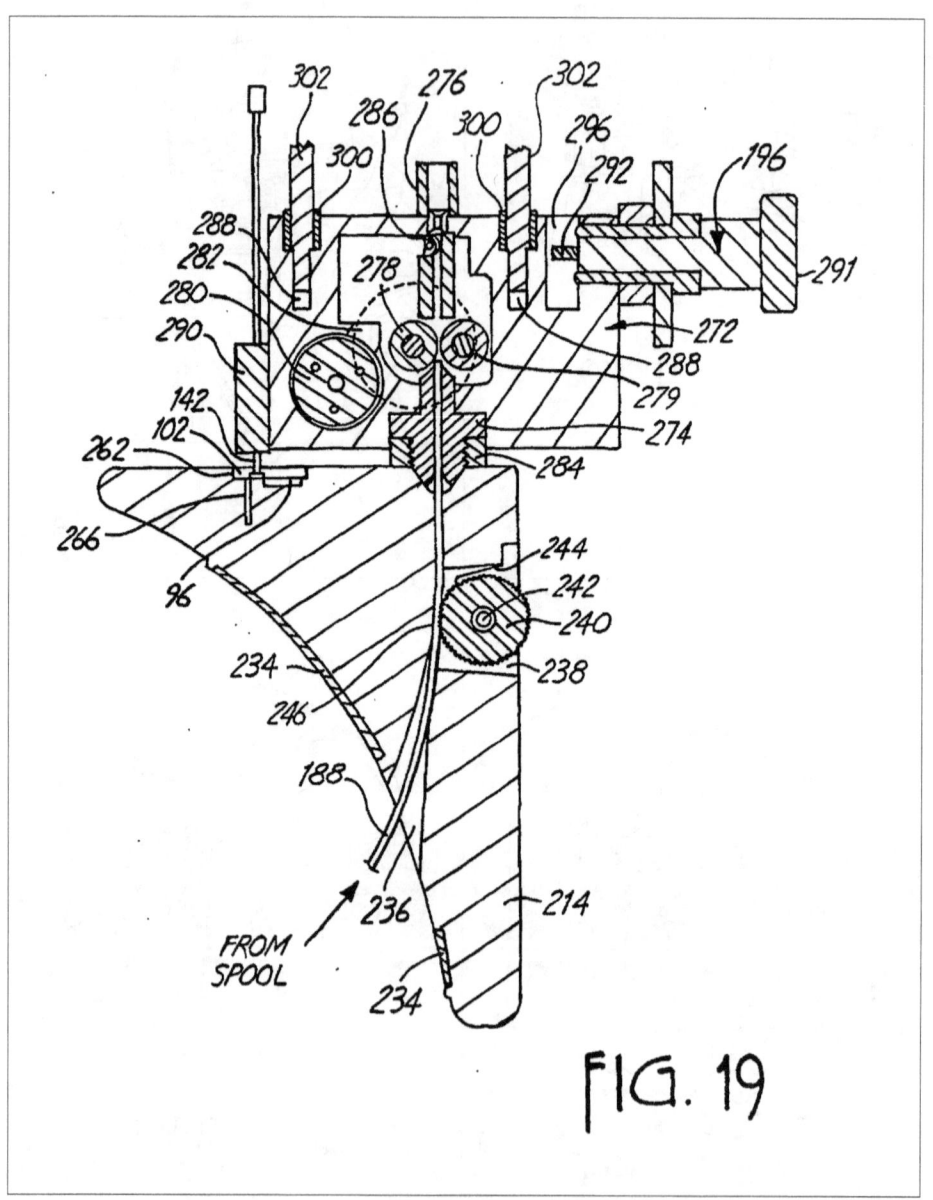

FIG. 19

CLAIMS

1. A filament cassette (44, 184) comprising:

   a chamber (59) containing a rotatable spool (54, 186) of coiled modeling filament (14, 188) made flowable when heated;
   a filament path (70, 236) leading from the chamber (59) to an exit orifice (72, 238); and
   a means (116, 278, 279, 280, 282) for advancing a strand of the filament (14, 188) from the spool (54, 186) along the filament path (70, 236); **characterized in that**:
   said chamber (59) contains a supply of desiccant (62); and
   said chamber (59) is air tight;

   wherein said filament cassette (44, 184) is used for supplying modeling filament to a three-dimensional modeling machine (40, 180).

2. The filament cassette of claim 1, wherein the means for advancing comprises:
   a pair of rollers (76, 78) mounted opposite one another along the filament path so as to grip the filament strand therebetween.

3. The filament cassette of claim 2, wherein each roller in said pair of rollers is passive and one roller in said pair is a follower roller (76) that is accessible to receive an external drive force.

4. The filament cassette of claim 3, wherein the follower roller (76) has a floating axis of rotation in a direction perpendicular to the filament path, allowing the follower roller to move away from the filament path in the absence of an external applied force, thereby relieving pressure on a filament strand in the filament path.

5. The filament cassette of claim 1, wherein the means for advancing comprises a knurled roller (240) mounted opposite a wall of the filament path so as to grip the filament strand therebetween.

6. The filament cassette of claim 5, wherein the knurled roller (240) is accessible to receive an external drive force.

7. The filament cassette of claim 1, wherein the means for advancing comprises a raised contour in a wall of the filament path over which a strand of filament is positioned, the raised contour being accessible such that an external propulsion force may be applied to the strand of filament.

8. The filament cassette of claim 7, wherein the raised contour is defined by the surface of an idler wheel.

9. The filament cassette of claim 1, wherein a retainer (84) positions the filament strand in the filament path (70) while blocking air flow along the filament path (70).

10. The filament cassette of claim 1, wherein the means for advancing is accessed through a door (250) having a compressible seal (258) on an interior surface thereof for preventing air flow to the chamber.

11. The filament cassette of claim 1, wherein the chamber and coiled filament are dried to a water content of less than 700 ppm.

12. The filament cassette of claim 1, wherein a removable seal (248) blocks air from entering the exit orifice.

84 Selected patents

13. The filament cassette of claim 1 and further comprising:
an electronically readable and writeable data store (96) mounted on the cassette so as to be accessible to an external controller and containing information about the filament.

14. A method for supplying modeling filament to a three-dimensional modeling machine, the method comprising the steps of:
inserting into a loading bay (42, 182) of the modeling machine (40, 180) a cassette (44, 184) according to any one of claims 1-13;
engaging a strand of the filament (14, 188) in the filament path (70, 236) of the cassette (44, 184); and
advancing the filament strand (14,188) out of the exit orifice (72, 238) of the cassette (44, 184) and into a conduit (140, 274) of the modeling machine.

15. The method of claim 14 and further comprising the step of preventing air flow to the chamber while filament (188) is withdrawn from the cassette (184).

16. The method of claim 14 or 15 and further comprising the steps of:
identifying that the filament (14, 188) remaining in the cassette (44, 184) has reached a predetermined minimum length; and
automatically driving the filament strand (14, 188) back out of the conduit (140, 274), in response to the minimum length identification, so that the cassette (44, 184) can be removed and replaced.

17. A method for assembling the filament cassette of any one of claims 1-13, comprising the steps of:
loading the spool (54, 186) of coiled filament (14, 188) into the chamber (59); and
sealing the cassette after the filament (14, 188) is loaded, to make the chamber (59) air tight.

18. The method of claim 17, and further comprising the step of:
heating the filament cassette (44, 184) in an oven until the chamber has a water content of less than 700 ppm, before performing the sealing step.

19. The filament cassette of claim 1, and further comprising:
a cavity (88) for aligning the cassette with a cassette receiver (46) of the modeling machine.

Grayscale rendering in 3D printing

Patent number	US20130095302 A1
Publication type	Application
Application number	US 13/478,233
Published	18. Apr. 2013
Application	23. May 2012
Priority	14. Oct. 2011
Inventors	Nathaniel B. Pettis, Adam G. Mayer, Anthony James Buser
Original Assignee	Nathaniel B. Pettis, Adam G. Mayer, Anthony James Buser

Classifications (9), Legal Events (2)

Comment:

The patent describes a method on how to use two different filaments in order to achieve a 3D structured surface or a truly colored 3D object on a printed 3D model.

The title of the publication „*Grayscale rendering in 3d printing*" is a bit misleading. The applicant Makerbot Inc. also admits that:

Accordingly, the term grayscale as used herein is intended to describe any value or array of values that specify portions of an image according to a controllable or selectable scale of values, and does not imply any specific color or translucence of build materials that are overlapped according to a "grayscale" image of such values

The invention however is less a grayscale apparatus, but a solution that allows to use a 2-component 3D print to achieve specific object properties, such as color or structured surface.

86 Selected patents

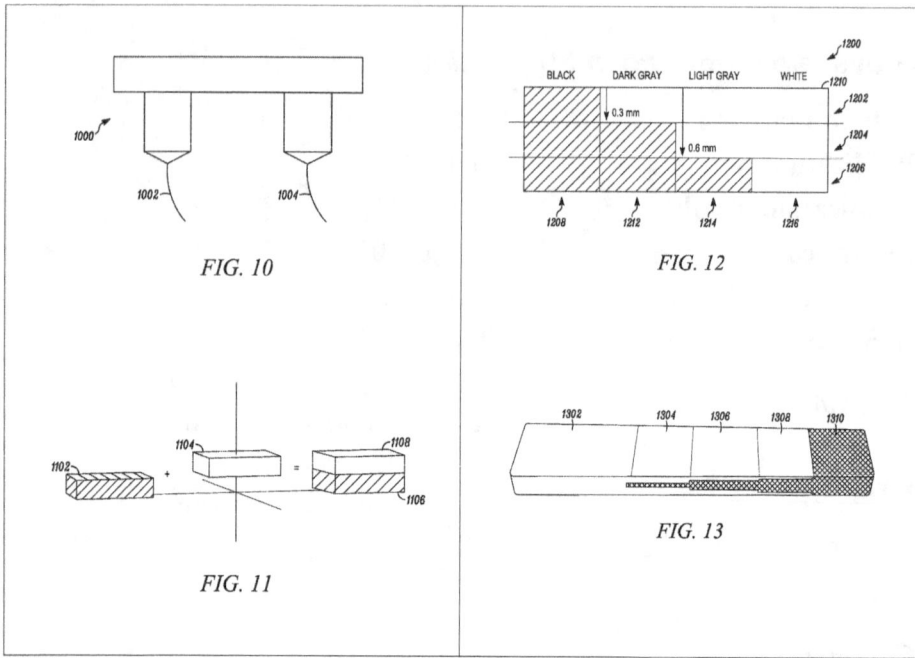

FIG. 10

FIG. 12

FIG. 11

FIG. 13

1. A method comprising: obtaining a grayscale pattern for an image, the grayscale pattern including a predetermined number of grayscale levels; determining a pattern for a plurality of two-dimensional layers of a first material and a second material to impart the grayscale pattern onto an exterior surface of an object, the first material being substantially opaque and the second material being substantially translucent; and fabricating the object with the plurality of two-dimensional layers using the first material and the second material according to the pattern.

2. The method of claim 1 wherein the image is a digital photograph.

3. The method of claim 1 wherein the predetermined number of grayscale levels includes three, four, or five grayscale levels.

4. The method of claim 1 wherein the first material is a black build material.

5. The method of claim 1 wherein the second material is a white build material.

6. The method of claim 1 wherein the exterior surface is a z-axis top or bottom surface of the object.

7. The method of claim 1 wherein the exterior surface is a sidewall of the object.

8. The method of claim 1 wherein fabricating the object includes extruding successive layers of material in two-dimensional patterns derived from a computer model of the object.

9. The method of claim 1 wherein the first material includes a colored material having at least one of a red color, a blue color, and a green color.

10. The method of claim 1 wherein the first material includes a colored material having at least one of a cyan color, a magenta color, a yellow color, and a black.

11. The method of claim 9 further

comprising a third material having a color different from the colored material.

12. The method of claim 1 wherein obtaining the grayscale pattern includes receiving the image in a digital image format and converting the image to a grayscale image conforming to the predetermined number of grayscale levels.

13. A structure comprising a lamination of multiple layers of at least two build materials, the structure including an exterior surface having a grayscale image comprising regions with three or more grayscale levels, each one of the three or more grayscale levels rendered using a different number and arrangement of layers of the at least two build materials, wherein the at least two build materials include an opaque build material and a translucent build material.

14. The structure of claim 13 wherein the at least two build materials include multiple overlaps of the opaque build material and the translucent build material in at least one region.

15. A system for additive fabrication comprising: a supply of two materials including a substantially opaque material and a substantially translucent material; an extruder controllable to selectively deliver one of the two materials; an x-y-z positioning system controllable to move the extruder relative to a build platform; and a controller configured to operate the extruder and the x-y-z positioning system to fabricate an object from the two materials, the controller including a processor configured to receive a digital image and to control delivery of the two materials in a manner that imparts a grayscale image of the digital image to an exterior surface of the object by selectively layering the substantially translucent material over the substantially opaque material to obtain one or more predetermined grayscale levels of the grayscale image.

16. The system of claim 15 wherein the digital image is a digital photograph.

17. The system of claim 15 wherein the digital image is a texture image for repeated instantiation on the exterior surface.

18. The system of claim 15 wherein the one or more predetermined grayscale levels includes three, four, or five grayscale levels.

19. The system of claim 15 wherein the substantially opaque material is a black build material.

20. The system of claim 15 wherein the substantially translucent material is a white build material.

21. The system of claim 15 wherein the exterior surface is a z-axis top or bottom surface of the object.

22. The system of claim 15 wherein the exterior surface is a sidewall of the object.

Description

RELATED APPLICATIONS

[0001] This application claims the benefit of U.S. Prov. App. No. 61/547,132 filed on Oct. 14, 2011, the entire content of which is incorporated herein by reference.

BACKGROUND

[0002] In an additive three-dimensional fabrication system, a physical object can be realized from a digital model by depositing successive layers of a build material that accumulate to provide the desired form.

[0003] There remains a need for techniques to render of grayscale images on exterior surfaces of printed three-dimensional objects.

88 Selected patents

SUMMARY

[0004] An additive three-dimensional fabrication process uses multiple build materials with different optical properties (e.g., color, opacity) at different surface depths to achieve grayscale-rendered images on exterior surfaces thereof.

BRIEF DESCRIPTION OF THE FIGURES

[0005] The invention and the following detailed description of certain embodiments thereof may be understood by reference to the following figures:

[0006] FIG. 1 is a block diagram of a three-dimensional printer.

[0007] FIG. 2 is a block diagram of a controller architecture for a three-dimensional printer.

[0008] FIG. 3 is a flowchart of a process for imparting surface texture to a three-dimensional object.

[0009] FIG. 4 is a flowchart of a process for fabricating an object with sub-pixel surface features.

[0010] FIG. 5 is a block diagram of a data structure describing an object for three-dimensional fabrication.

[0011] FIG. 6 shows an extrusion of a build material.

[0012] FIG. 7 shows an extrusion of a build material.

[0013] FIG. 8 shows an extrusion of a build material.

[0014] FIG. 9 depicts an exterior surface of an object fabricated from a digital model using a varying deposition rate.

[0015] FIG. 10 shows a multi-extruder.

[0016] FIG. 11 shows a basic fabrication building block for achieving grayscale affects.

[0017] FIG. 12 depicts a multilayer structure and corresponding grayscale exterior surface effects.

[0018] FIG. 13 depicts a grayscale surface with interdigitated layers.

[0019] FIG. 14 shows a flow chart of a process to fabricate a structure with grayscale images on an exterior surface.

Selected patents 89

Smothing method for layered deposition modeling

Patent number	EP1501669 B1
Publication type	Grant
Application number	EP20030716969
Published	24. Nov. 2010
Application	4. Apr. 2003
Priority	17. Apr. 2002
Also published as	CA2482848A1, 9 et al»
Inventors	JR. William R. c/o STRATASYS INC. PRIEDEMAN, 1 et al»
Applicant	Stratasys, Inc.

Drawings

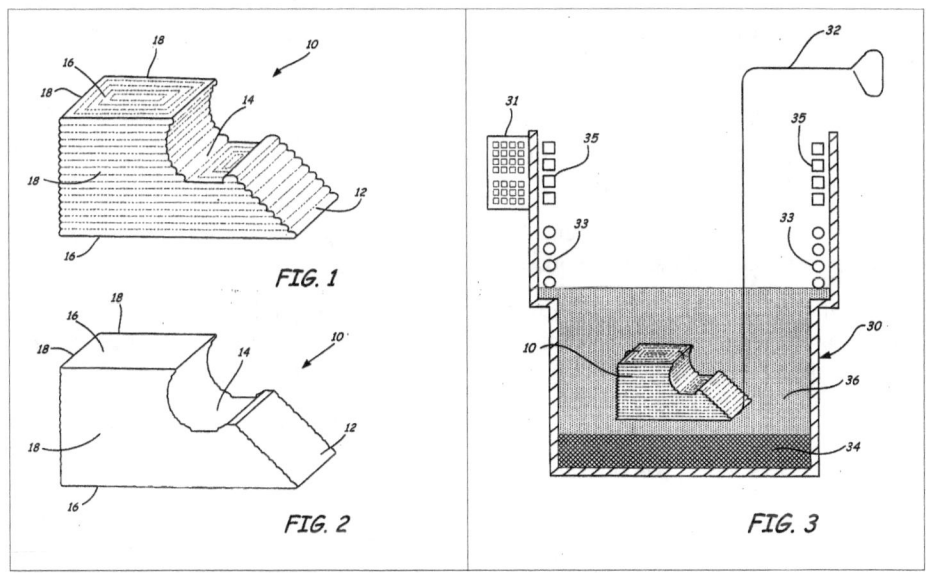

FIG. 1

FIG. 2

FIG. 3

CLAIMS

1. A method for making a three-dimensional object comprising the steps of: building an object from a polymeric or wax modeling material using a layered manufacturing rapid prototyping technique; and smoothing an object surface by exposing the object to vapors of a solvent that transiently softens the modeling material.

2. The method of claim 1, wherein the layered manufacturing technique is fused deposition modeling.

3. The method of claim 1, where the modeling material is a thermoplastic resin.

4. The method of claim 3, wherein the thermoplastic resin comprises at least about 50 weight percent of an amorphous thermoplastic selected from the group consisting of ABS, polycarbonate, polyphenylsulfone, polysulfone, polystyrene, polyphenylene ether, amorphous polyamides, acrylics, poly(2-ethyl-2-oxazoline), and blends thereof.

5. The method of claim 4, wherein the solvent is selected from the group consisting of methylene chloride, an n-Propyl bromide solution, perchloroethylene, trichloroethylene, and a hydrofluorocarbon fluid.

6. The method of claim 1, wherein the modeling material is selected from the group consisting of thermoplastics, green metals dispersed in a polymeric binder, green ceramics dispersed in a polymeric binder, and jetting wax.

7. The method of claim 6, wherein the modeling material is glassfilled nylon.

8. The method of claim 1, and further comprising the step of: selecting a length of time during which the object is to be exposed to the solvent vapors as a function of concentration of the solvent vapors, prior to the smoothing step.

9. The method of claim 8, and further comprising the step of: reducing the concentration of solvent vapors so that the selected exposure time will increase.

10. The method of claim 1, and further comprising the step of: masking selected portions of the object surface with a substance that will inhibit smoothing of the selected portions, prior to the step of smoothing the object surface.

11. The method of claim 10, wherein the masking substance is applied using an automatic process.

12. The method of claim 11, wherein the automatic process is a jetting process.

13. The method of claim 11, wherein the automatic process is a fused deposition modeling process.

14. The method of claim 11, and further comprising the step of: identifying the selected portions of the object surface for masking accordingly to their geometry.

15. The method of claim 14, and further comprising the step of: identifying the selected portions of the object surface for masking accordingly to their radii of curvature.

16. The method of claim 11, and further comprising the step of: identifying the selected portions of the object surface using a software algorithm that creates a digital representation of the surface area to be protected.

17. The method of claim 16, wherein digital data identifying the surface area to be protected is stored in an s.tl file.

18. The method of claim 1, and further comprising the step of: ~~~ 13 creating a digital mask of selected portions of the object surface for which smoothing is not desired, using a haptic input interface.

19. The method of claim 1, wherein the building step comprises pre-distorting certain object features so that said features will obtain a desired geometry following the smoothing step.

20. The method of claim 19, and further comprising the steps of: providing an

initial object representation in a digital format, the initial object representation having a surface geometry; and modifying the initial object representation to pre-distort certain features of the surface geometry, producing a modified object representation; wherein the object built in the building step has a geometry defined according to the modified object representation; and wherein the desired geometry attained following the smoothing step approximately matches that of the initial object representation.

21. A method for eliminating surface roughness of an object built from a modeling material using a layered manufacturing rapid prototyping technique, comprising the step of: reflowing a surface of the object by exposing the object to vapors of a solvent that transiently softens the modeling material.

22. The method of claim 21, where the modeling material is a thermoplastic resin.

23. The method of claim 22, wherein the thermoplastic resin comprises at least about 50 weight percent of an amorphous thermoplastic selected from the group consisting of ABS, polycarbonate, polyphenylsulfone, polysulfone, polystyrene, polyphenylene ether, amorphous polyamide, methyl methacrylate, poly(2-ethyl-2-oxazoline), and blends thereof.

24. The method of claim 23, wherein the solvent is selected from the group consisting of methylene chloride, an n-Propyl bromide solution, perchloroethylene, trichloroethylene, and a hydrofluorocarbon fluid.

25. The method of claim 21, wherein the modeling material is selected from the group consisting of thermoplastics, green metals dispersed in a polymeric binder, green ceramics dispersed in a polymeric binder, and jetting wax.

26. The method of claim 25, wherein the modeling material is glass-filled nylon.

27. The method of claim 21, and further comprising the step of: masking selected portions of the object surface with a substance that will inhibit smoothing of the selected portions, prior to the step of reflowing the surface.

28. The method of claim 27, wherein the masking substance is applied using an automatic process.

29. The method of claim 28, wherein the automatic process is a jetting process.

30. The method of claim 28, wherein the automatic process is a fused deposition modeling process.

31. The method of claim 28, and further comprising the step of: identifying the selected portions of the object surface for masking accordingly to their geometry.

32. The method of claim 31, and further comprising the step of: identifying the selected portions of the object surface for masking accordingly to their radii of curvature.

33. The method of claim 28, and further comprising the step of: identifying the selected portions of the object surface using a software algorithm that creates a digital representation of the surface area to be protected.

34. The method of claim 33, wherein digital data identifying the surface area to be protected is stored in an .stl file.

35. The method of claim 28, and further comprising the step of: identifying the selected portions of the object surface

for masking using a haptic input interface.

36. A method for making a three-dimensional object comprising the steps of: providing an initial object representation in a digital format, the initial object representation having a surface geometry; modifying the initial object representation to pre-distort certain features of the surface geometry, producing a modified object representation; building an object as defined by the modified object representation, from a modeling material using a layered manufacturing technique; and vapor smoothing surfaces of the object to produce a finished object, the finished object having a surface geometry that approximately matches that of the initial object representation.

37. The method of claim 36, and further comprising the step of: identifying features of the surface geometry for pre-distortion according to their radii of curvature.

Selected patents 93

A digitally active 3-D object creation system

Patent number	US8454345 B2
Publication type	Grant
Application number	US 12/836,582
Published	4. June 2013
Application	15. Juli 2010
Priority	16. Jan. 2003
Also published as	CA2513291A1, 109 et al»
Inventors	Kia Silverbrook
Original Assignee	Silverbrook Research Pty Ltd

Patent citations (26), Classifications (20), Legal Events (2)

Comment:

The applicant describes a method is designed to print multiple layer of a 3D model in one pass.

The usage of multiple nozzle does not only allow to print an object in different colors and with different properties in one model, but he also sketches a machine that is able to print all required components, such as electronics etc. in one process.

FIELD OF INVENTION

[0001] This invention relates to the creation of objects using digital additive manufacturing and more particularly to creating working objects that may be electrically and/or mechanically active.

CO-PENDING APPLICATIONS

[0002] Various methods, systems and apparatus relating to the present invention are disclosed in the following co-pending applications filed by the applicant or assignee of the present invention simultaneously with the present application:

[0003] DAM01S, DAM02US, DAM03US, DAM04US, DAM05US, DAM06US, DAM07US, DAM08US, DAM09US, DAM11US, DAM12US, DAM13US, DAM14US.

[0004] The disclosures of these co-pending applications are incorporated herein by cross-reference. Each application is temporarily identified by its docket number. This will be replaced by the corresponding USSN when available.

94 Selected patents

BACKGROUND

[0005] Digital additive manufacturing is a process by which an object is defined three dimensionally by a series of volume elements (hereinafter referred to as voxels). The object is then produced by creating/laying down each voxel one at a time, in rows at a time, swaths at a time or layers at a time.

[0006] There exists systems that use modified inkjet type technology to 'print' material onto a substrate, so building the object. However, these systems typically utilize a single scanning printhead and are only useful for producing non-working models.

SUMMARY OF INVENTION

[0007] In the present invention we digitally define objects as a series of voxels and have a production line that creates objects by creating each voxel. The production line simultaneously creates different portions of objects with each portion produced by a separate subsystem. In the preferred embodiments each portion is for different products and so the system builds up multiple objects simultaneously. The finished objects may be of identical or of different designs. The portions may be of any shape that may be digitally described. Portions produced by different subsystems may have different shapes.

[0008] In the preferred embodiments each and every voxel has the same dimension. However, a product may be defined by voxels of more than one size.

[0009] The portions are preferably created or laid down onto one or more substrates. In the preferred embodiments one or more substrates are provided, each having a substantially planar surface upon which material is deposited. Each of the surfaces preferably moves in it's own plane past the subsystems but does not otherwise move relative to the subsystems. Each substrate need not have a planar surface upon which material is deposited and the surface may be of any shape desired. The substrate may move past the subsystems at a constant velocity along a path or may move in steps. The substrate may also be caused to rotate about one or more axes, as it moves between subsystems, as it moves past subsystems, as it is stationary or in combinations of these. In the preferred embodiments a continuous substrate moves past the subsystems of the production line at a substantially constant velocity.

[0010] The portions of the object produced by successive subsystems preferably lie on top of each other but could be spaced apart from each other, positioned end on end, adjacent to each other or in any other configuration. As an example, a substrate having a cylindrical surface may be caused to rotate about its axis as it moves past a subsystem, so that material deposited extends in a helix on the cylindrical surface.

[0011] The portions are preferably layers of the object and the layers are preferably two dimensional, i.e. they lie in a flat plane. However, the layers need not be planar. The layers may have a constant thickness. Layers having differing thickness within the one layer are within the scope of the invention. Similarly objects may be made with multiple layers that do not have the same thickness characteristics.

[0012] In the preferred embodiments each layer is planar, is made up of voxels of constant size and all layers have the same dimensions. Alternate layers may be offset relative to each other. Preferably alternate layers are offset by half a voxel in one or both of two mutually orthogonal directions.

[0013] Because voids may be formed in the object, when we refer to a 'layer' we mean a layer as defined, which may include voids, not a continuous layer of material or materials.

[0014] In preferred embodiments each layer is created by one or more printheads. In the preferred embodiments the printheads are arranged along a longitudinally extending production line and one or more substrates move past the printheads, and apart from the first layer, the printheads print onto a previously printed layer of material(s). The printheads for all layers operate simultaneously and so whilst the first printhead is printing a first layer of a first set of one or more products, the second printhead is printing a second layer of a second set of one or more products and the third printhead is printing a third layer of a third set. Thus if we have a product 1000 layers high we have 1000 different subsystems, one for each layer. These 1000 subsystems operate to simultaneously produce 1000 different layers of 1000 sets of products.

[0015] In the preferred embodiments the printheads extend across the width of the substrate and are capable of printing across the full substrate width simultaneously i.e. they do not scan or raster when printing but are stationary. This enables a substrate to be moved past the printheads at a substantially constant speed, with the printheads printing rows of material onto the substrate. The substrate speed is matched to the row width and printhead cycle time so that the substrate has moved the width of the rows printed for each printhead cycle. Thus the next row or rows printed by each printhead will be printed next to a previously printed row or rows. In the preferred embodiments the printheads each print two rows simultaneously for increased substrate speed.

[0016] Whilst substrate width printheads are preferred, scanning type printheads may be utilized to simultaneously produce multiple layers of objects.

[0017] The terms "printhead", "print" and derivatives thereof are to be understood to include any device or technique that deposits or creates material on a surface in a controlled manner.

[0018] Each layer is printed by one or more printheads. We refer to the printhead or printheads for a layer as a 'layer group'. As used in the description and claims it is to be understood that a layer group may have only one printhead that prints one material and the use of "group" is not to be taken to require multiple printheads and/or multiple materials.

[0019] Whilst the layer groups may have multiple printheads, each layer group preferably prints only one layer at any one time, which may be made of one material or multiple materials. The number of printheads in each layer is usually determined by the number of materials to be printed. In the preferred embodiments each material is printed by a separate

96 Selected patents

printhead and any additional printheads are only to enable a single layer to have multiple materials within it. This is because the materials being printed have a relatively high viscosity compared to water based inks and so require large supply channels. Thus in the description it is assumed that each printhead only prints one material. Thus if the system is capable of printing N different materials, at one printhead per material, this requires N printheads per layer. However, this is not to preclude printheads that print multiple materials.

[0020] However, because each printhead could print more than one material or multiple printheads could print the same material, there does not have to be a one to one ratio between the number of printheads and the number of different materials. It is not critical that all the layer groups are identical, and in some embodiments it is desirable that different layer groups print different numbers of materials or different combinations of materials.

[0021] It will be appreciated that for production efficiency more than one printhead in a layer group may print the same material. Where the refill rate of the printheads for different materials is substantially the same, speed increases can only be achieved when all materials have the same number of printheads. However if one material requires a much longer refill time, provision of two or more printheads for that material alone may allow increased substrate speed.

[0022] When different materials are printed, they may need to be printed at different temperatures and so in preferred embodiments the printheads of a layer group may be maintained at different temperatures.

[0023] Even if only one material is used there are advantages in printing material compared to molding. For example, it is possible to create voids in the finished product. The voids may be of any complexity that may be digitally described. Thus, any pattern of dots may be missing from the object created.

[0024] The number of separate products that may be printed simultaneously depends on the printhead width, the product size across the substrate, the product size along the substrate and the longitudinal spacing between products.

[0025] The preferred systems are capable of printing most materials that are required but there are circumstances where a discrete object may be incorporated into products. Examples of such discrete objects include semiconductor microchips, which can be manufactured in more appropriate materials and in much smaller feature sizes than in the current systems of the invention. For semiconductor devices, the device speed is dependant on feature size and materials used. Whilst preferred embodiments of the invention can produce organic semiconductors, these are relatively slow compared to conventional inorganic semiconductors. Thus, for example, where a high speed integrated circuit is required, insertion of a separately manufactured integrated circuit chip will be appropriate, as opposed to printing a low speed circuit. Mechanically active objects may also be inserted where printing cannot satisfactorily produce them. In

Selected patents 97

embodiments that create three dimensional products, the printing process may create the cavities into which such discrete devices may be inserted.

[0026] The material(s) printed by the printheads may be hot melts. Typical viscosities are about 10 centipoise. The materials that may be printed include various polymers and metals or metal alloys. It is thus possible to print wires, in both two and three dimensions in products. The material solidifies to a solid, either by freezing or by other processing to form solid voxels. As used in the description and claims the terms cured, curing or derivatives are to be understood to include any process that transforms material or materials in one state to the same or different material or materials in a solid state. Different materials may require different curing techniques or curing conditions.

[0027] The preferred printhead is a Micro Electro Mechanical System (MEMS) type printhead in which a material is ejected from a chamber under the control of a movable element. Reference is made to the following patent specifications that disclose numerous such MEMS type printheads or printhead components:

98 Selected patents

Drawings:

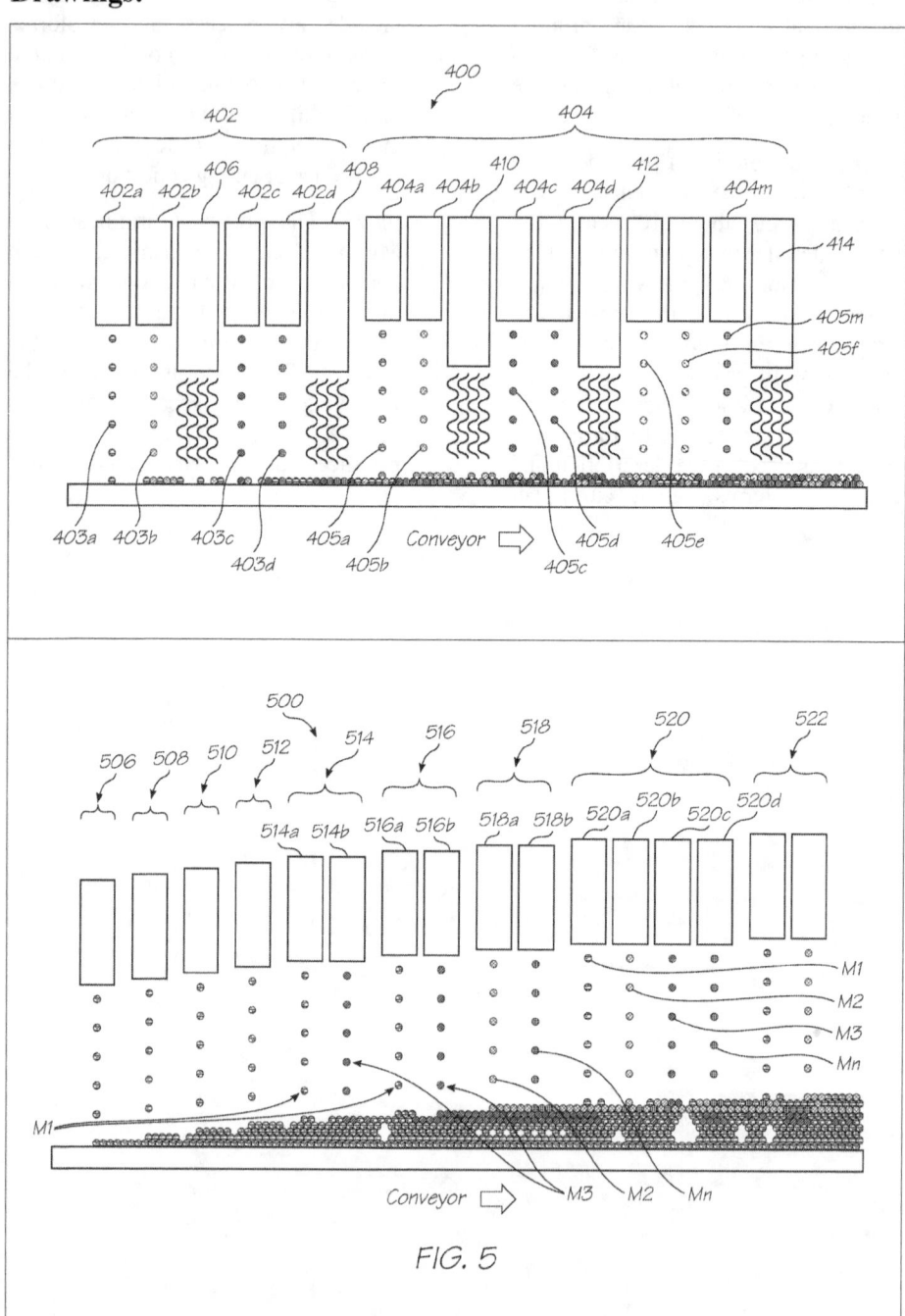

FIG. 5

Selected patents 99

Printable support structure from silicone + polymer

Original title (Material and method for three-dimensional modeling)

Patent number	US7534386 B2
Publication type	Grant
Application number	US 11/985,387
Published	19. May 2009
Application	15. Nov. 2007
Priority	20. Apr. 1999
Fee status	Paid
Also published as	CN1666217A, 6 et al»
Inventors	William R. Priedeman, Jr.
Original Assignee	Stratasys, Inc.

Patent citations (90), Classifications (51), Legal Events (3)

External links: USPTO, USPTO assignment, Espacenet

Comment:

The inventor describes a method using a dual extractor with a thermoplastic compound(A) and a silicon based material mix(B), where (B) does act as support structure material Several problems have to be solved to achieve this. The support material for instance has to withstand similar temperatures as the main material. The patents names the compositions and the results from testing variation along with the supplier of these chemicals..

Surprisingly the mix of thermoplastics such as Nylon, Peek, PEAK or ABS and 10% silicone was able to prevent the nozzle from clogging. Usually a nozzle has a maintenance free operation for around 3.5 Kg of print material. With the addition of 10% silicone the inventors observed up to 20 Kg operation without nozzle clogging. This effect was not the goal of the invention.

100 Selected patents

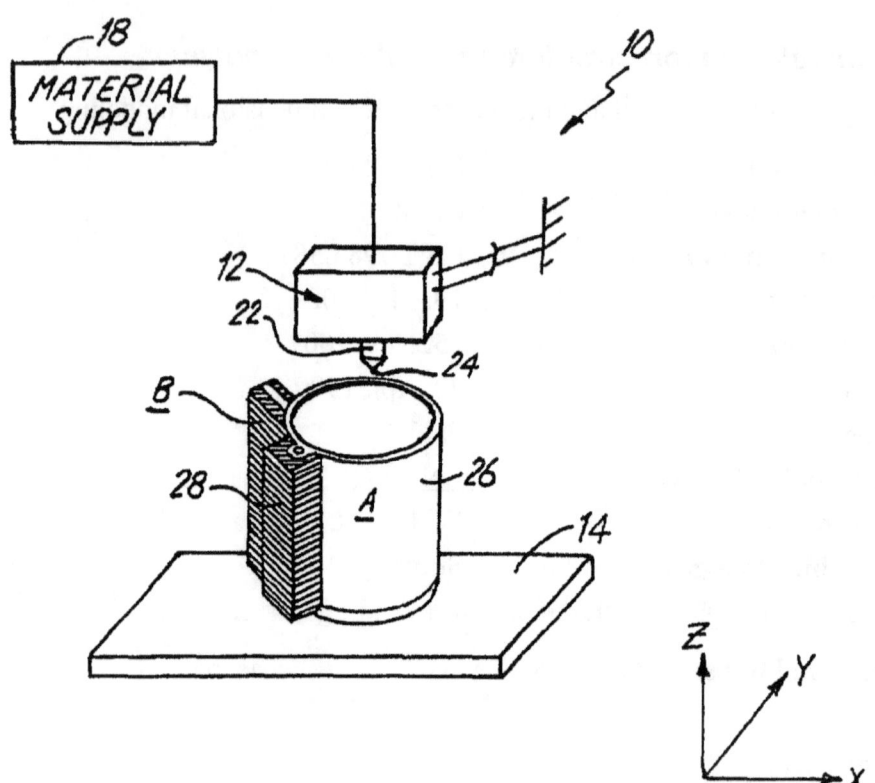

SUMMARY

A three-dimensional model and its support structure are built by fused deposition modeling techniques, wherein a thermoplastic material containing silicone is used to form the support structure and/or the model. The thermoplastic material containing silicone exhibits good thermal stability, and resists build-up in the nozzle of an extrusion head or jetting head of a three-dimensional modeling apparatus. The silicone contained in a support material acts as a release agent to facilitate removal of the support structure from the model after its completion.

SUMMARY

The present invention relates to a thermoplastic material for use in layered-deposition three-dimensional modeling. The thermoplastic material has a heat deflection temperature greater than about 220° C., a suitable melt flow for extrusion, and includes a base polymer and a silicone release agent constituting about 0.5 percent by weight to about 10 percent by weight of the thermoplastic material.

BRIEF DESCRIPTION OF THE DRAWINGS

FIG. 1 is a diagrammatic illustration of a model and a support structure therefor formed using layered extrusion techniques.

DETAILED DESCRIPTION

The present invention is described with

reference to a deposition modeling system of the type shown in FIG. 1. FIG. 1 shows an extrusion apparatus 10 building a model 26 supported by a support structure 28 according to the present invention. The extrusion apparatus 10 includes an extrusion head 12, a material-receiving base 14 and a material supply 18. (..)

A modeling material A is dispensed to form the model 26, and a support material B is dispensed in coordination with the dispensing of modeling material A to form the support structure 28. For convenience, the extrusion apparatus 10 is shown with only one material supply 18. It should be understood, however, that in the practice of the present invention, the modeling material A and the support material B are provided to the extrusion apparatus 10 as separate feedstocks of material from separate material supplies. The extrusion apparatus 10 may then accommodate the dispensing of two different materials by: (1) providing two extrusion heads 12, one supplied with modeling material A and one supplied with support material B (..)

To properly support the model under construction, the support material B must bond to itself (self-laminate). The support materials B must form a weak, breakable bond to modeling material A (co-laminate), so that it can be separated from the completed model without causing damage to the model. Where the support structure is built up from the base, support material B must additionally bond to the base (..)

To produce a dimensionally accurate model, the modeling and support materials must exhibit little shrinkage upon cooling in the conditions of the build envelope. Any shrinkage of the support material B must match that of the modeling material A. A shrink differential in the materials would cause stresses and bond failures along the model/support structure joint. (..)

Testing of Materials:

The following are examples of material formulations which were tested for use as support materials in a very high-temperature modeling environment (i.e. build chamber temperature of 200° C. or greater). The material formulations were tested as support materials for a polyphenylsulfone modeling material. Specifically, in each case, the polyphenylsulfone modeling material is Radel™ R 5600 NT (available from BP Amoco). This polyphenylsulfone resin has a heat deflection temperature of 236° C., and a melt flow in the range of 20-30 gms/10 min. at 400° C. under a 1.2 kg load. Example 3 embodies the present invention, while Example 1 and 2 are comparative examples.

All of the materials tested met the rheology criteria discussed above. In each case, techniques conventional in polymer chemistry were used to compound the component materials. The exemplary materials were successfully formed into modeling filament of a very small diameter, on the order of 0.070 inches, and used in a filament-fed deposition modeling machine.

EXAMPLE 1

Models of various sizes were built in a build chamber having a temperature of about 200-225° C., using the polyphenylsulfone modeling material and a support material comprising a blend of polyphenylsulfone and amorphous polyamide. In some cases, the support material further included polysulfone. Weight percent ranges of the various component materials were between about 60 and 90 weight percent polyphenylsulfone, and between about 10 and 40 weight percent amorphous polyamide blend, or between about 60 and 90 weight percent polyphenylsulfone, between about 1 and 40 weight percent polysulfone and between about 10 and 40 weight percent amorphous polyamide blend. A particular exemplary resin tested is a blend of 50 weight percent Radel™ R 5600 NT polyphenylsulfone (available from BP Amoco), 25 weight percent Udel™ P 1710 NT 15 polysulfone (available from BP Amoco), and 25 weight percent EMS TR 70 amorphous polyamide (available from EMS-Chemie AG of Switzerland). This resin has a heat deflection temperature of 224° C. and a melt flow similar to that of the modeling material. The support material was extruded from a liquifier having a temperature of about 350° C. to form a support structure for a model built using the polyphenylsulfone resin.

The support material according to this example was satisfactory for models that took less than about 20 hours to build, but failed for models that had a longer build time. It was observed that the support material exhibited thermally instability after about 20 hours in the build chamber. The thermally instability manifested by the material becoming dark and eventually blackening, and becoming strongly adhered to the model. Desirably, a material will survive build times of up to about 200 hours, to permit the building of large and complex parts. Thus, while the support material of the present example was found satisfactory for supporting small parts, it is not suitable for more general high-temperature use.

EXAMPLE 2

Test models were built in a build chamber having a temperature of about 200-225° C., using the polyphenylsulfone modeling material and a support material which comprised various resins of polyethersulfone, polyphenylsulfone or polyetherimide (i.e., Ultem™). These materials exhibited favorable thermal stability, but could not be broken away from the model. The support material containing polyphenylsulfone adhered very strongly to the model. The support material containing polyetherimide adhered fairy strongly to the model, and the support material containing polyethersulfone, while exhibiting the least adherence to the model, adhered too strongly for suitable use.

EXAMPLE 3

Large and small polyphenylsulfone models were built in a build chamber having a temperature of about 200-225° C., using a support material comprising a polyethersulfone base polymer and a silicone release agent. For convenience, commercially available compounds were used to provide a "masterbatch" containing silicone, which was compounded with the base polymer. Various masterbatches were tested, which included polypropylene, linear low-density polyethylene, and high-impact polystyrene. Additionally, various silicones were tested, ranging in viscosity from about 60,000 centistokes (intermediate viscosity) to 50 million centistokes (very high viscosity). The very high viscosity silicones have a high molecular weight, while the lower viscosity silicones have a lower molecular weight.

It was found that intermediate viscosity silicone was a much better release agent than the very high viscosity silicone, and that the high-impact polystyrene masterbatch released more easily from the polyphenylsulfone modeling material than did the other masterbatches tested. In a preferred embodiment, the masterbatch contained about 75 weight percent of a high-impact polystyrene copolymer and about 25 weight percent of a 60,000 centistoke (cSt) viscosity silicone. In this embodiment, the support material comprised between about 90-95 weight percent polyethersulfone, between about 3-8 weight percent high-impact polystyrene, and between about 1-3 weight percent silicone. This composition was demonstrated using BASF, Ultrason E-1010 polyethersulfone and Dow-Corning MB25-504 styrene butadiene copolymer containing hydroxy-terminated poly dimethyl siloxane (i.e. hydroxy-terminated silicone). This material was extruded from a liquifier having a temperature of about 420° C. to successfully form a support structure for a model built using the polyphenylsulfone resin. The support structure satisfactorily released from the model after its construction.

The support material of the present example exhibited a tensile strength of between 5000 psi and 12,000 psi, exhibited a shrinkage typical of amorphous polymers (less than 0.010 inch/inch), a melt flow in the range of about 5-30 gms/10 min. under a 1.2 kg load at a temperature of up to 450° C., and a heat deflection temperature of about 232° C.

Discussion of Results

It was demonstrated that adding a small amount of silicone to a base polymer weakened the bond between the base polymer and the modeling material, enabling use of the polymer to form a support structure that could be broken-away from the model. An intermediate viscosity silicone (on the order of about 104-105 centistokes) provided good release characteristics, although it is expected that a variety of silicones can be used to advantage in the present invention.

As the silicone release agent exhibited thermal resistance at temperatures of 225° C. for over 200 hours, the present invention is particularly useful in supporting models made from high-temperature thermoplastics in a very hot environment. Heretofore, there have been no known materials suitable for building a support structure by layered deposition modeling techniques in an environment hotter than about 180° C.

While the composition of the present invention was demonstrated using a polyethersulfone base polymer, the silicone release agent can be added to a variety of other base polymers to likewise lessen adhesion of the support structure to the model. A base polymer is selected based upon various physical, thermal and Theological properties demanded by the deposition modeling process. For high-temperature processes, silicone added to a polyphenylsulfone or polyetherimide base polymer will exhibit good thermal stability. Other potential base polymers for use in various build environments include polyphenylenes, polycarbonates, high-impact polystyrenes, polysulfones, polystyrenes, acrylics, amorphous polyamides, polyesters, nylons, PEEK, PEAK and ABS. Where adhesion between a base polymer and a modeling material is higher, a greater amount of silicone can be added. A suitable amount of silicone will weaken but not destroy the bond between the support structure and the model, providing adhesion sufficient to support the model under construction. It is expected that up to about 10 weight percent silicone may be desired in some cases.

While a high-impact polystyrene copolymer was used in demonstrating the present invention, such co-polymer is but one example of a copolymer which may be included in the composition of the present invention. The high-impact polystyrene masterbatch was used as a matter of convenience in compounding the silicone with the base polymer. Those skilled in the art will recognize that various masterbatches may be used (e.g., one made with the base polymer of the support material), that other techniques for compounding may be used which do not require a masterbatch (e.g., liquid silicone could be added directly to the base polymer), and that various other co-polymers may be included in the thermoplastic composition, in various amounts, to satisfy processing demands of a given application.

An unexpected benefit of the thermoplastic material containing silicone is that this material resisted build-up in the nozzle of the extrusion head liquifier. This attribute of the material, though unintended, is highly desirable. Typically, the liquifier of an extrusion-based layered deposition modeling machine needs to be replaced after extrusion of only about 7 pounds of material, due to an unacceptable build up of material in the nozzle. Resistance to clogging of the material containing silicone was observed to surpass that of any materials heretofore known in the art. The nozzles of liquifiers used to extrude the thermoplastic material containing silicone extruded over 40 pounds of the material before needing replacement. Nozzle life was thus extended by over 400 percent. Hence, silicone was demonstrated to provide the thermoplastic with characteristics desirable for modeling materials as well as support materials.

Resistance to nozzle clogging was demonstrated with compositions that included as little as 0.75 weight percent silicone. For modeling materials, the amount of silicone in the material may thus be kept very small, between about 0.5 weight percent and 2 weight percent, to prolong the liquifier life without degrading the strength of the modeling material. As will be recognized by those skilled in the art, the higher viscosity silicone, which has a lesser release ability, may be beneficial as an additive to the modeling material. As will be further recognized by those skilled in the art, where silicone is contained in both the modeling and support material, a reduced amount of silicone in the support material may be preferred.

Also as will be recognized by those skilled in the art, the modeling material A and support material B may include inert and/or active filler materials. The fillers can provide enhanced material properties which may be desirable depending upon the intended use of the resulting model. For instance, fillers can provide RF shielding, conductivity, or radio opaque properties (useful for some medical applications). Fillers can alternatively degrade material properties, but this may be acceptable for some uses. For instance, an inexpensive filler can be added to the modeling material A or support material B to decrease the cost of these materials. Fillers can also change thermal characteristics of the materials, for instance a filler can increase the heat resistance of a material, and a filler can reduce material shrinkage upon thermal solidification. Exemplary fillers include glass fibers, carbon fibers, carbon black, glass microspheres, calcium carbonate, mica, talc, silica, alumina, silicon carbide, wollastonite, graphite, metals and salts.

Filler materials which will assist in removal of the support structure can also be used in the composition of the present invention. For instance, a filler material that swells when contacted by water or another solvent will tend to be useful in breaking down the support structure. A filler material that evolves gas when contacted by water or another solvent will likewise tend to be useful in breaking down the support structure.

Those skilled in the art will recognize that innumerable other additives may also be to modify material properties as desired for particular applications. For instance, the addition of a plasticizer will lower the heat resistance and melt flow of a thermoplastic material. The addition of dyes or pigments can be done to change color. An antioxidant can be added to slow down heat degradation of material in the extruder.

The modeling and support materials A and B of this foregoing examples may be molded into filament, rods, pellets or other shapes for use as a modeling feedstock, or it may be used as a liquid feedstock without prior solidification. Alternatively, the mixture may be solidified and then granulated.

It is noted that the modeling material A and support material B of the foregoing examples are moisture sensitive. It has been demonstrated that exposure of these materials to a humid environment will significantly degrade model quality, thus, maintaining dry conditions is important. In order for the materials of the present invention to build accurate, robust models by fused deposition techniques, the material must dried. Particularly suitable apparatus for building up three-dimensional objects using the high temperature, moisture-sensitive materials of the present invention are disclosed in pending U.S. application Ser. Nos. 09/804,401 and 10/018,673, which are incorporated by reference herein. The '673 application discloses a modeling machine having a high-temperature build chamber, and the '401 application discloses a moisture-sealed filament cassette and filament path for supplying moisture-sensitive modeling filament in a filament-fed deposition modeling machine.

For the modeling material A and support material B of the foregoing examples, an acceptable moisture content (i.e. a level at which model quality will not be impaired) is a level less than 700 parts per million (ppm) water content (as measured using the Karl Fischer method). The '401 application discloses techniques for drying the filament provided in the a filament cassette. One method for drying the material is to place a cassette containing the material in an oven under vacuum conditions at a suitable temperature (between 175-220° F. is typical) until the desired dryness is reached, at which time the cassette is sealed. The cassette may then be vacuum-sealed in a moisture-impermeable package, until its installation in a machine. An expected drying time is between 4-8 hours to reach less than 300 ppm water content. Another method is to dry the material by placing packets of desiccant in the cassette without use of the oven. It has been demonstrated that placing packets containing Tri-Sorb-molecular sieve and calcium oxide (CaO) desiccant formulations in the cassette and sealing the cassette in a moisture-impermeable package will dry the material to a water content level of less than 700 ppm, and will dry the material to the preferred range of 100-400 ppm. This desiccant-only drying method has advantages over the oven-drying method in it requires no special equipment, and is faster, cheaper and safer than oven drying. Suitable Tri-Sorb-molecular sieve desiccant formulations include the following: zeolite, NaA; zeolite, KA; zeolite, CaA; zeolite, NaX; and magnesium aluminosilicate.

The '401 application further discloses a filament delivery system and an active drying system which will preserve the dryness of the material when it is loaded in the modeling machine. The drying system creates an active moisture barrier along a filament path from the cassette to the extrusion head, and purges humid air from the modeling machine. The drying system continuously feeds dry air or other gas under pressure to the filament path, disallowing humid air from remaining in or entering the filament path, and is vented at or near the end of the filament path.

Volumetric feed control for flexible filaments

Publication number	WO1997037810 A1
Publication type	Application
Application number	PCT/US1997/005590
Publication date	16 Oct 1997
Filing date	3 Apr 1997
Priority date	8 Apr 1996
Also published as	US6085957
Inventors	John S Batchelder, Robert L Zinniel
Applicant	Stratasys Inc

Patent Citations (7), Referenced by (6), Classifications (14), Legal Events (6)

External Links: Patentscope, Espacenet

Comment:

The method describes how to continuously measure the diameter of a filement with various means. From purely mechanical solutions to optical methods incorporation two light emitting sources in a 90° angle and more.

108 Selected patents

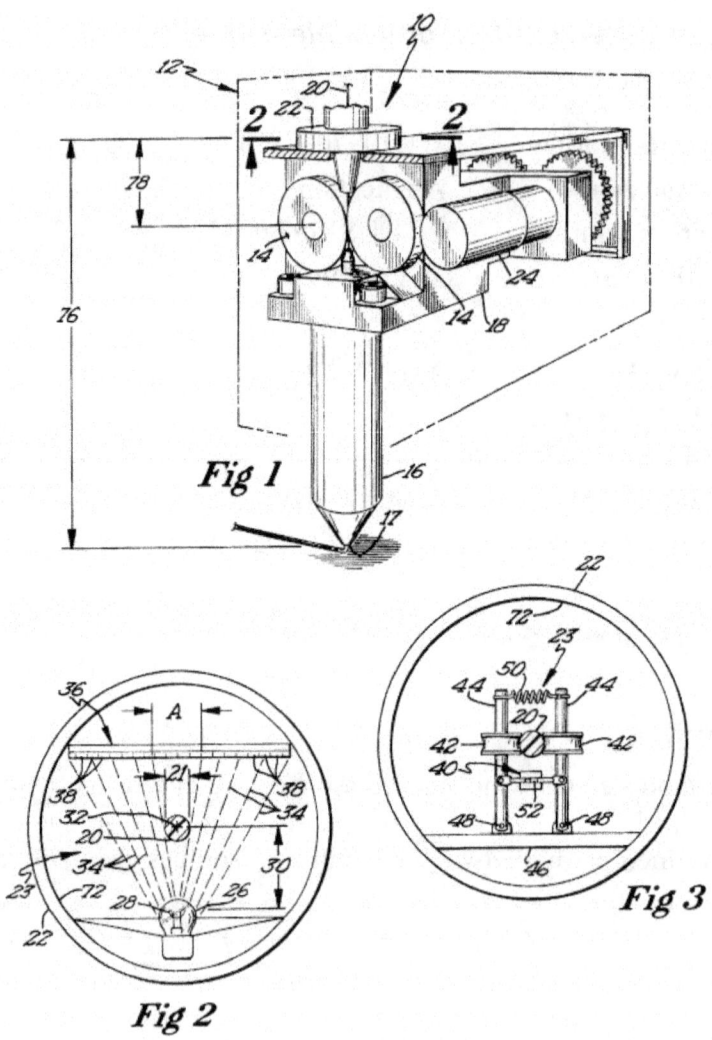

Fig 1

Fig 2

Fig 3

BRIEF SUMMARY OF THE INVENTION

It is an object of the present invention to provide a volumetric feed control system that will allow for an increased tolerance range in build element effective cross section, in other words, a loosening of the strictness of the tolerance requirements.

It is another object of the present invention to improve the constancy of the flow rate of fluid delivered through the application tip of a three-dimensional modeling machine.

It is yet anotner object of the present invention to provide a feed control system suitable for installation on an existing three-dimensional modeler including the type disclosed in U.S. Patent No. 5,121,329 to Crump, which is hereby incoφorated by reference, and which will require little modification of existing equipment. The present invention achieves these objects by providing a system for continuously measuring, computing, and monitoring the effective cross section of a build material element such as a filament as the element is fed to the melting unit or application tip of the modeling machine, and adjusting the speed at which the element is fed to the melting unit or the application tip to ensure a more constant flow rate of fluid at the application tip. Build material element is fed to a modeling machine by an advancement mechanism including a motor. The motor can be a stepper motor or a DC servo motor. In the present invention, the build element is advanced to the dispensing head by the advancement mechanism. The effective cross section of the element is determined through the use of sensing means and a central processing unit. Various configurations for determination of effective cross section may be used, for example infrared emitter and detector pairs, tungsten filament and infrared detector arrays, pinch rollers and linear variable differential transformers (LVDT), and capacitive measurement. There is usually a spatial gap between the sensing means and the application tip of the three-dimensional modeler. Therefore, a lag response exists in the system. A variance in filament cross section will not immediately affect the volume of filament material present at the application tip. To combat this delay, the distances between the sensing means and the application tip as well as between the sensing means and the center of the modeler advancement mechanism are provided to the central processing unit. The sensing means provide continuous signals to the central processing unit which can then compute the effective cross section of the filament. The motor of the advancement mechanism is connected to the central processing unit to allow the central processing unit to know the speed of the motor at all times. Since the central processing unit knows the speed of the motor and receives measurements from the sensing means, the effective cross section of the element may be continuously computed. Necessary changes to motor speed and hence feed roller speed and the proper times to effect the changes in speed may therefore be controlled by the central processing unit to ensure that the lag response is continuously and properly compensated. The volumetric feed control apparatus of the present invention will allow the tolerance of flexible filament to be increased. In other words, the filament diameter accuracy level required by the present invention is less than that previously required by the prior art. The reason for this is the use of more accurate methods of providing a constant flow rate of filament to the modeling machine application tip. This relaxed tolerance requirement will considerably cut the manufacturing costs of filament, and therefore of models created by modeling machines.

Further, any existing system using a roller feed method of feeding a flexible filament to a modeler may easily use the present invention. Insertion of the sensing means into an existing system may be easily accomplished. The central processing unit may be located anywhere, provided that proper connections are made to the sensors and to the motor controlling the advancement mechanism. No changes other than the drive control of the motor, and the possible addition of an encoder feedback to the motor are necessary.

110 Selected patents

Typically, the build material element is configured in the shape of a cylindrical filament, normally wound on a spool or stored in a roll. However, the element may be supplied in a wide variety of configurations, including ribbons, tubes, extrusions of triangular, trapezoidal, or pentagonal shape, and the like. The build material element may also be supplied in discrete quantities, and need not be wound on a spool.

These and other objects and benefits of the present invention will become apparent from the following detailed description thereof taken in conjunction with the accompanying drawings, wherein like reference numerals designate like elements throughout the several views.

DESCRIPTION OF THE DRAWINGS

Fig. 1 is a perspective view of an embodiment of the volumetric feed control in place on a machine;

Fig. 2 is a view of an embodiment of the sensing system of Fig. 1, taken along line 2-2 thereof;

Fig. 3 is a view of an alternative embodiment of the sensing system of Fig. 2; Fig. 4 is a view of another alternative embodiment of the sensing system of Fig. 2; Fig. 5 is a view of yet another alternative embodiment of the sensing system of Fig. 2; and Fig. 6 is a partial block diagram of a control system for the volumetric feed control.

DESCRIPTION OF THE PREFERRED EMBODIMENT

Referring now to the drawings, Fig. 1 shows the volumetric feed control 10 in place on a three-dimensional modeling machine 12, the machine 12 having an element advancement mechanism such as feed rollers 14, a dispensing head 16 with an application tip 17, and a frame 18. A build material element such as filament 20 is fed to machine 12 from a build element source, not shown, which may be a spool or roll of material, or another such storage device. Build material is often formed as a filament such as filament 20, but may take other configurations. Such other configurations include those of different cross sections. Further, the build material element may be supplied in discrete quantities, and need not be wound in a roll or on a spool.

Volumetric feed control 10 may include dimension control ring 22 and DC servo motor 24 with encoder feedback. Dimension control ring 22 contains sensing means 23 to determine the effective cross section of a build material element such as filament 20 being fed through the dimension control ring 22.

Cross sectional area is often used to estimate volume. Also used are diameter measurements. These methods of determining volume only work when no anomalies are present. Such methods of measurement, especially using conventional instruments and techniques, fail to take into account that if only a diameter measurement is made, a volume computation is meaningless if the element being measured is hollow. The effective cross section is a measurement that takes into account such factors as the cross sectional area of the element, known quantities such as length, width, and diameter, and other information, such as whether the element is hollow, oblong, or the like. The use of effective cross section reduces the possibility for miscalculation due to various physical factors of the element. A more accurate volume calculation may then be made. The sensing means 23 is operatively connected to a central processing unit 74, and continuously gathers data and feeds information signals measuring the build

Selected patents 111

material element being fed therethrough to the central processing unit 74. The central processing unit is also operatively connected to a motor 24, which may be a DC servo motor or a stepper motor. Motor 24 is in turn operatively connected to feed rollers 14 or an other element advancement mechanism which may be used on the modeling machine. The central processing unit 74 controls the speed at which the motor 24 turns, and therefore the speed at which the advancement mechanism rotates to pull the build material element through the dimension control ring 22. Central processing unit 74 adjusts the speed of motor 24 in order to provide a constant flow rate of build material element to dispensing head 16 and application tip 17.

Sensing means 23 need not be housed in a dimension control ring 22. It may be mounted at any place in which it will be positioned to make measurements on element 20.

Sensing means 23 is preferably positioned between any driving contact means such as feed rollers 14 and the application tip 17. This is because the driving contact means may affect the effective cross section of the element due to forces imparted by the feed rollers 14 or other mechanical driving means. Sensing means 23 may even be incoφorated into the element advancement mechanism, such as by mounting the feed rollers to communicate with a linear variable differential transformer as described below.

Referring now also to Figs. 2-4, various embodiments of the sensing means 23 may be seen. In Fig. 2, filament 20 is shown substantially centered in dimension control ring 22. As has been mentioned, dimension control ring 22 is not required. The sensing means 23 may be mounted elsewhere. Although in this configuration it is preferred that filament 20 be centered in dimension control ring 22, it is not necessary. In Fig. 2, a tungsten halogen lamp 26 is oriented with its lamp filament 28 parallel to and a fixed predetermined distance 30 from the axis 32 of filament 20. The emitted light 34 from the lamp 26 creates a shadow of the filament 20 on a linear CCD array 36. The shadow width is designated as letter A (Fig. 2). Shadows of different widths A will cause a variation in the number of array pixels 38 that are illuminated by the light 34 from lamp 26. The width 21 of filament 20 may then be determined using standard clocking and preamplification techniques known in the art and not further described herein. These measurements are used to generate an effective cross section of filament 20. Referring to Fig. 3, a sensing means 23 using a three-coil linear variable differential transformer (LVDT) 40 and a pair of dimension rollers 42 is shown. Dimension rollers 42 are mounted to shafts 44. Each shaft 44 is flexibly attached to rigid mount 46 by a suitable mounting apparatus, such as pins 48. Rigid mount 46 is attached to the interior surface 72 of the dimension control ring 22, but may also be attached at any fixed point on the frame of the modeling machine. The dimension rollers 42 are biased toward each other by spring 50 attached between shafts 44. Each shaft 44 also carries an attachment for LVDT 40 which is attached therebetween. The terminals of LVDT 40 are operatively connected to rollers 42, one terminal to each roller. As has been described above, tf oilers 42 may be used with multiple functions, such as to also serve as feed rollers for eicment advancement, or encoding the element velocity. Filament 20 passes between dimension rollers 42. As the filament diameter changes, the

112 Selected patents

dimension rollers 42 respond by moving, causing motion of the shafts 44. The movements of the dimension rollers 42 cause the core 52 of LVDT 40 to change position within LVDT

40. Sense circuits known in the art may be employed to translate the relative changes in core 52 position and inductance in the LVDT coils to an analog voltage which may be used to compute the effective cross section of the filament 20.

Fig. 4 shows a third embodiment of the sensing means 23 used in the dimension control ring 22 or alternatively mountable directly to the modeling machine. In this embodiment, the filament effective cross section is calculated using information from a capacitive sensor 54.

The sensor 54 is comprised of a pair of conducting plates 56 sandwiching a thin insulator 58 there between. A typical insulator 58 is mylar, approximately 0.002 inches in thickness. Insulator 58 lies in a plane 60 through which a hole 62 is drilled, the hole 62 being coaxial with the axis 32 of build filament 20 and coplanar with plane 60, and exposing the conductive plates 56. The diameter 64 of hole 62 is slightly larger than the diameter of the largest filament 20 expected to be used with the modeling machine. A capacitance meter 66 is attached to the conductive plates 56. Changing diameter of the filament 20 will cause a change in capacitance that may be translated in known fashion to the cross sectional area of the filament. This method of determining the effective cross section of the filament 20 is independent of its cross sectional shape, since the capacitive sensor 54 essentially measures the percentage of the hole 62 that is filled with filament 20 as opposed to air. The capacitance measurement scheme may also be used to detect the presence of absorbed water in the filament 20, since the filament 20 material and water have different capacitive properties. Yet another alternative embodiment (Fig. 5) of the sensing means 23 comprises at least one set of emitter/ detector pairs 68, 70 spaced 180 degrees apart around the axis of the filament 20. The emitter/detector pair 68, 70 is situated so that the filament 20 will pass through the beam from emitter 68 as the filament 20 is advanced by feed rollers 14. The emitter 68 sends out a light signal or beam that may be partially occluded by filament 20 and which is detected by the opposite detector 70. If the filament 20 changes in size, the intensity of the beam detected by the detector 70 will change, allowing a measurement which may be used to calculate the filament effective cross section. Preferably, a plurality of emitter/detector pairs are spaced at equal intervals around the axis of filament 20 in order to more accurately detect and measure the effective cross section of the filament 20 as it is advanced by the advancement mechanism. Other types of sensors are also compatible with the volumetric feed control 10, and could be used in place of the emitter/detector pairs. Such other sensors include but are not limited to opto-electric sensors, miniature CCD cameras, fiber optic sensors, mechanical bladder ring sensors, or pinch roller sensors. All could send information that may be used to determine the effective cross section of the flexible filament to the central processing unit 74. The various sensing means 23 described above each send a signal corresponding to the filament effective cross section to central processing unit 74. The central processing unit 74 computes the effective cross section and the required feed speed of the filament 20 to provide a constant flow rate of build material to the application tip 17 of the dispensing head 16, and adjusts the speed of motor 24 which controls the speed of filament feed by controlling the speed of the advancement mechanism such as feed rollers 14. This adjustment ensures that any changes in the effective cross section of the filament 20 will result in a corresponding change in the speed at which the filament 20 is fed. If further accuracy of effective cross section measurement and testing of properties of the filament 20 is desired, two or more sensing means may be combined or used in sequence to determine multiple properties of the filament 20 and provide a reference for averaging computed values. For example, an LVDT sensing means as described above may be used along with a capacitive sensor as also described above, in order to determine both the outer dimension and the water content of the filament 20. Consequently, the tolerance of a filament with nominal diameter of 0.070 inches can be increased substantially from +/- 0.0015 inches.

Another way to increase the accuracy of the effective cross section is to more closely monitor the effective velocity of the element. Although the rotational speed imparted by the element advancement mechanism provides a good approximation of the element velocity, the approximation may be in error due to a number of factors. The element advancement mechanism itself often requires a groove such as that shown in Fig. 3 on rollers 42 in order to seat the build material element properly. The angular velocity of the rollers and accordingly the linear velocity imparted by the rollers differs at the outer periphery and at the central most portion of the groove. To combat such inaccuracies, the element advancement mechanism may be encoded for element velocity. When such an account is made of effective element velocity, this measure may be combined with effective cross section to more accurately compute the volumetric flow rate. Build material elements may be fabricated in a variety of cross sectional shapes and geometries, including ribbons, tubes, extrusions of triangles, trapezoids, pentagons, and other polyhedra. The measurement techniques described above may be adapted to these alternative geometries. In operation, the volumetric feed control 10 works as follows. The sensing means 23 sends measurement signals to central processing unit 74. Central processing unit 74 uses the signals to continuously compute the effective cross section of the build element. In response to this known quantity, central processing unit 74 is able to adjust the feed speed of the build element by adjusting the speed of motor 24 controlling the feed rollers 14 that advance the build element toward the dispensing head 16 and application tip 17. The adjustment is made so that a constant flow rate of build material is fed to the dispensing head

16.A time lag exists between the computation of build element effective cross section and the arrival of the particular measured portion of the element at the application tip

17. Consequently, a change in effective cross section of the build element at the sensing means 23

does not immediately translate to a change in volume of material at the application tip 17. The

change in build element effective cross section will affect the volume of material at the

application tip at some point in time after it passes the sensing means 23.

To account for this lag, the central

processing unit 74 must know the distance 76

between the application tip 17 and the sensing means 23, as well as the distance 78 between the sensing means 23 and the center of feed rollers 14. The connection of motor 24 to the central processing unit allows it to know or compute at all times both the effective cross section of the build element and the speed of the feed rollers 14. The central processing unit

74 can therefore correct for the lag response in the system and provide a constant volume of material at the application tip 17 regardless of variances in the effective cross section of the build element.

The detailed description outlined above is considered to be illustrative only of the principles of the invention. Numerous changes and modifications will occur to those skilled in the art, and there is no intention to restrict the scope of the invention to the detailed description. The preferred embodiment of the invention having been described in detail, the

scope of the invention should be defined by the following claims.

Selected patents 115

Auto tip calibration in an extrusion apparatus

Patent number	US20070228592 A1
Publication type	Application
Application number	US 11/397,012
Published	4. Oct. 2007
Application	3. Apr. 2006
Priority	3. Apr. 2006
Also published as	CN101460290A, 5 et al»
Inventors	James Comb, Benjamin Dunn, Hans Erickson, Jason Wanzek
Original Assignee	Stratasys, Inc.

Referenced by (8), Classifications (6), Legal Events (2)

External links: USPTO, USPTO assignment, Espacenet

Comment:

The invention describes a 2-stage method for auto calibrating 3D printers. At first, a defined test object is printed at a predefined position of the printbed. Next, a mechanical or optical measuring tip will report the position and dimension of the test object back to the software, which will then use this data to correct any possible offset.

116 Selected patents

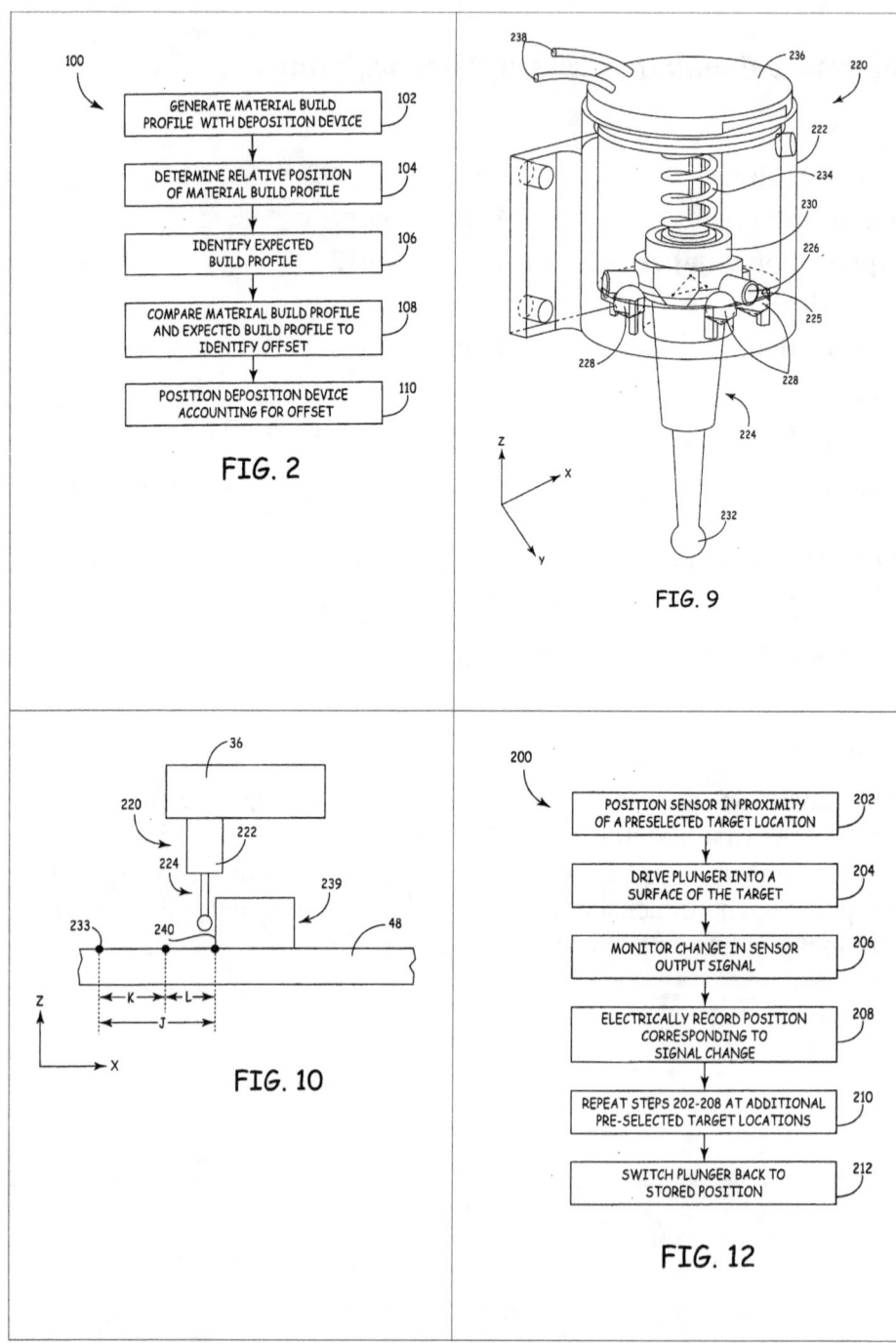

Selected patents 117

Rapid prototype injection molding

Patent number	US20050173839 A1
Publication type	Application
Application number	US 10/511,787
PCT Number	PCT/US2003/011854
Published	11. Aug. 2005
Application	17. Apr. 2003
Priority	17. Apr. 2002
Also published as	CN1652915A, 6 et al»
Inventors	Steven Crump, William Priedeman Jr,Jeffery Hanson
Original Assignee	Stratasys, Inc.

Referenced by (2), Classifications (17), Legal Events (2)

External links: USPTO, USPTO assignment, Espacenet

Comment:

The invention describes a method that uses a conventional 3D FDM printer to perform a plastic mold injection process in two steps.

In the first step the injection mold is printed by the FDM printer.

The patent names PEEK as preferred material.

Then using conventional thermoplastic with a lower melting point the mold is filled slowly and with low pressure.

As a result the injected and hardened model can be removed from the mold and the mold can be reused for additional makings of the object.

118 Selected patents

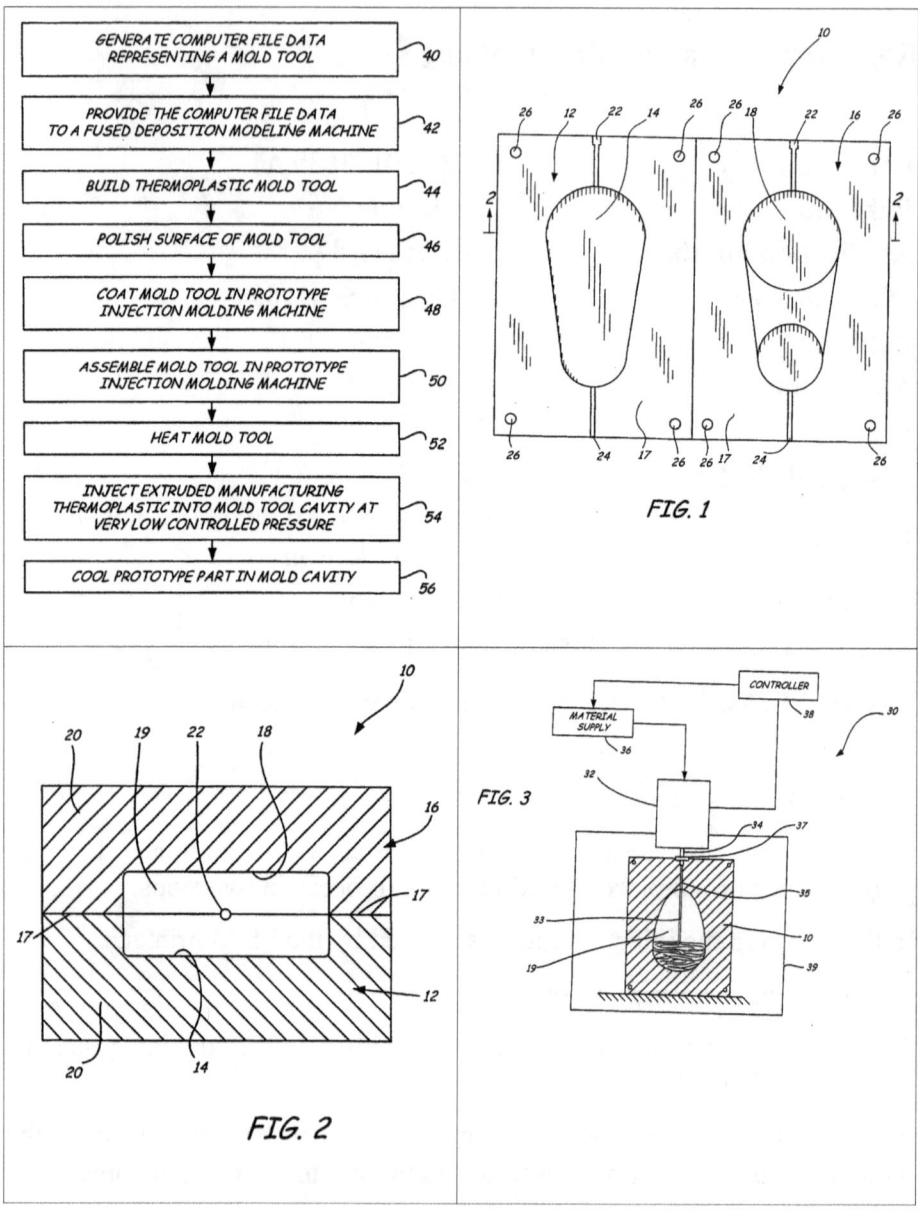

FIG. 1

FIG. 2

FIG. 3

The exemplary mold tool 10 is formed from a non-conductive thermoplastic material that will sustain the temperature and pressure of the injection molding process, so as to produce at least one prototype plastic injection molded part. An exemplary thermoplastic comprises at least 50 weight percent of a thermoplastic selected from the group consisting of polycarbonate, polystyrene, acrylics, amorphous polyamides, polyesters, polyphenylsulfone, polysulfone, polyphenylene ether, nylon, PEEK, PEAK, poly(2-ethyl-2-oxazoline), and

Selected patents 119

blends thereof. The thermoplastic resin may contain various fillers, additives and the like, as will be understood by those skilled in the art. A particularly preferred thermoplastic for use in creating a mold tool by fused deposition modeling is a polyphenylsulfone-based resin.

FIG. 3 shows an exemplary rapid prototype injection molding apparatus 30 in accordance with the present invention, in the process of making a prototype part. The apparatus 30 comprises an extrusion head 32 having a dispensing tip 34, a material supply 36, a controller 38, a modeling envelope 39, and a hollow sprue 35. The mold tool 10 is assembled and positioned in the apparatus 30. Prior to assembly of the mold tool 10, the mold surfaces 14 and 18 are created with a release agent that facilitates removal of a completed part from the mold tool 10. Suitable release agents include dry film lubricants, and others that will be recognized by those skilled in the art. The mold tool 10 in mounted in the modeling envelope 39. Sprue 35 is placed in the sprue channels 22, such the a dispensing end of the sprue 35 is directed into the mold cavity 19. The sprue 35 has an entry 37 at a top end thereof, designed to mate with the downward-facing extrusion head tip 34. The sprue entry 37 receives and attached to the extrusion head tip 34, thereby providing a flow path from the extrusion head 32 into the mold cavity 19. Preferably, an insulator is provided for the extrusion head tip 34, so that the tip 34 will not cause melting of the prototype part as it is being formed. Also, a pressure transducer (not shown) is placed in the sprue to monitor pressure in the mold cavity so that a predetermined pressure may be maintained.

The apparatus 30 may be a fused deposition modeling machine. It should be understood, however, that unlike fused deposition modeling, the process of the present invention involves no translational movement of the extrusion head. The extrusion head 32 may be of any type which receives a thermoplastic material and dispenses the material in a molten state through a dispensing tip at low flow rates and low pressure. Suitable extrusion heads have been developed for fused deposition modeling, and include a liquifier pump, a piston pump and a screw pump. Each of these extrusion heads developed for three-dimensional modeling receives a feedstock of thermoplastic in solid form, and heats the thermoplastic material to a desired temperature for extrusion.

In the exemplary embodiment, the extrusion head 32 receives a supply of production thermoplastic material for creating the molded prototype part from the material supply 36, at a rate controlled by the controller 38. Where the extrusion head 32 of the exemplary embodiment is a liquifier pump, the material supply 36 comprises spooled flexible filament and the extrusion head 32 carries a set of feed rollers for advancing the filament into the extrusion head at the controlled rate. Liquifier pumps are disclosed, for example, in U.S. Pat. No. 6,004,124. Where the extrusion head 32 of the exemplary embodiment is a piston pump, the material supply 36 comprises cylindrical feed rods of thermoplastic material fed in a batch process. A piston pump extrusion head is disclosed in U.S. Pat. No. 6,067,480. Where the extrusion head 32 of the exemplary embodiment is a screw pump, the material supply 36 comprises pellets of thermoplastic material. A screw pump extrusion head is disclosed, for example, in U.S. Pat. No. 5,312,224. Two-stage extrusion heads are also known in the art, and can also be used in practice of the present invention.

120 Selected patents

A extrusion pump is disclosed in U.S. Pat. No. 5,764,521, wherein the feedstock received from material supply 36 is pressurized in a two-stage process which may take various forms.

The extrusion head 32 may include an ultrasonic vibrator for creating a thixotropic flow at the dispensing tip exit, such as is disclosed in U.S. Pat. No. 5,121,329. The ultrasonic energy would reduce the injection pressure while increasing the flow rate of the production thermoplastic.

For the production of a prototype part, production thermoplastic is provided from the material supply 36 to the extrusion head 32, which heats the production thermoplastic to an extrusion temperature and dispenses molten extruded material 33 through sprue 35 and into the mold cavity 19. Production thermoplastics that may be used in the present invention include, without limitation, ABS, polycarbonate, polystyrene, acrylics, amorphous polyamides, polyesters, polyphenylsulfone, polyphenylene ether, nylon, PEEK, PEAK, and blends thereof. The production thermoplastic may, of course, include various fillers, additives and the like. Shrink characteristics of the mold tool plastic are matched to the shrink characteristics of the production thermoplastic, which can be achieved by using amorphous thermoplastics. Also, the production thermoplastic must have a heat deflection temperature lower than a heat deflection temperature of the plastic which forms the mold tool, so that the mold tool will maintain its shape.

FIG. 4 shows a flow diagram which summarizes an exemplary method of producing a prototype injection molded part in accordance with the present invention, using a mold tool made by fused deposition modeling. A CAD tool is used to generate computer file data representing a mold tool, in a step 40. The data is provided to a fused deposition modeling machine, in a step 42. The mold tool is built in the fused deposition modeling machine, in layers defined by the computer file data, in a step 44. In a step 46, the mold surfaces and/or mating surfaces of the mold tool are smoothed to remove ridges unintentionally created in the formation of the mold tool.

In a preferred embodiment, the smoothing is done in a vapor smoothing process, which is the subject of International Application No. PCT/US03/_____ entitled "Smoothing Method For Layered Deposition Modeling," filed Apr. 4, 2003, assigned to the same assignee as the present application, and hereby incorporated by reference as if set forth fully herein. As is disclosed in said co-pending application, the surfaces of the mold tool can be smoothed by placing the mold tool in a vaporizer and exposing it to vapors of a solvent until a desired surface finish is obtained. The solvent is selected to be compatible with the material which forms the mold tool. Suitable solvents will react with the material so as to soften and flow the material at the object surfaces. A preferred solvent for use with a wide range of amorphous thermoplastics is methylene chloride. Other suitable solvents will be recognized by those skilled in the art, for instance, an n-Propyl bromide solution (e.g., Abzol®)), perchloroethylene, trichloroethylene, and a hydrofluorocarbon fluid sold under the name Vertrel®. Vapor smoothing will also serve to seal the surfaces of the mold tool. As is taught in said co-pending application, certain mold features may be identified for solvent masking or for pre-distortion prior to the vapor smoothing step, and the computer file data representing the mold tool may include data identifying said features. Alternatively, smoothing can be done by applying a liquid solvent. Other alternative smoothing techniques include sanding, grinding, and thermal ironing.

The mold surfaces of the mold tool are then coated with a release agent, in a step 48 (a soluble mold tool may not need a release agent). Suitable release agents include dry film lubricants, and others that will be recognized by those skilled in the art. If needed, sprue and vent channels and alignment holes are machined into the mold tool prior to step 48. The mold tool is assembled in an prototype injection molding apparatus according to the present invention, without the addition of any conductive fill material or layers, in a step 50. The fused deposition modeling machine used to build the mold tool may be used also as the prototype injection molding apparatus.

In step 50, the sprue is positioned in the mold tool and attached to a dispensing tip of an extrusion head. The mold may be clamped to a fixture to hold it in place, using a clamp or other means. A clamping force of less than or equal to about 10 tons will ensure office compatibility of the injection process. The mold tool is then heated to a predetermined temperature, in a step 52.

Injection molding is then performed, in a step 54. Production thermoplastic is injected from an extrusion head of the molding apparatus into the mold tool, at low speed and low pressure. If an ultrasonic vibrator is used in the extrusion head, a thixotropic flow of thermoplastic will be injected. During the injection, pressure is preferably monitored, such as by a pressure transducer placed in the mold cavity or sprue. A system controller can adjust the extrusion flow rate based upon pressure reading from the transducer, to maintain the pressure within a target range. The target pressure will typically be less than 5000 psi and may be set at less than 500 psi, to as low as less than 20 psi (near-zero pressure).

Filling the mold cavity will typically take about 1-2 hours. During this time, the temperature of the mold and the production thermoplastic remain approximately constant, as the plastic mold is a thermal insulator having a high thermal resistance. In the exemplary embodiment, the mold tool is heated prior to the injection step 54, to provide isothermic conditions. Various techniques may be used to heat the mold, as will be recognized by those skilled in the art. A temperature sensor may be placed in the mold cavity, and temperature of the thermoplastic flow, the mold tool, and/or the build environment can then be adjusted as needed to maintain isothermic conditions. Maintaining the temperature of the mold tool at approximately the extrusion temperature of the production thermoplastic prevents premature solidification of the production thermoplastic, so that the mold cavity can fill completely before the prototype part hardens. It should be understood, however, that some materials and process parameters may provide isothermic conditions without the need for pre-heating the mold, in which case step 52 may be omitted. Also, it may be desirable to heat the mold cavity and inner mold surface, rather than heating the entire mold.

During (and prior to) the injection step 55, a vacuum may be drawn upon the mold tool. This may be done, for example, by placing the mold tool in a vacuum chamber. The vacuum will remove gases from the mold tool and the sprue, through the porosity of the mold or the vent. The vacuum will assist in pulling the injected material into the mold cavity. The vacuum will also facilitate filling the mold cavity more fully and consistently than would be achieved under normal atmospheric conditions, resulting in a void-free part.

When the mold cavity is filled, injection of material into the mold cavity is terminated and the prototype part is allowed to cool inside the mold tool, in a step 56. Cooling may take from 1 to 2 hours. Pressure may be placed on the mold tool during cooling, to compensate for shrinkage of the mold tool and the prototype part. If desired, active cooling may be used to speed the cooling process. Also, monitoring of pressure in the mold cavity may be continued during cooling. Cooling in the mold tool may be allowed to continue until the prototype part reaches room temperature, or the part may be removed when it is substantially cool.

Using the method of the present invention, a prototype plastic injection molded part can be produced within a 24-hour time period. Up to 50 prototype injection molded parts could be produced within 48 hours.

It should be understood that a mold tool for use in carrying out the present invention need not be limited to a thermoplastic mold build by a deposition modeling process. Rather, any non-conductive plastic mold tool compatible with the injection process may be utilized, including, for example, mold tools formed by stereolithography, thermoset mold tools, and mold tools formed by a machine-removable process (e.g., CAM/CNC). A plastic material forming the mold tool may include various fillers, additives and the like.

Although the present invention has been described with reference to preferred embodiments, the invention is defined by the claims. Workers skilled in the art will recognize that changes may be made in form and detail without departing from the spirit and scope of the invention.

For example, in one alternate embodiment, the mold tool is transparent and a photopolymer is used to form the prototype part. The photopolymer is injected into the mold cavity and cured by exposure to light. In another embodiment, thermoset reaction injection molding techniques are employed. Two or more reactant materials are mixed together to form a thermoset resin, which is injected into the mold tool. The resin is cured to form the prototype part by applying heat to the mold tool.

Melt flow compensation for filaments

Original title:"Extrusion apparatus and melt flow compensation method used in said extrusion"

Patent number	US6547995 B1
Publication type	Grant
Application number	US 09/960,133
Published	15. Apr. 2003
Application	21. Sept. 2001
Priority	21. Sept. 2001
Fee status	Paid
Also published as	CN1291829C, CN1555306A, EP1427578 A1,EP1427578A4, EP1427578B1,US200 30064124, WO2003026872A1,
Inventors	James W. Comb
Original Assignee	Stratasys, Inc.

Patent citations (7), Referenced by (30), Classifications (12),Legal Events (10)

External links: USPTO, USPTO assignment, Espacenet

Comment:

Heated filament will expand. As it cools down it shrinks again. This leads to unwanted scaling errors. The invention describes a theoretical model that calculates the effect on the model and corrects the required amount of building material before the printing starts.

124 Selected patents

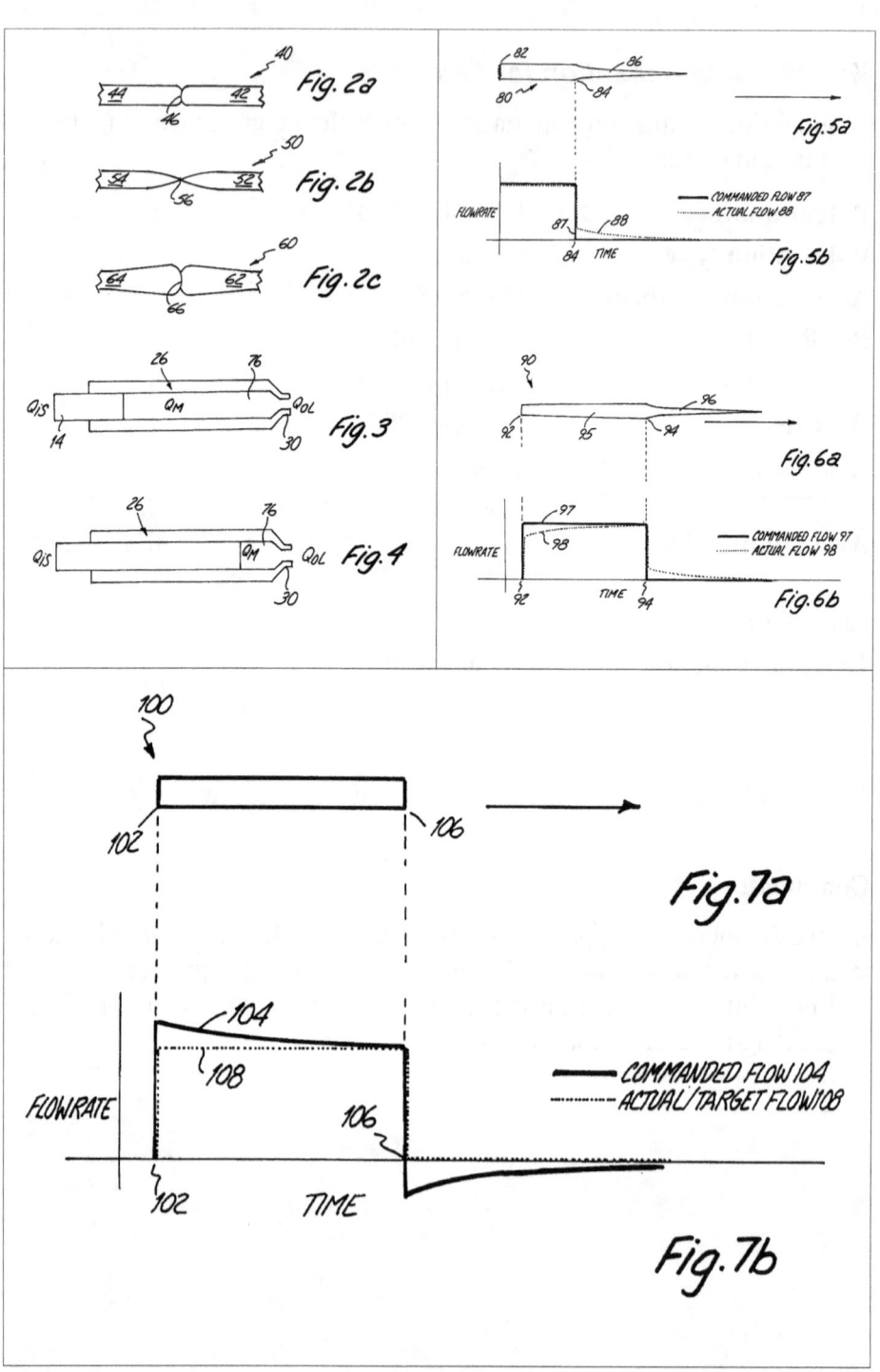

BACKGROUND OF THE INVENTION

This invention relates to the fabrication of three-dimensional objects using extrusion-based layered manufacturing techniques. More particularly, the invention relates to supplying solid modeling material to a liquifier carried by an extrusion head, and extruding the material in a flowable state in a predetermined pattern in three dimensions with respect to a base.(..)

One type of rapid prototyping system of the prior art drives the motion of the extrusion head at a constant velocity along a tool path comprising a poly-line. A poly-line is a continuous curve of straight-line segments defined by a list of X-Y coordinate pairs at each vertex. The head velocity is preselected so as to accomplish the general goal of moving the extrusion head quickly along the poly-line while minimizing the displacement from the tool path. As a result, the head velocity must be set to be slow enough that the deviation will not exceed the maximum allowable following error for the largest deflection along that poly-line. Using a constant head velocity along a tool path, bead width remains fairly constant but errors arise at start points and end points of the tool path, for instance, at the location of a "seam" (i.e., the start and end point of a closed-loop tool path).

Another type of prototyping system of the prior art varies the extrusion head speed to increase the throughput of the modeling machine. The extrusion head speeds up along straight-aways in the tool path, and slows down where there are deflection angles or vertices. U.S. Pat. No. 6,054,077 describes one such technique for varying the extrusion head speed, using X-Y trajectory profiling that follows the exponential step response of the liquifier pump. The velocity profile of the extrusion head looks like a "shark tooth", while the pump profile follows a step function.

It has been observed that the variable velocity systems of the prior art introduce greater bead width error, and also have seam errors. It would be desirable to reduce errors in bead width and seam quality so as to achieve a desired extrusion profile, while allowing the higher throughput of a variable rate system.

BRIEF SUMMARY OF THE INVENTION

The present invention is a liquifier pump control method and apparatus which reduces bead width errors and seams errors observed in the prior art by accounting for thermal expansion of the modeling material in the liquifier. The melting of modeling material is accompanied by its expansion. The present invention recognizes that the melt expansion produces unanticipated extruded flow rates from the liquifier during transient conditions. The present invention predicts a melt flow component of the extruded flow rate produced by the thermal expansion of the modeling material, and compensates for the predicted melt flow in a commanded flow rate.

BRIEF DESCRIPTION OF THE DRAWINGS

FIG. 3 is a graphical representation of a liquifier operating at a minimum flow rate.

FIG. 4 is a graphical representation of a liquifier operating at a maximum flow rate.

FIG. 5a is a view of an extrusion profile extruded by a prior art liquifier pump operating at a steady state and then turned off.

FIG. 5b is a graphical representation of the amount of flow produced by the liquifier pump of FIG. 5a.

(..)

The present invention recognizes that melt expansion of the modeling material is a significant cause of errors in the desired extrusion profile, such as the seam errors illustrated in FIGS. 2b and 2 c. Utilizing the present invention, the melt flow component of the extruded flow rate is predicted and is compensated for by adjusting the input rate of solid material, resulting in significantly reduced errors in bead width and seams.

The melt flow compensation of the present invention takes into account the flow history of the liquifier to command a flow rate that will account for melt flow. FIG. 3 is a graphical representation of a cross-section of the liquifier 26 operating at a minimum flow rate. FIG. 4 is a graphical representation of a cross-section of liquifier 26 operating at a maximum flow rate. The filament 14 is fed into the liquifier 26 at an input (or commanded) flow rate QiS, heated in the liquifier 26 to a liquid 76 at a melting rate QM, and extruded out of the tip 30 of liquifier 26 at an output flow rate QoL. As illustrated, at higher flow rates, more of the liquifier 26 contains solid modeling material in the form of filament 14, as compared to melted modeling material (liquid 76). This is due to limited melt capacity of the liquifier. If the input flow rate, QiS, were to go from a higher to a lower rate, the amount of liquid 76 in the liquifier 26 will increase and the output flow rate, QoL, will include a melt flow component, QMFL, that is taken into account by the present invention by way of a downward adjustment of the commanded input flow rate, QiS.

In order to account for melt flow, the melt flow characteristic of a given operating system may be modeled by an equation. The melt rate of a solid rod of material in a cylindrical liquifier has been observed to be approximately exponential. For a step increase in solid material input rate, the rate of melting increases exponentially to an asymptotic value equal to the input rate of solid material. When the liquifier pump is turned on, the melt flow rate of material from the liquifier increases approximately exponentially. Conversely, when the liquifier pump is turned off, the melt flow rate exponentially decreases to zero. Accordingly, melt flow can be predicted by an exponential equation dependent upon a melt flow time constant of the liquifier.

(..)

What is claimed is:

1. In an extrusion apparatus having a liquifier which receives a solid element of a material that exhibits thermal expansion, heats the material, and deposits a flow of the material through a dispensing tip thereof along a predetermined tool path at an output rate, said apparatus using a material advance mechanism to supply the solid element of material to the liquifier at an input rate which controls the output rate, a method for matching the output rate to a predetermined target output rate which is selected to achieve a desired extrusion profile of the material deposited along the tool path, comprising the steps of:

predicting a melt flow component (QMF) of the output rate for a time step corresponding to a segment of the tool path, the melt flow being a rate of flow attributed to thermal expansion of the material heated in the liquifier; and

commanding the input rate (QiS) for that

time step so as to compensate for the predicted melt flow.

2. The method of claim 1, and further comprising the step of:

repeating the steps of predicting and commanding for subsequent time steps.

3. The method of claim 1, wherein the melt flow is predicted as a function of a melt flow time constant of the liquifier (τMF) and a percent thermal expansion of the material (%MF).

4. The method of claim 3, wherein predicting the melt flow component (QMF) of the output rate at the time step comprises adding the melt flow component from a previous time step (QMF t−1) to a predicted change in the melt flow component from the previous time step (ΔQMF), and wherein the input rate (QiS) for the time step is commanded according to the equation QiS=(1+%MF)(QTarget−QMF) where Qtarget is the predetermined target output rate.

5. The method of claim 4, wherein the predicted change in the melt flow component is given by the difference equation

$\Delta Q\,MFS = \%\,MF \star Q\,iS\,t-1\,1 + \%\,MF - Q\,MFS\,t-1 \star \Delta\,t\,\tau\,MF$,

$$\Delta Q_{MFS} = \frac{\%_{oMF} * Q_{iS_{t-1}}}{1 + \%_{oMF}} - Q_{MFS_{t-1}} * \frac{\Delta t}{\tau_{MF}}.$$

where QiS t−1 is the input rate from the previous step, and Δt is the duration of a time step.

6. The method of claim 1, wherein the melt flow over time is predicted using an exponential model.

7. The method of claim 6, wherein the exponential model is a function of a melt flow time constant of the liquifier (τMF) and a percent thermal expansion of the material (%MF).

8. The method of claim 7, wherein the exponential model of melt flow over time is given by the equation

Q MFS = % MF $\star$ Q iS 1 + % MF $\star$ (1 - 1 - t τ MF),

$$Q_{MFS} = \frac{\%_{oMF} * Q_{iS}}{1 + \%_{oMF}} * \left(1 - e^{\frac{-t}{\tau_{MF}}}\right).$$

for a step change in QiS from zero.

9. An extrusion apparatus comprising:

a liquifier which receives a solid element of a material that exhibits thermal expansion, heats the material, and deposits a flow of the material through a dispensing tip thereof along a predetermined tool path at an output rate;

a material advance mechanism which supplies the solid element of material to the liquifier at an input rate (QiS) that controls the output rate;

a control for providing control signals to the material advance mechanism, the control signals commanding operation of the material advance mechanism so that the input rate compensates for a predicted melt flow component (QMF) of the output rate.

10. The extrusion apparatus of claim 9, wherein the control contains an algorithm for predicting the melt flow component as a function of a melt flow time constant of the liquifier (τMF) and a percent thermal expansion of the material (%MF).

11. The extrusion apparatus of claim 10, wherein the algorithm comprises calculating a predicted change in the melt flow component (QMF) from a previous time step to a next time step according to the difference equation

ΔQ MFS = % MF ⋆ Q iS t - 1 1 + % MF - Q MFS t - 1 ⋆Δ tτ MF ,

$$\Delta Q_{MFS} = \frac{\%_o MF * Q_{iS_{t-1}}}{1 + \%_o MF} - Q_{MFS_{t-1}} * \frac{\Delta t}{\tau_{MF}}.$$

where QiS t−1 is the input rate at the previous time step, QMFS t−1 is the melt flow component of the output rate of solid material at the previous time step, and Δt is the duration of a time step.

12. The extrusion apparatus of claim 9, where melt flow over time is predicted using an exponential model.

13. The extrusion apparatus of claim 12, wherein the exponential model of melt flow over time is given by the equation

Q MFS = % MF ⋆ Q iS 1 + % MF ⋆ (1 - tτ MF) ·

$$Q_{MFS} = \frac{\%_o MF * Q_{iS}}{1 + \%_o MF} * \left(1 - e^{\frac{-t}{\tau_{MF}}}\right).$$

Water soluble rapid prototyping support and mold material

Publication number	US6228923 B1
Publication type	Grant
Application number	US 09/096,100
Publication date	8 May 2001
Filing date	11 Jun 1998
Priority date	2 Apr 1997
Fee status	Paid
Also published as	EP1078327A1, EP1078327A4, US6437034, US20010025073, WO1999060507A1
Inventors	John Lang Lombardi, Dragan Popovich, Gregory John Artz
Original Assignee	Stratasys, Inc.
Export Citation	BiBTeX, EndNote, RefMan

Patent Citations (16), Non-Patent Citations (5), Referenced by (56), Classifications (22), Legal Events (10)

External Links: USPTO, USPTO Assignment, Espacenet

Comment:

A rather long winded patent text, that – after closer inspection – reveals interesting information on the invention, as well as on some secondary aspects of this application. This text has been shortened, check the original document if interested in more details.

SUMMARY OF THE INVENTION

In the present invention, a unique thermoplastic polymer material, i.e., poly(2-ethyl-2-oxazoline) (referred to hereafter as "PEO"), is used as a polymer layer material as well as a support material in a freeform fabrication process. More specifically, PEO is melt extruded by a freeforming apparatus in layer form. The PEO layers solidify upon cooling and complicated shaped parts can be freeform fabricated by precisely and sequentially depositing polymer layers upon one another until the desired component is produced. Thus, prototypes can be directly freeformed by an extrusion freeforming apparatus using PEO as a raw material.

In addition, in the present invention, PEO

is used as a support material for use in rapid prototype processes such as extrusion freeform fabrication or a fused deposition modeling process. In particular, many parts which are fabricated by these processes have complicated overhang geometries which require the use of a support material that prevents the sagging of deposited molten, prototype material layers before cooling and solidification.

It has been discovered that a major advantage of PEO over other materials is that PEO is a high strength, rigid thermoplastic polymer that is easily and accurately extruded and has a good slump resistance at temperatures less than about 200° C. PEO also has the added benefits in that it is essentially an amorphous polymer that does not undergo significant shrinkage upon solidification. Polyethylene oxide, another commercially available water soluble thermoplastic, on the other hand, undergoes approximately 15-20% shrinkage due to crystallization upon solidification. Shrinkage on the order of this magnitude puts a great deal of stress and may induce warpage in freeformed support material layers. PEO also has high degree of interlayer adhesion when freeformed. Polyethylene oxide has negligible interlayer adhesion when freeformed. A major benefit of using PEO is that it has all of the above properties coupled with high water solubility. Rapid prototype parts can therefore be fabricated using PEO as a support material and the PEO support can be easily washed away with water from the completed prototype part without employing toxic and environmentally detrimental solvents, which may also dissolve the desired polymer prototype part. It is believed that PEO is the only commercially available non-ionic water soluble thermoplastic material (sold under the tradename Aquazol by Polymer Chemistry Innovations Inc., of Tucson, Ariz.) that has all of the above properties. PEO is also very tacky and many materials readily adhere to it, thereby making PEO an excellent rapid prototyping support material.

Furthermore, PEO is not as hygroscopic compared to other commercial water soluble polymers including polyvinyl alcohol and polyethylene oxide, and thus PEO possess significantly greater dimensional stability in ambient humid atmosphere compared to these other polymers. Moreover, PEO can be extruded at higher temperatures without decomposing and having its melt viscosity change with time.

In another aspect of the present invention, PEO is used as a fugitive mold material for casting ceramic slurries, e.g. for ceramic green body fabrication, and also preparing polyurethane or epoxy parts by pouring reactive mixtures of these liquid precursor materials into a mold which is precision machined from bulk PEO stock. Thus, in accordance with the present invention, parts can be subsequently extracted from the mold by placing the entire part in a water bath after the slurry or precursors are cured so that the water dissolves the PEO and leaves the fabricated polymer or green ceramic part behind.

This unique polymer PEO, not heretofore suggested for use as a extrusion freeform fabrication material, greatly facilitates the extrusion freeform fabrication of parts, as well as for casting ceramic slurries.

(..)

Samples were tested along the writing direction. This simply denotes the bead direction with respect to the mechanical testing equipment. The equipment used was a model 1011 Instron apparatus with a

Selected patents 131

load cell capacity of 1000 pounds. The 1011 Instron apparatus uses vertical specimen loading and wedge-action type grips. The cross head speed for all specimens was 0.2 inches per minute.

Tensile moduli, strength, 0.2% yield strength, and elongation or strain to fracture were calculated.

Discussion of Results

The values contained in Table I resulted from averaging the test samples' measured properties of interest.

The mechanical properties of the materials prepared in this work are compared with other free formed polymer materials in Table I. The PEO is more than 30 percent stronger and between 2 to 3 times stiffer than any of the presently available water soluble polymer materials. These properties represent a substantial improvement in the art.

TABLE I

Comparison of Materials Properties from Commercial SFF Systems

σ tensile E tensile ε break

System	Material	Grade	(psi)	(ksi)	(%)
3D	Epoxy	XB5170	2,400	130	9
DTM	Nylon-11	LN4000	5,200	200	32
Stratasys	ABS		5,000	360	50
ACR	PEEK	450 FC	36,374	1195	3
ACR	Poly-ethylene oxide (200,000 MW)	Union Carbide Polyox WSR-N80	3,000	40-70	500
ACR (200,000 MW)	PEO	Aquazol 200	4,000	230	1.9
ACR	PEO	Aquazol 50	900	150	0.9

(50,000 MW)

where in MW = molecular weight

SFF = Solid Free-Forming

3D = 3D Systems of Valencia, California

DTM = DTM Corporation of Austin, Texas

Stratasys = Stratasys of Eden Prairie, Minnesota

ACR = Advanced Ceramics Research, Inc. of Tucson, Arizona

PEO in Filament Applications

PEO has been found to be not only useful as cylindrical feed rod material, but also as filament feed material in yet another preferred embodiment of the present invention. It has been discovered that PEO is an excellent filament feed material that can be freeformed using fuse deposition modeling processes taught in U.S. Pat. No. 5,340,433 and U.S. Pat. No. 5,121,329 because it is water soluble and can be washed away easily, is a stiff material is thermally stable, and adheres well to other materials, including other layers of PEO. Therefore, PEO filament feedstock can be used as a support material in fuse deposition modeling of polymer prototype parts. (..)

The polymer material comprising PEO can be used as a support for free formed layers of other material. Further, the method of the present invention can be used to make an article of manufacture that is a free form three-dimensional object comprising a plurality of filament layers of PEO. The present invention further includes a thermoplastic polymer in the form of an extrudable object comprising a filament of PEO.

Further it has now been discovered that PEO can be blended with a variety of polar thermoplastics, fillers, and plasticizers to modify its physical properties. These additives enable the PEO polymer to be extruded into tough, flexible geometries (including Stratasys

132 Selected patents

Fused Deposition Modeller (FDM) filament form).

The polymer material comprising PEO can also include an inorganic filler, which in turn can be comprised of at least one soluble salt.

The PEO can be blended with at least one inert filler. The inert filler can be selected from the polymer filler group consisting of calcium carbonate, glass spheres, graphite, carbon black, carbon fiber, glass fiber, talc, wollastonite, mica, alumina, silica, and silicon carbide.

The typical extrusion temperature of the polymer in the head member can be in the range of about 120-410° C., and is preferably in the range of 150-290° C., and most preferably approximately 180° C.

As a further example, the modulus of PEO can be decreased by the addition an alcohol plasticizer. Preferably the alcohol plasticizer is in an amount of 0.5 to 45 wt. % alcohol plasticizer to the PEO. Preferred alcohol plasticizers are water soluble and have structures composed of multiple hydroxyl groups (i.e., ethylene glycol, glycerol, or 200-10,000 MW Union Carbide PEG polyethylene glycols). 600 MW PEG is a preferred plasticizer due to its combination of low viscosity and low melting point. These plasticizers decrease the rigidity of PEO and enable it to be drawn into flexible filament feedstock that can be extruded by a Stratasys Fused Deposition Modeller (FDM). Furthermore, PEG plasticizers are miscible with water and are believed to enhance the overall water solubility and dissolution rate of the freeformed plasticized PEO material.

PEG plasticized PEO filament is highly tacky in humid atmosphere, which makes it difficult to uniformly spool as feed material through the Stratasys FDM dispensing head. Consequently, its formulation must be modified to decrease its tackiness as well as enhance its strength. Addition of 0.25-5 wt. % of polar wax has been shown to decrease filament tackiness. The polar wax can be selected from the group consisting of compounds having alcohol, acid, ester or amide functional groups. Thus, in the present invention it is contemplated that among the various compounds that can be used include, but are not limited to amide waxes, including oleamide and stearamide, stearic acid, and stearate/oleate esters. In particular, an ethoxylated fatty alcohol known under the tradename of Unithox 420 (Baker Petrolite Corporation, Tulsa, Okla.) has been found to reduce filament tackiness. The structure of Unithox 420 is given below:

CH3CH2(CH2CH2)xCH2CH2(OCH2CH2)yOH

where x/y ranges from 4-10, but the preferred ratio is about 5.2.

Unithox 420 is believed to be uniformly soluble in the PEG plasticized PEO at elevated temperatures but phase separates from the mixture and migrates to the extruded filament surface upon cooling. This leaves a slightly waxy, low tackiness surface upon the cooled filament.

Polar homopolymers and copolymers containing polar functional groups, either pendant to or present in its main chain, can be added to PEG plasticized PEO formulations in order to increase the strength and toughness of the filament. Examples of polar homopolymers and copolymers that can be added to the PEG plasticized poly(2-ethyl-2-oxazoline) include Nylon 12, amorphous nylon copolymer of terephthalamide/isophthalamide/hexamethylenediamide, Nylon 6/Nylon 12 copolymer, polyvinylformal, polyvinylbutyral, and polyesters. These polymers also decrease the tendency of the filament to fracture when it is fed through the rollers on the Stratasys FDM head. Examples of polyamides include Nylon 12 (Grilamid L16) and an amorphous nylon copolymer of terephthalamide/isophthalamide/hexamethylenediamine (Grivory G16), both manufactured by EMS American Grilon Inc., Sumter, S.C., and Nylon 6/Nylon 12 Copolymer (Vestamelt 430P-1), made by Huls/Creanova Inc., Somerset, N.J. These polyamides can be present in amounts ranging from 0.5-35 wt. % based upon the total mass of PEG plasticized PEO.

Specific examples of water soluble plasticized PEO compositions that can be extruded into flexible filament and successfully extruded through a Stratasys FDM head are presented below:

EXAMPLE I

Calcium Carbonate* 22.3 wt. %

PEO (200K MW) 65.0

PEG (600 MW) 8.6

Grilamid L16 4.1

EXAMPLE II

Calcium Carbonate* 59.1

PEO (50K MW) 26.9

PEG (600 MW) 11.1

Vestamelt 430P-12.9

EXAMPLE III

Calcium Carbonate* 26.1

PEO (200K MW) 57.5

PEG (600 MW) 10.0

Grilamid L16 4.9

Unithox 1.5

EXAMPLE IV

Calcium Carbonate* 22.4

PEO (50K MW) 60.9

PEG (600 MW) 6.9

Grivory G-16 Nylon 6.7

Unithox 420 3.1

EXAMPLE V

CaCO3 59.25

PEO (200K MW) 26.25

PEG (600 MW) 10.80

Polyvinylbutyral** 3.70

EXAMPLE VI

CaCO3 25.98

PEO (200K MW) 58.96

PEG (600 MW) 8.35

Phenoxy PKHM 301*** 3.70

Unithox 420 1.52

EXAMPLE VII

CaCO3 26.09

PEO (200K MW) 59.23

PEG (600 MW) 8.39

Tyril 125**** 4.76

Unithox 420 1.53

*Calcium Carbonate filler was a submicron precipitated powder known under the tradename of Multifex MM 1007/056, made by Specialty Minerals

Inc., Adams, MA.

**Polyvinylbutyral used is known under the tradename Butvar B-98, made by Monsanto Company of St. Louis, MO.

***Phenoxy PKHM 301 is a linear thermoplastic phenoxy resin oligomer blend obtained from Phenoxy Specialists (Division in InChem Corp.), Rock Hill, SC.

****Tyril 125 is a styrene-acrylonitrile (SAN) copolymer manufactured by Dow Chemical Corp., Midland, MI. Preferred SAN copolymers have an amount ranging from about 20-40 wt. % acrylonitrile repeat units present in the polymer chains.

Examples VI and VII are believed to provide the most preferred embodiments of the present invention in that they are the easiest to formulate, and both exhibit excellent fluidity characteristics. Thus, it is preferred that the polar polymer added to the PEO is a polar polymer selected from the group consisting of compounds having nitrile functional groups (like Example VII) or compounds having ether and hydroxyl functional groups (like Example VI). Further, the linear thermoplastic phenoxy resin oligomer blend of Example VI and the styrene-acrylonitrile copolymer of Example VII each exhibited a high degree of thermodynamic compatibility with PEO polymers.

Those of skill in the art will recognize various changes to the methods, materials, component ratios, and apparatus are possible without departing from the spirit and scope of the invention. Thus, the invention is to be limited only by the claims and equivalents thereof.

Selected patents 135

Dispenser

136 Selected patents

3D print under water

Original title: "Device and method for the production of three-dimensional objects"

Patent number	CN1450953 A
Publication type	Application
Application number	CN 00819378
Published	31. Oct. 2001
Application	17. Apr. 2000
Priority	17. Apr. 2000
Also published as	CN1450953A, 6 et al»
Inventors	Hendrik John, Ruediger Landers, Rolf Muelhaupt
Applicant	Envision Technologies Gmbh

Patent citations (1), Referenced by (8), Classifications (12), Legal Events (2)

External links: DPMA, Espacenet

Comment:

The rather bulky patent text does reveal some interesting details at second look.

The principle of this invention makes use of the effect, that certain silicons cure immediately after the got in contact with water. Here the inventor uses a syringe that deposits silicone below the water surface.

The silicone can be mixed with other ingredients in order to achieve desired material properties. Since the curing goes so fast the inventor claims that his methods makes the use of support structures obsolete.

It is also proposed to use living cells as component of the printing material.

The author of this book raises the question, whether the syringe will not clog due to cured silicone under these conditions.

Check the claims for the detailed information on the composition of the silicone material.

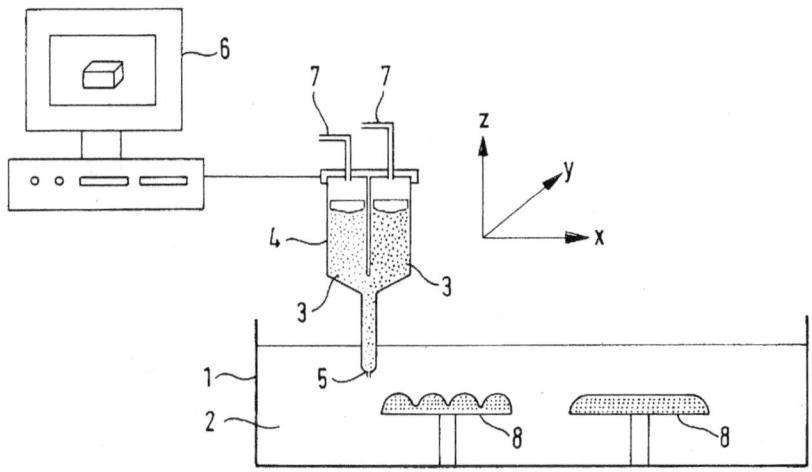

SUMMARY

The present invention relates to manufacturing apparatus and method for three-dimensional object. Apparatus includes a means for medium (2) of the container (1) and a three-dimensional positioning for the material (3) into the medium (2) the dispenser (4), materials (3) adding medium (2) leads to the formation of solid structure within. By the container (1) within a first material (2) filling height below the platform (8) along the XYZ direction dispenser added material (3), resulting in a three-dimensional object.

CLAIMS

1 The method of manufacturing three-dimensional object, comprising a container (1) of preparing a non-gaseous medium (2); the three-dimensional motion of a distributor (4) of the outlet (5) positioned on the medium (2) ; A solution consisting of one or more composition of the material (3) through the distributor (4) into the medium (2), the time, the material (3) into the medium (2) within the post-curing, or Media (2) caused by the contact to form a solid structure; And, the distributor (4) moving to the corresponding three-dimensional object areas, to form a three-dimensional solid structures.

(2) as claimed in claim 1, wherein the container (1) of preparing a medium (2) in a predetermined filling height, and the dispenser outlet (5) is less than the media (2) of the filling height positioned in the container (1) inside.

3 according to claim 1 or claim 2, wherein the medium (2) has a density selected for the material (3) has a density substantially the same compared to large or too small to not by much more.

4 according to one of claims 1 to 3, wherein, wherein the material (3) is formed leaving gaps, overlaps or spiral microdots, or form one or more pieces of fine, of which, one or a a plurality of fine pieces individually or conjointly, continuous or of allotment, spirally

wound or linearly, with continuous or discontinuous material flow ingredients.

5 according to one of claims 1 to 4, the method, wherein the use of materials (3) for liquid or ointment-like composition, said material (3) the ingredients of droplets or micro-beam.

6 according to one of claims 1 to 5, wherein, wherein said material (3) to include the ingredients of the core and a shell.

7 according to one of claims 1 to 6, the method, wherein the implementation of the medium (2) and / or materials (3) precipitation; or to implement a controlled precipitation, to form a three-dimensional object around the sub-structure of the cortex; or, medium (2) for containing one or more of the precipitated material (3) and the precipitant material (3) precipitation.

8 according to one of claims 1 to 7, wherein, wherein said material (3) contains co-reactive components which react with each other, and / or, the first medium (2) contains a co-reactive component which the material (3) the reaction of one or more components.

9 according to the method of claim 8, wherein the implementation of the interfacial polymerization, polycondensation or polyelectrolyte complex formation.

A process according to one of claims 1 to 9, wherein, wherein, by removing the core / shell of the core material (3), or by interfacial polymerization and removing the implementation of the interface can not afford the polymerization reaction material (3) , the formation of micro-pores or micro-channels.

11 according to one of claims 1 to 10 wherein wherein the first medium (2) through a material (3) is formulated into, by material (3) or the material (3) dissolved together with melted , curing, or bonding; or the material (3) into the medium with (2), by the medium (2) or the medium (2) dissolved together with, melting, solidification or bonding.

12 according to one of claims 1 to 11, said method, wherein as medium 2 with liquid, gelatinous, thixotropic, ointment, powder, the presence of a particulate or solid material, and / or as material (3) using a liquid, a gel, an ointment-like material.

13 according to one of claims 1 to 12, wherein, wherein the medium (2) from the group consisting of water, gelatin, an aqueous solution of a polyamine and mixtures thereof selected from the group; And, material (3) that contains a liquid at room temperature The oligomers and polymers, oligomers and polymer melt, the reactive oligomer and the polymerization, monomers, gels, pastes, plastisols, solutions, with reactive components of the two-component systems, their dispersions and mixtures selected from the group; and / or

14 according to the method of claim 13, wherein the material (3) as a gel with one or more one-component or two-component silicone rubber as a paste using one or more of the filling of one or more of organic and inorganic filler oligomers and polymers, as well as a reactive component of a two component system with one or more isocyanate / polyamide systems; or as material (3) the use of one or more urethane oligomer.

15 according to one of claims 1 to 14, said method, wherein the medium (2) or the material (3) contains an inorganic and an organic filler.

16 according to one of claims 1 to 15, said method, wherein as medium (2) use of

one or more monomers, of one or more monomers added to the base body of a fibrous structure and / or frame structure, and, then, one or more monomers.

17 according to one of claims 1 to 16 wherein, wherein the medium (2) and the material (3) through the use of the rheological properties of organic and inorganic nano filler adjusted.

18 according to one of claims 1 to 17, said method, wherein in the first and / or second material (3) containing biologically active substances.

19 according to the method of claim 18, wherein the one or more types of cells are discharged in the space provided exact position, to constitute a three-dimensional structure can be accurately adjusted.

20 according to the method of claim 19, wherein the three-dimensional structure equipped with holes, for supplying nutrients and eliminate metabolites.

21 according to one of claims 1 to 20 wherein the method is characterized as follows: in the medium (2) and the material (3) addition of a system comprising a delay medium (2) at one of its component materials (3) or a component of the reaction between the substance (10).

22 according to the method of claim 21, characterized in that: said material (10) added to the material (3).

23 according to claim 21 or claim 22, characterized as follows: by adding a substance (10), medium (2) or a component of the material (3) or a component of the reaction between the time (t) delayed so long, and the material (3) into the medium (2) within the adhesion after curing has been cured before the material (3) to form a solid structure or cause.

24. For implementing according to one of the forefront of all the method claimed in claim The apparatus includes a means for medium (2) of the container (1), a three-dimensional motion for the material (3) into the medium (2) within the dispenser (4), wherein said distributor (4) has an outlet (5), the outlet (5) can be positioned in the container (1) within a first material (2) below the filling height.

25 as claimed in claim 24, wherein said outlet (5) designed as a one-dimensional nozzle or include one by one control, individual heating and / or two-dimensional nozzle valve nozzle groups, as well as said distributor (4) for one or more materials (3) a container for each component.

26 according to claim 25 wherein the apparatus, it is set to the medium (2) and / or materials (3) maintained in a predetermined state, or in the discharge for heating or cooling through the material (3) of each component container and / or container (1) or / or one or more nozzles, causing a hot purposefully induced response.

27 in accordance with one of claims 1 to 23 or in accordance with the method and claims 25 to 26 of the application apparatus according to one of biological or pharmaceutical active substance, bio-medical or biological activity of the three-dimensional object.

28 according to claim 27, wherein, the use of proteins, growth factors and living cells as biological or pharmaceutical active substance, the use of hyaluronic acid, gelatine, collagen, alginic acid and its salts, chitosan and its salts as an additive or as a precursor material..)

140 Selected patents

Other methods

Selected patents 141

3D print, multicolor, with multiple materials

Original title:"Layer manufacturing of a multi-material or multi-color 3-D object using electrostatic imaging and lamination"

Patent number	US20020145213 A1
Publication type	Application
Published	10. Oct. 2002
Application	10. Apr. 2001
Priority	10. Apr. 2001
Also published as	US6780368
Inventors	Bor Jang, Junhai Liu
Original Assignee	Jang Bor Z., Junhai Liu

Referenced by (18), Classifications (24), Legal Events (4)

External links: USPTO, USPTO assignment, Espacenet

Comment:

The inventor presents a process of printing 3D objects, that resembles a laser printer. A powder a ionized powder transferring mechanism and a binder and a UV light source for curing are the main components for this system.

142 Selected patents

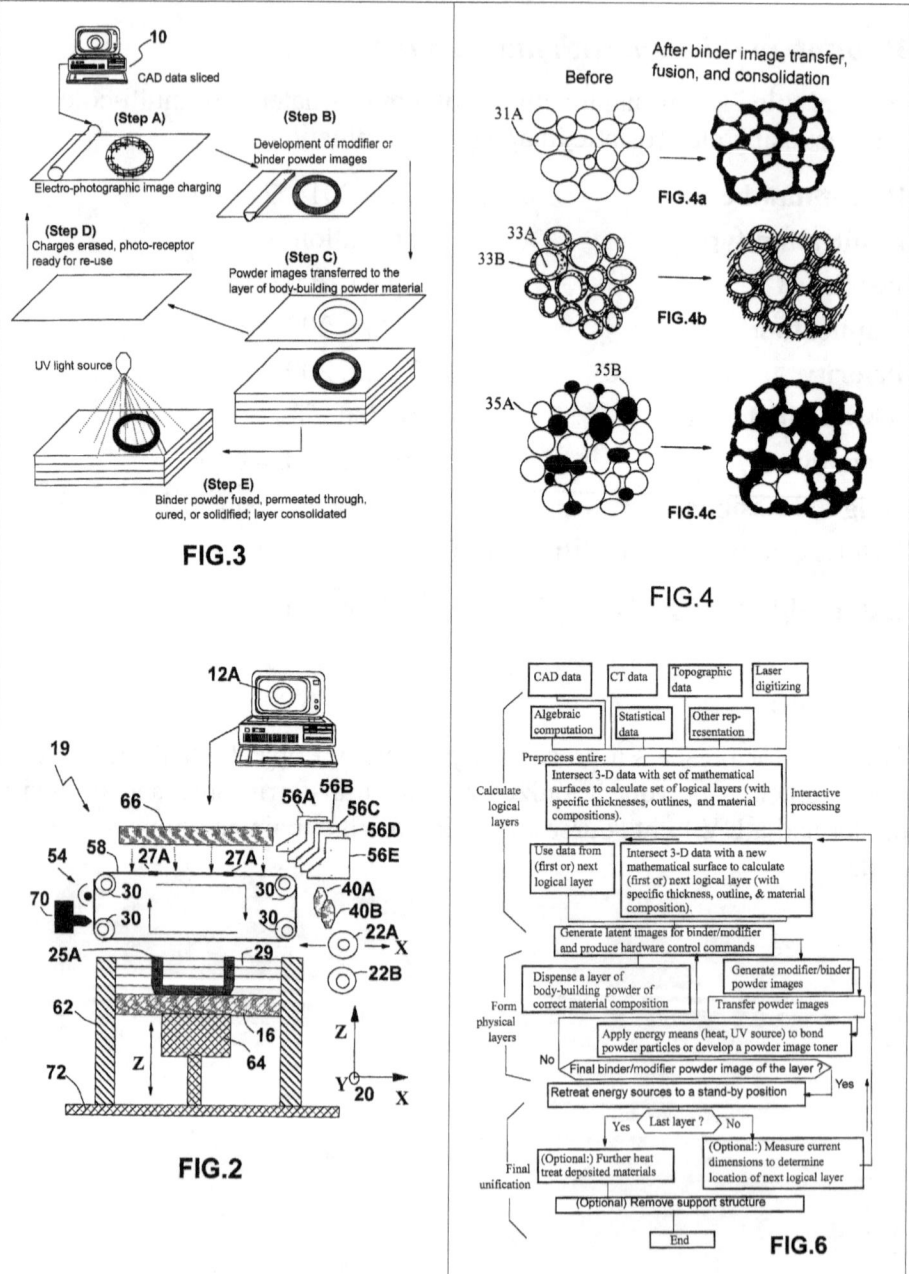

Selected patents 143

FIELD OF THE INVENTION

A solid freeform fabrication method and related apparatus for fabricating a three-dimensional, multi-material or multi-color object from successive layers of a primary body-building powder, at least a modifier powder and a binder powder in accordance with a computer-aided design of the object, the method including: (a) feeding a first layer of the primary body-building powder to a work surface; (b) operating an electrophotographic powder deposition device to create at least a modifier powder image and a binder powder image in accordance with this design; (c) transferring these powder images in a desired sequence to the first layer of a primary body-building powder; (d) applying energy sources to fuse the binder powder, forming a binder fluid that permeates through the first layer of a primary body-building powder for bonding and consolidating the powder particles to form a first cross-section of the object; (e) feeding a second layer of a primary body-building powder onto the first layer and repeating the operating, transferring, and applying steps to form a second cross-section (possibly of a different material composition distribution or color pattern) of the object; (f) repeating the feeding, operating, transferring, and applying steps to build successive layers of materials in a layer-wise fashion in accordance with the design for forming the multiple-layer, multi-material object; and (g) removing un-bonded powder particles, causing the 3-D object to appear.

BACKGROUND OF THE INVENTION

[0002] Layer manufacturing (LM) or solid freeform fabrication (SFF) or is a new fabrication technology that builds an object of any complex shape layer by layer or point by point without using a pre-shaped tool such as a die or mold. This process begins with creating a Computer Aided Design (CAD) file to represent the geometry or drawing of a desired object. This CAD file is converted to a proper solid interface format such as the stereo lithography (.STL) format. The geometry file is further sliced into a large number of thin cross-sectional layers with each layer being comprised of coordinate point data. In a commonly used layer-wise data format called Common Layer Interface (CLI), the contours (shape and dimensions) of each layer are defined by a plurality of line segments connected to form polylines on an X-Y plane of a X-Y-Z orthogonal coordinate system. The layer data are converted to tool path data normally in terms of computer numerical control (CNC) codes such as G-codes and M-codes. These codes are then utilized to drive a fabrication tool for defining the desired areas of individual layers and stacking up the object layer by layer along the Z-direction.

(..)

[0003] The SFF technology makes it possible to convert a CAD image data directly into a three-dimensional (3-D) physical object. The technology has been widely used in applications such as verifying CAD database, evaluating engineering design feasibility, testing part functionality, assessing aesthetics, checking ergonomics of design, aiding in tool and fixture design, creating conceptual models and marketing tools, producing medical or dental models, generating patterns for investment casting, reducing or eliminating engineering changes in production, and providing small production runs.

144 Selected patents

[0004] The SFF techniques may be divided into three categories: layer-additive, layer-subtractive, and hybrid (combined layer-additive and subtractive). A layer additive process involves adding or depositing a material to form predetermined areas of a layer essentially point by point; but a multiplicity of points may be deposited at the same time in some techniques, such as of the multiple-nozzle inkjet-printing type. These predetermined areas together constitute a thin cross-section of a 3-D object as defined by a CAD geometry. Successive layers are then deposited in a predetermined sequence with a layer being affixed to its adjacent layers for forming an integral multi-layer object. A 3-D object, when sliced into a plurality of constituent layers or thin sections, may contain features that are not self-supporting and in need of a support structure during the object-building procedure. These features include isolated islands in a layer and overhangs. In these situations, additional steps of building the support structure, also on a layer-by-layer basis, will be required of a layer-additive technique. An example of a layer-additive technique that normally requires building a support structure is the fused deposition modeling (FDM) process as specified in U.S. Pat. No. 5,121,329; issued on Jun. 9, 1992 to S. S. Crump.

[0005] A layer-subtractive process involves feeding a complete solid layer of a material to the surface of a support platform and using a cutting tool (normally a laser) to cut off or somehow degrade the integrity of the un-wanted areas of this solid layer. The solid material in these un-wanted areas of a layer becomes a part of the support structure for subsequent layers. These un-wanted areas are hereinafter referred to as the "negative region" while the remaining areas that constitute a cross-section of a 3-D object are referred to as the "positive region". A second solid layer of material is then fed onto the first layer and bonded thereto. The same cutting tool is then used to cut off or degrade the material in the negative region of this second layer. These procedures are repeated successively until multiple layers are laminated to form a unitary object. After all layers have been completed, the unitary body (or part block) is removed from the platform, and the excess material (in the negative region) is removed to reveal the 3-D object. This "decubing" procedure is known to be tedious and difficult to accomplish without damaging the object. An example of a layer-subtractive technique is the well-known laminated object manufacturing (LOM), disclosed in, for instance, U.S. Pat. No. 4,752,352 (Jun. 21, 1988 to M. Feygin).

[0006] A hybrid process involves both layer-additive and subtractive procedures. An example can be found with the Shape Deposition Manufacturing (SDM) process disclosed in U.S. Pat. No. 5,301,863 issued on Apr. 12, 1994 to Prinz and Weiss. Such a process is complicated and difficult to operate. It also requires the operation of heavy and expensive equipment.

[0007] Another good example of the layer-additive technique is the 3-D powder printing technique (3D-P) developed at MIT; e.g., U.S. Pat. No. 5,204,055 (April 1993 to Sachs, et al.) and U.S. Pat. No. 6,007,318 (Dec. 28, 1999 to Russell, et al.). This 3-D powder printing technique involves dispensing a layer of loose powders onto a support platform and using an ink jet to spray a computer-defined pattern of liquid binder onto a layer of uniform-composition powder in a point-by-point fashion. The binder serves to bond together the powder particles on those areas (positive region) defined by this pattern. Those powder particles in the un-wanted areas (negative region) remain loose or separated from one another and are removed at the end of the build process. Another layer of powder is spread over the preceding one, and the process is repeated. The "green" part made up of those bonded powder particles is separated from the loose powders when the process is completed. This procedure is followed by binder removal and impregnation of the green part with a liquid material such as epoxy resin and metal melt. Although several nozzle orifices may be employed to dispense several droplet streams at the same time, this 3D-P process remains to be essentially a point-by-point process, being characterized by a slow build speed.

[0008] This same drawback is true of the selected laser sintering (SLS) technique (e.g., U.S. Pat. No. 4,863,538, Sep. 5, 1989 to C. Deckard, U.S. Pat. No. 4,938,816, Jul. 3, 1990 to J. Beaman, et al., and U.S. Pat. No. 5,316,580, May 31, 1994 to Deckard). The SLS technique involves spreading a full-layer of loose powder particles and uses a computer-controlled, high-power laser to partially melt these particles within predetermined areas (positive region) in a point-by-point fashion. Commonly used powders include thermoplastic particles, thermoplastic-coated metal particles, metal-coated ceramic particles, and mixtures of high-melting and low-melting powder materials. These point-wise procedures are repeated for subsequent layers, one layer at a time, according to the CAD data of the sliced-part geometry. The loose powder particles in the negative region of each layer are allowed to stay as part of a support structure. The sintering process does not always fully melt the powder, but allows molten material to bridge between particles. Commercially available systems based on SLS are known to have several drawbacks. One problem is that the need to use a high power laser makes the SLS an expensive technique and un-suitable for use in an office environment. Again, the spot-by-spot or point-by-point laser scanning is a very slow procedure, resulting in a low object-building speed.

[0009] In U.S. Pat. No. 5,514,232, issued May 7, 1996, Burns discloses a method and apparatus for automatic fabrication of a 3-D object from individual layers of fabrication material having a predetermined configuration. Each layer of fabrication material with desired shape and dimensions is first deposited on a carrier substrate in a deposition station. The fabrication material along with the substrate are then transferred to a stacker station. At this stacker station the individual layers are stacked together, with successive layers being affixed to each other and the substrate being removed after affixation. Lamination-based LM techniques that require radiation curing of solid sheet polymer materials layer by layer can be found in U.S. Pat. No. 5,174,843 (Dec. 29, 1992 to M. Natter) and No. 5,352,310 (Oct. 4, 1994 to M. Natter). Natter's technique is limited to high-energy radiation-curable polymer materials in a solid sheet form. Disclosed in U.S. Pat. No. 5,183,598 (Feb. 2, 1993 to J-L Helle, et al.) is a process that includes preparing thin sheets of a fiber- or screen-reinforced matrix material. In these composite sheets, the matrix material exhibits the feature that its solubility in a specific solvent can be changed when the material is exposed to a specific radiation. Selected areas of individual sheets are radiated to reduce the solubility. The un-irradiated portion (the negative region) of individual layers remains soluble in the solvent. The stack of sheets are affixed together to form an integral body, which is immersed in the solvent that causes the desired object to appear. This process exhibits the following shortcomings:

[0010] (1). A high-power radiation source (e.g., a high-power laser beam) is required. High energy radiation sources and their handling equipment (for reflecting, focusing, etc) are expensive. Furthermore, they are not welcome in an office environment.

[0011] (2). When a screen is used as the reinforcement, the screen in the negative region is difficult to get dissolved in the solvent particularly if this screen is made of metal or ceramic materials. A strong acid is needed in dissolving a metal screen.

[0012] Lamination-based LM techniques that involve transferring thin sections of powders, prepared by electrophotographic or electrostatic attraction, to a stacking station are disclosed in U.S. Pat. No. 5,088,047 (Feb. 11, 1992 to D. Bynum), U.S. Pat. No. 5,593,531 (Jan. 14, 1997 to S. M. Penn), and U.S. Pat. No. 6,066,285 (May 23, 2000 to Kumar). In Bynum's process, a drum-shaped electrophotographic element is first prepared. A light image corresponding to a cross-section of an object generated by a computer is projected into this element by line-by-line laser scanning, coordinated with rotational speed of the drum to selectively dissipate the charge thereon, thereby creating an electrostatic latent image on the element. The element, along with the latent image thereon, is then rotatably transferred to a plurality of developer stations, which respectively apply forming powders (toner) to different areas of the electro-photographic element. For each layer, at least two developer stations are needed to apply two different powders to the positive and negative regions, respectively, for building the object cross-section (positive region) and the support structure (negative region). These areas of powders are then electrostatically attracted to a surface of an endless flexible belt, which carries these patterned powders to a fixing station where the powder particles in the positive region are made tacky by the application of heat or solvent vapor. The tackified lamina is then transferred to a stacking station and laid up onto a support platform or a previous layer to form a layer of both the object cross-section and support structure. The above steps are repeated in the same sequence to lay up multiple laminas to form a block of laminas. The powder materials in the negative regions for forming the support structure are usually made of lower melting materials and can be removed by heat from this block at the end of the build process to reveal the desired 3-D object. A fundamentally similar process is disclosed in Penn's patent and Kumar's patent. The processes specified in these three patents (U.S. Pat. Nos. 5,088,047, 5,593,531, and 6,066,285) have the following drawbacks:

[0013] (1) At least two toner developing stations are required, one for forming the part (object) and the other for the support structure. For every layer of the same object-building material, two different types of powders have to be precisely deposited electrostatically, in sequence and in registration, onto complementary areas of a layer. This is difficult to accomplish without suffering cross-contamination.

[0014] (2) It is well-known in the art of electrophotography that most of the conductive particles (e.g., metal powders) do not work well with charging devices.

This effectively eliminates the freeform formation of many metallic parts if metal particles are the primary body-building material of the part being built. In contrast, the presently invented method provides an effective way of eliminating this limitation, making our method so much more versatile. In this method, we make use of a simple powder-feeder to supply and evenly spread up a layer of a primary object body-building powder material (e.g., metal), analogous to the powder-feeding step in afore-mentioned SLS and 3D-P processes. We then use electrophotography techniques to form, develop, and transfer toner images of a binder powder (to bond or sinter together the underlying primary body-building powder particles) and a plurality of property modifying powders (modifier powders, e.g., coloring agent), simultaneously or in sequence. The binder and modifier powders collectively occupy only a small fraction of the object cross-section being built.

[0015] (3) These three prior art electrophotography methods are limited to loose powders as the starting primary body-building materials. Other forms of material such as a porous substrate (e.g., comprising fiber preform as a reinforcement for a composite) can not be used in these processes.

[0016] (4) Penn's and Kumar's methods are essentially limited to the fabrication of an object of homogeneous material composition and are not easily or readily adapted for the preparation of a multi-material or multi-color object in which the material composition or color pattern can be varied from point to point. Bynum's method, in principle, allows for variation of material composition or color pattern from point to point, like in the case of the traditional 2-D printing process that involves developing and transferring multi-color toner images to a sheet of paper. In real practice, however, the electrostatic attraction in a traditional electrophotography system can only handle a thin layer of light-weight toner powder at a time, up to 10 µm or less in thickness. It would take an extremely long time to build up a 3-D model of, say, 100 mm in thickness. In contrast, in our method, the powder feeder can feed layers of heavy- or light-weight powder of which the layer thickness can be varied from very thin to very thick. With the primary body-building powder occupying the majority of the object volume (typically 70% to 95%), the electrophotography device is required to provide only a small amount of binder and modifier powders at a time. Further, in our method, in the negative region of a layer where the primary body-building powder receives no binder, the powder particles serve to provide the needed support structure. It is not necessary to carry out the extra steps of developing a support structure toner image and transferring this image to the negative region of a layer (where the positive region of the layer is already deposited with the image material) in such a fashion that the two complementary regions of different materials must perfectly match (in registry) in shapes and thickness.

[0017] Despite these shortcomings of the afore-mentioned three patents, the concept of adapting electrophotography techniques for transferring powder materials in a LM system has proven to be very useful.

[0018] Due to the specific solidification mechanisms employed, many LM techniques are limited to producing parts from specific polymers. For instance, Stereo Lithography (SLa) and Solid Ground Curing (SGC) rely on ultraviolet (UV) light induced curing of photo-

148 Selected patents

curable polymers such as acrylate and epoxy resins. The photo-curable polymer in these two cases constitutes the vast majority of the material in the resulting 3-D object. Any other ingredient such as an additive or reinforcement represents at best a minority phase in the structure. The photo-curable polymer in the resulting structure is a "host" while any additive, if present, is just a guest. The host provides the basic structural integrity of the 3-D object. Unfortunately, photo-curable polymers alone normally do not have good mechanical strength and toughness.

[0019] The above state-of-the-art review has indicated that all prior-art layer manufacturing techniques have serious drawbacks that prevent them from being more widely implemented.

[0020] Therefore, an object of the present invention is to provide an improved layer-additive method and apparatus that can be used for producing a multi-material or multi-color 3-D object.

[0021] Another object of the present invention is to provide a computer-controlled method and apparatus for producing a part on a layer-by-layer, but not point-by-point basis (hence, with a high build speed).

[0022] It is a further object of this invention to provide a computer-controlled object building method that does not require heavy and expensive equipment such as a high-power laser system.

[0023] It is another object of this invention to provide a method and apparatus for building a CAD-defined object in which the support structure is readily provided during the layer-adding procedure.

[0024] Still another object of this invention is to provide a layer manufacturing technique that places minimal constraint on the range of materials that can be used in the fabrication of a 3-D object. Further, the material composition or color of the object can be varied from spot to spot and/or from layer to layer.

SUMMARY OF THE INVENTION

[0025] The Method

[0026] The objects of the invention are realized by a method and related apparatus for fabricating a three-dimensional, multi-material or multi-color object on a layer-by-layer basis (but not point-by-point) and in accordance with a computer-aided design (CAD) of this object. The object is made from at least a primary body-building powder material, a binder powder, and at least a property-modifying material in fine powder form (hereinafter referred to as modifier powder). This modifier powder can contain a colorant. The design contains data on the geometry (shape and dimensions) and material composition distribution (and/or color pattern). The data preferably is sliced into layer-wise data sets with each set defining the geometry and material composition of a constituent cross-section of the object. Basically, the method includes, in combination, the following steps:

[0027] (a) providing a work surface on a support platform that lies substantially parallel to an X-Y plane of an X-Y-Z Cartesian coordinate system defined by three mutually orthogonal X-, Y- and Z-axes;

[0028] (b) feeding a first layer of a primary body-building powder material to the work surface (e.g., by using a traditional powder feeder commonly used in selected area sintering and 3-D powder printing processes);

[0029] (c) operating an electrophotographic powder deposition means to create transferable powder toner images of a binder powder and at least a modifier powder in accordance with the CAD design; (A plurality of modifier powders may form separate toner images or may be combined to form one composite toner image.)

[0030] (d) transferring the transferable modifier and binder powder images, one image at a time, in a desired sequence onto the first layer of the primary body-building powder material;

[0031] (e) applying energy means to fuse said binder powder, allowing the resulting fused binder fluid to permeate downward through the first layer of primary body-building material for bonding and consolidating the particles in the first layer to form a first cross-section of the object; (Bonding and consolidating are hereinafter collectively referred to as sintering in the present context.)

[0032] (f) feeding a second layer of a primary body-building powder material onto the deposited first layer and repeating the operating, transferring, and applying steps to form a second cross-section of the object; (The material distribution and color pattern in the second cross-section may be different from those of the first cross-section.)

[0033] (g) repeating the feeding, operating, transferring, and applying steps to build successive layers of possibly varying material compositions and/or color patterns in a layer-wise fashion in accordance with the CAD design for forming multiple layers of the object; and

[0034] (h) removing un-bonded powder particles, causing the 3-D object to appear.

[0035] In this instant method, the steps of applying energy means could include pre-heating a layer of primary body-building powder material to a temperature above the melting point of the binder powder. This is done so that the binder powder, when transferred and deposited onto the predetermined areas (positive region) of a corresponding pre-heated body-building material powder layer, will be quickly melted to become a fluid that permeates through the gaps between fine particles of the body-building material powder. This binder fluid, when solidified, will bond and consolidate the powder particles in the positive region, leaving the powder particles in the negative region un-bonded (free from binder). The particles in the negative region stay as part of a support structure. As one can easily see, in this method, any material that can be made into a fine powder form can be used as a primary body-building material and can be easily fed and evenly spread up to form a layer. This is a very significant advantage over other prior art electrophotography-based LM techniques.

[0036] The binder powder could include a resin composition that can be cured or hardened with heat, ultra violet light, electron beam, ion beam, plasma, microwave, X-ray, Gamma ray, or a combination thereof. Alternatively, the binder powder could include a lower-melting material that can be readily fused to become a fluid. Once permeating through a layer of primary body-building powder material for providing bridges between particles, the binder fluid can be cooled down to below the melting point of the binder material and be solidified. Preferably, the steps of applying energy means are carried out in such a manner that successive layers are affixed together to form a unitary body of the 3-D object. This can be easily accomplished by allowing the fused binder fluid to have sufficient time to permeate through the current layer of body-building powder material and reaching the top surface of the previously deposited layer.

[0037] In the instant invention, the working principle of the electrophotographic powder deposition means can be selected from a range of electrostatic printer or photocopier mechanisms. For instance, electrophotographic powder deposition means can include, but not limited to (1) planar capacitor dot matrix charging device and (2) combined corona discharging/thin photoconductive charge receptor/scanning laser imaging devices. The electrophotographic powder deposition means is characterized by the following features:

[0038] (4) It provides a 2-D pattern or "latent image" of electrostatic charges to attract fine powder particles of the binder composition and/or modifiers to form these binder/modifier particles into a toner "image" (thin section of powder particles) in selected areas of a powder layer; these areas being programmable and predetermined by a computer. These areas, corresponding to the positive region of a layer, are defined by the layer data of a CAD design for the object to be built. A full area of the binder powder and/or modifier powder is formed and transferred to deposit onto a layer of body-building powder material, equivalent to a process of "photo-printing". The binder powder "photo-printed" to the positive region of a body-building powder material layer will help sinter the particles therein, forming a cross-section of the 3-D object. The modifier powder image transferred to the same region of a layer will impart desired physical properties (e.g., color appearance) to this layer. The primary body-building powder particles in other areas of the same layer, not receiving any binder powder composition, will remain as isolated, loose particles that serve as part of a support structure. As opposed to the case of conventional selected laser sintering (SLS) in which a laser beam is used to sinter the powder spot by spot (essentially point by point), the presently invented method builds the part area by area (up to one full layer at a time). This is also in sharp contrast to operating an inkjet printhead to print adhesive onto a layer of powder in a point-by-point fashion in a conventional 3D powder printing (3D-P or MIT) process.

[0039] (5) The binder powder, once deposited, is melted in such a manner that the binder fluid flows around to provide a bridge between primary body-building particles in the positive region. The binder can bond together these particles to impart sufficient strength and rigidity to the layer for easy handling and for maintaining the part dimensional accuracy during the formation of subsequent layers. If the binder contains a photo-curable adhesive composition, the pre-heat energy intensity and the energy of the imposing light source (heat and light constituting the energy means) should be provided in such a fashion that successive layers can be affixed together to form a unitary body of the 3-D object.

[0040] (6) If the binder contains a heat-fusible material composition, a complete body-building powder layer can be pre-heated by other heat sources (e.g., infrared, IR) disposed near the object-building zone to a temperature (Tpre) sufficient for melting the binder composition. After a selected duration of time, this heat source may be switched off to allow the binder fluid (already permeating through a layer) to solidify. If the layer of primary body-building material is already mixed with component compositions of a binder (excluding a photo-initiator, for instance), the electro-photographic powder deposition means may be used to transfer an image of the photo-initiator powder to the positive region of the layer. The pre-heat temperature Tpre may be so chosen that it is capable of promoting the curing reaction once initiated by the photo-initiator along with an incident light, but insufficient for initiating the curing reaction of the binder compositions by the pre-heat alone. This auxiliary heat would help accelerate the cure reaction and significantly reduce the light intensity requirement that would otherwise be imposed upon the light source. In this favorable situation, the light source can be just based on an ordinary ultraviolet (UV) light source. No expensive high-power laser beam, electron beam, X-ray, Gamma-ray or other high-energy radiation is necessary.

[0041] (7) The physical sizes of the binder powder image forming area (electrostatically charged substrate area of a photo-receptor, for instance) of this electrophotographic powder deposition means are preferably sufficient to cover the complete envelop of a primary body-building powder layer so that a complete cross-section of the 3-D object can be built in one binder powder image transfer. This is one of the advantages over the case of conventional selected laser sintering (SLS) which requires aiming a laser beam to one spot at a time (spot being micron- or sub-millimeter-sized). It would take a much longer time for a laser beam to fuse and sinter the particles of a complete cross-section in a spot-by-spot or point-by-point fashion. Further, since binder powder image can be exactly identical to the desired cross-section of a layer, this instant invention also has a significant advantage over the conventional 3D-P process, which involves ejecting adhesive droplets essentially point by point to cover the positive region, a slow process indeed.

[0042] In the presently invented method, the photo-curable binder may consist of such adhesive compositions as a base resin, a hardening or cross-linking agent, a photo-initiator, a photo-sensitizer, and possibly with additional catalyst and/or reaction accelerator. All of these compositions, if in a powder form, may be mixed together to form a complete binder adhesive mixture. This binder mixture is then attracted by the electro-photographic means to form into a binder image, which is transferred and deposited onto a powder layer. Alternatively, one or more compositions may be included as secondary ingredients in the primary body-building powder material to be dispensed one layer at a time by a powder feeder (powder-dispensing means) while the remaining composition(s) may constitute the binder powder image.

[0043] The powder inside a powder feeder may comprise a primary body-building material (fine particles), additives (physical or chemical property modifiers), and secondary ingredients (selected compositions of a binder adhesive). In this method, the primary body-building powder may be composed of one or more than one type of fine particles. These fine powder particles could be of any geometric shape, but preferably spherical. The particle sizes are preferably smaller than 100 µm, further preferably smaller than 10 µm, and most preferably smaller than 1 µm. The size distribution is preferably uniform. The primary body-building powder may be selected from the following three basic types of powders:

[0044] Type A: fine particles of a primary

body-building material only. In this type, only primary body-building materials in a fine particle form are included as the ingredients in the powder; no binder composition being included. All binder compositions are present as a binder powder to be formed into an image by the electro-photographic means. The primary body-building materials can be selected from polymers, ceramics, glass, metals and alloys, carbon, and combinations thereof. The polymers may be thermoplastic (e.g., polyvinyl chloride) or thermosetting (e.g., polyimide oligomer or prepolymer powder). The binder, including all selected compositions, will be deposited over the positive region of a complete layer and allowed to permeate through the gaps between fine particles in a layer of primary body-building powder. The binder (if an adhesive) in the positive region (corresponding to the desired cross-section) of a layer will be at least partially cured (chemically cross-linked or otherwise hardened) to bond together the primary body building particles. The binder (if containing a fusible material composition) will be heated to become a fluid which, once permeated through a layer, will be cooled to solidify. No binder will be deposited to the negative region and, hence, the fine particles in this region will remain loose and will stay as part of a support structure.

[0045] Type B: fine ceramic, metallic, glass, or polymeric particles (as primary body-building materials) each coated with a thin layer of coating comprising selected binder adhesive compositions. Once a layer of these coated solid particles is deposited, the remaining compositions of a binder adhesive are then deposited, melted, and allowed to permeate through the gaps between these primary body-building particles. These remaining compositions are then in contact or reacted with the selected binder compositions in the coating to make a complete binder adhesive. The binder adhesive, only existing in the positive region of a layer, is then at least partially cured by heat and/or UV light or any other energy means to bond together body-building particles, leaving the particles in the negative region loose and un-bonded.

[0046] Type C: a mixture of fine particles of primary body-building materials (e.g., a silicon dioxide powder) with at least one binder adhesive composition also in a fine powder form. The other remaining binder adhesive compositions are electro-photographically formed into a binder image, deposited onto a layer of Type C powder mixture, and allowed to flow around the fine particles and react with the at least one binder adhesive composition. The complete binder adhesive formulation in the positive region of this layer is then at least partially cured to provide inter-particle bonding for those primary body-building particles in the positive region. Again, the adhesive will not enter the negative region and the powder particles in this region will remain loose and physically separable.

[0047] In each powder type, additional ingredients may be added to impart desired physical and/or chemical properties to the object being built. These ingredients may contain a reinforcement composition selected from the group consisting of short fiber, whisker, and particulate reinforcements such as a spherical particle, ellipsoidal particle, flake, small platelet, small disc, etc. These ingredients may also contain, but not limited to, colorants, anti-oxidants, anti-corrosion agent, sintering agent, plasticizers, etc. Any of these ingredients, when intended to be used in each and

Selected patents 153

every layer of the 3-D object, may preferably be included in the primary body-building powder to be dispensed by a traditional powder feeder. Those ingredients that are to be deposited only at selected spots of a layer or selected layers (but not all layers) of an object may be included as a part of a modifier powder. These ingredients will then be electrophotographically formed into a modifier powder image (toner) and transferred to a corresponding cross-section of a primary body-building powder, before or after the binder powder image is transferred. Alternatively, selected ingredients may be combined with a binder powder to form a composite binder-modifier powder image.

[0048] Many prior-art powder-dispensing means or feeders are available for feeding layers of powder materials, one layer at a time. The moving and dispensing operations of the powder-dispensing means and the operation of an electrophotographic powder deposition means are preferably conducted under the control of a computer. This can be accomplished by (1) first creating a computer-aided design of the 3-D object on a computer with the design containing information on both the geometry and material composition distribution of the object with the geometry including a plurality of data points defining the object, (2) generating programmed signals corresponding to each of the data points, collected into layer-wise data sets, in a predetermined sequence; (3) generating plural powder images (comprising a binder powder image and at least a modifier powder image) and transferring/depositing these binder/modifier powder images to corresponding areas of a layer of body-building powder material responsive to these programmed signals, (4) moving the powder-dispensing means and the work surface relative to each other (in Z-direction, e.g.) in response to these programmed signals. The signals for moving may be advantageously prescribed in accordance with the G-codes and M-codes that are commonly used in computer numerical control (CNC) machinery industry, but other motion control codes may also be used. The signals for forming a powder image may be created by any image formation means commonly used in an electrostatic printer or photo-copier.

[0049] In order to produce a multi-material 3-D object in which the material composition of the primary body-building powder can vary from layer to layer, the presently invented method may further comprise the steps of (1) creating a geometry of the 3-D object on a computer with the geometry including a plurality of layer-wise sets of data points defining the object; each of the data sets being coded with a selected material composition, (2) generating programmed signals corresponding to each of the data sets in a predetermined sequence; and (3) operating the powder-dispensing means in response to the programmed signals to dispense and deposit powders of selected body-building material compositions, with the material compositions varying possibly from layer to layer. In order to achieve a point-to-point variation in material composition or color, each data point may be coded with a material composition or color. Such a material distribution or color pattern can be physically achieved by using the color electrophotography steps to form and transfer multi-material or multi-color powder images to corresponding layers of a primary body-building powder. The virtual reality modeling language (VRML), which is capable of building the geometry of a 3-D object with rich material composition and/or color information, is particularly useful as a CAD tool in the practice of the present invention.

[0050] To further ensure the part accuracy and compensate for the potential variations in part dimensions (thickness, in particular), the present method may be executed under the assistance of dimension sensors. These sensors may be used to periodically measure the dimensions of the object being built while a computer is used to determine the thickness and outline of individual layers intermittently in accordance with a computer aided design representation of the object. The computing step includes operating the computer to calculate a first set of logical layers with specific thickness and outline for each layer and then periodically re-calculate another set of logical layers after periodically comparing the dimension data acquired by the sensor with the computer aided design representation in an adaptive manner.

[0051] The Apparatus

[0052] Another embodiment of this invention is a solid freeform fabrication apparatus for automated fabrication of a 3-D object. This apparatus includes:

[0053] (1) a work surface to support the object while being built;

[0054] (2) powder-dispensing means at a predetermined initial distance from the work surface; the dispensing means having an outlet directed to the work surface for feeding successive layers of powder onto the work surface, one layer at a time, with the powder including at least a primary body-building material;

[0055] (3) an electrophotographic powder deposition means at a distance from the work surface; the electrophotographic powder deposition means having an imaging surface directed to the work surface for feeding successive layers of binder/modifier powder images onto the corresponding layers of primary body-building materials, one layer at a time;

[0056] (4) energy means at a distance from the work surface for providing fusion, cooling, curing, and/or bonding energy to successive layers being built; and

[0057] (5) motion devices coupled to the work surface, electrophotographic powder deposition means, and powder-dispensing means for moving the electrophotographic and dispensing means with respect to the work surface so that the binder/modifier powder image plane is substantially parallel to a plane defined by first and second directions (X- and Y-directions) and in a third direction (Z-direction) orthogonal to the X-Y plane to dispense multiple layers of powder and then transferring binder/modifier powder images, one layer at a time, for forming the 3-D object. Preferably, the work surface is lowered by one layer thickness distance vertically in the Z-direction after one layer is built to get ready for receiving powders of the next layer.

[0058] In order to automate the object-fabricating process, the present apparatus is preferably equipped with a computer-aided design computer and supporting software programs operative to (a) create a three-dimensional geometry of the 3-D object, (b) convert this geometry into a plurality of data points defining geometry and material composition of the object, and (c) generate programmed signals corresponding to each of the data points in a predetermined sequence. The apparatus also includes a three-dimensional motion controller electronically linked to the computer and the motion devices. The electrophotographic powder deposition means is also preferably electronically connected to the computer, optionally through an electrophotography controller. The motion controller is operated to actuate the motion devices and the electrophotography controller is operated to activate the electrophotographic powder deposition means to generate a binder and/or modifier powder image, both being responsive to the programmed signals for the data points received from the computer.

[0059] The apparatus preferably includes dimension sensors that are electronically linked to the computer. The sensors periodically provide layer dimension data to the computer. In the mean time, the supporting software programs in the computer act to perform adaptive layer slicing to periodically create a new set of layer data, including the data points defining the object, in accordance with the layer dimension data acquired by the sensors means. New sets of programmed signals corresponding to each of the new data points are generated in a predetermined sequence.

[0060] Specifically, the motion devices are responsive to a CAD-defined data file which is created to represent the 3-D preform shape to be built. A geometry (drawing) of the object is first created in a CAD computer. The geometry is then sectioned into a desired number of layers with each layer being comprised of a plurality of data points. These layer data are then converted to form an image for attracting binder powder particles and also converted to machine control languages that can be used to drive the operation of the motion devices and powder-dispensing devices. These motion devices operate to provide relative rotational and translational motions of the powder-dispensing device and the electrophotographic powder deposition means with respect to the work surface. The motion devices further provide relative movements of the work surface in the Z-direction, each time by a predetermined thickness distance.

ADVANTAGES OF THE INVENTION

[0061] The process and apparatus of this invention have several features, no single one of which is solely responsible for its desirable attributes. Without limiting the scope of this invention as expressed by the claims which follow, its more prominent features will now be discussed briefly. After considering this brief discussion, and particularly after reading the section entitled "DESCRIPTION OF THE PREFERRED EMBODIMENTS" one will understand how the features of this invention offer its advantages, which include:

[0062] (1) The present invention provides a unique and novel method for producing a three-dimensional object on a layer-by-layer basis under the control of a computer. This method does not require the utilization of a pre-shaped mold or tooling.

[0063] (2) Most of the layer manufacturing methods, including powder-based techniques such as 3-D printing (3DP) and conventional selective laser sintering (SLS), are normally limited to the fabrication of an object in a point-by-point fashion and, hence, are very slow. In contrast, the presently invented method allows the fabrication of a part one complete layer at a time due to the full-field sized programmable, electrophotographic powder deposition device being capable of precisely forming a thin layer of binder powder corresponding to the positive region of a layer. Therefore, the presently invented method can be order-of-magnitude faster than the conventional SLS and 3DP.

[0064] (3) The presently invented method provides a computer-controlled process which places minimal constraint on the variety of materials that can be processed. In the present method, both the primary body-building powder material and the modifier powder may be selected from a broad array of materials including various organic (including polymers) and inorganic substances (including ceramic, metal, glass, and carbon based materials) and their mixtures. This is in sharp contrast to both Stereo Lithography (SLa) and Solid Ground Curing (SGC), which solely rely on ultraviolet (UV) light-curable polymers such as acrylate and epoxy resins as the primary body-building material. The photo-curable polymer in both SGC and SLa represents the vast majority of the material in the resulting 3-D structure and is the "matrix" or "host" that accommodates any additive or reinforcement that might exist in the structure. The host basically provides the structural integrity of the 3-D object. The cured resin will not be removed or otherwise disintegrated. In the instant invention, the binder adhesive provides only a vehicle for tentatively holding together other otherwise loose powder particles. This binder or adhesive constitutes only a minority material phase of the resulting 3-D structure. In the cases of ceramic, glass, or metal powder particles, this cured adhesive will be burned off leading to the formation of a somewhat porous structure. This porous structure is then either sintered at a high temperature to produce a solid body or impregnated with another liquid material (e.g., metal melt) to form a composite or hybrid material object. This final structure will contain no low-temperature material such as the polymeric adhesive (only metal and/or ceramic, e.g.). Both metal and ceramic materials can be used in a much higher temperature environment.

[0065] In terms of the variety of materials, the presently invented method also presents several advantages over the prior-art electrophotographic powder deposition based SFF techniques. For instance, these prior-art techniques are normally limited to the formation of thin, light weight powder images only and are not able to form a thicker layer of heavier powders such as ceramic and metallic particles due to the limited electrostatic attractive force between charges and solid powder particles. Further, it is normally very difficult to charge electrically conductive materials such as metals and, hence, the prior-art electro-photographic methods are not effective in building parts from metallic powders. In contrast, in the practice of our method, one is free to choose any light-weight, non-conductive binder powder composition to be electrophotographically formed and transferred to a layer of primary body-building powder. Individual layers of a heavier and/or conductive primary body-building powder such as a metal or ceramic material can be deposited by using other more simple and easy-to-perform powder-dispensing means (such as those successfully used in SLS and 3D-P), which are not limited by the relatively weak electrostatic attractive forces.

[0066] (4) The present method provides an adaptive layer-slicing approach and a thickness sensor to allow for in-process correction of any layer thickness variation. The present invention, therefore, offers a preferred method of layer manufacturing when part accuracy is a desirable feature.

[0067] (5) The method can be embodied

using simple, inexpensive, and field-proven photo-copier mechanisms, so that the fabricator apparatus can be relatively small, light, inexpensive and easy to maintain. No high-power laser beam (to fuse and sinter a thicker layer of powder) is required.

[0068] (6) In the present method, a support structure naturally exists when a layer of body-building powder is fed. No additional tool is needed to build the support structure. This is in contrast to most of the prior-art layer-additive techniques that require a separate tool to build a support structure point by point, thereby slowing down the part-building process.

DESCRIPTION OF THE PREFERRED EMBODIMENTS

[0075] In the drawings, like parts have been endowed with the same numerical references. FIG. 1 illustrates one preferred embodiment of the presently invented apparatus for making a three-dimensional object. This apparatus is equipped with a computer 10 for creating a CAD drawing 12 (geometry and color pattern) of an object (shown as a coffee cup) and, through a hardware controller 14 (including signal generator, amplifier, and other needed functional parts) for controlling the operation of other components of the apparatus. These other components include at least a powder-dispensing means 22, an electrophotographic powder deposition means (of which a photo-receptor 18 and a binder powder image 27 being shown in FIG. 1), an energy means (UV source 40, as an example), and a work surface 16 on an object-supporting platform. The hardware controller 14 may comprise a UV light source controller, electrophotographic device controller, powder-dispensing device controller, and motion controller. The powder-dispensing means 22 provides successive layers of a primary body-building powder material onto the work surface 16 one layer at a time. A plurality of powder-dispensing means (one of the powder feeders being shown as 22 in FIG. 1) may be used to feed successive layers of different primary body-building powders. The electrophotographic powder deposition means (with its photo-receptor and hoppers, e.g.) creates a thin section (image 27) of binder powder with a predetermined shape and dimensions in accordance with a computer aided design (CAD) data of an object and then transfers this binder powder image onto a layer of the primary body-building powder material. The electrophotographic powder deposition means may also produce thin sections of modifier powders with predetermined geometry and material composition distribution (or color pattern) and transfer these modifier powder (toner image) layers onto their corresponding layer of a primary body-building powder material. This transfer of modifier powder images may be conducted before or preferably after the binder powder image is transferred to the same layer of a primary body-building material. The energy means 40 may comprise developer means to "develop" these modifier images (e.g., by setting the colorant-containing resin in a color toner composition) before these colored images are transferred to the surface of a primary body-building layer. If the modifier powders contain other types of additives but no colorant, these powder "images" (thin sections) do not have to be developed and can be transferred to predetermined areas of a primary body-building powder to modify physical properties thereto before, after, or concurrently with the binder powder image transfer step.

[0076] Optional temperature-regulating means (e.g., heaters, coolers, and temperature controllers; well-known in the art, not shown herein) and pump means (not shown) may be used to provide a protective atmosphere and a constant temperature over a zone surrounding the work surface where a part 24 is being built. The heaters may be used to pre-heat the body-building material powder so that when the binder powder is deposited onto a positive region 25 of a layer, the binder powder can be quickly melted and be capable of permeating through the gaps between body-building powder particles in this positive region. The binder fluid provides bridges between these particles and, when the binder is solidified, these particles are bonded and consolidated together. Solidification is accomplished by exposing the binder to an energy means (e.g., heat and/or UV light to cure or harden the binder if the binder is an adhesive) or by exposing the binder fluid to a lower temperature environment below the melting point of the binder. A motion device (not shown) is used to position the work surface 16 with respect to the powder-dispensing device 22, the electro-photographic means (including photo-receptor 18), and the energy means (e.g., light source 40). After a layer of body-building powder, binder and modifier materials is deposited and a cross-section of the 3-D object is built, the powder feeder 22 and the work surface 16 are shifted away from each other by a predetermined distance to get ready for dispensing a next layer of powder. Preferably, it is the work surface that is lowered vertically in the Z-direction so that other devices (including the powder feeder 22, the electro-photographic means, and the energy means will not have to move up in the Z-direction, defined in the Cartesian coordinate system 20 (FIG. 1).

[0077] Electro-photographic Powder Deposition Means

[0078] In one preferred embodiment, the electro-photographic powder deposition means 19, as indicated in FIG. 2, includes a continuous loop photo-receptor belt 58, with means such as motor-powered rollers 30 to drive the belt 58. The belt 58 has a thin layer of photo-conductive or photo-receptive material coated on one side of the belt. The photo-conductive coating is electrically non-conducting unless exposed to a light source. A powder image transferring cycle begins with charging the photo-receptor of the belt by using a charging device 54, of a type known in the art such as a corona charging device. The charged photo-receptor belt is then driven to be positioned before an image projector 66, which creates a latent image 27A of the desired cross-section of the 3-D object (e.g., a cross-section 12A of a coffee cup shown on a CAD computer monitor) by projecting light onto the region to be charged. The image may be formed in a known manner using CRT displays or lasers, as in a laser printer regulated by a computer. The belt 58 is then moved so as to pass by or near a binder powder delivery device 56A. Powder delivery devices are also well-known in the art. A plurality of additional powder delivery devices 56B, 56C, 56D, 56E, etc. may be used to provide different modifier powders (e.g., for cyan, magenta, yellow, and black toner image powders, respectively). A thin layer of preferably charged binder or modifier powder is attracted onto the charged areas (e.g., 27A) of the latent image formed on the belt 58 by image projector 66. Commonly used techniques for transferring the powder to the belt include the use of a magnetic brush device and a triboelectric charging device. This thin layer of binder or modifier powder image is then moved to just above a layer of primary body-building powder material already deposited on a work surface or a previously built layer (e.g., 25A plus 29) supported by this work surface. The primary body-building powder material is preferably pre-charged with charges of a polarity opposite to that in the binder or modifier powder to facilitate binder powder transfer from the belt to the current layer of a primary body-building powder. This work surface 16 sits on a build platform 64 which provides for precise alignment. The platform and the work surface move up and down so that when the binder or modifier powder image is brought into the correct position, the current layer of primary body-building powder material can be brought into a near-contact position with the belt 58 to receive the binder powder therefrom. The image area of the belt 58, after releasing the binder powder, then passes into the belt cleaning device 70, thereby completing one complete electrophotographic powder deposition cycle. Different modifier powders may be formed into separate modifier toner powder images and transferred in a desired sequence to the corresponding layer of a primary body-building powder. Alternatively, different modifier powders may be combined into one composite toner image which is then transferred to the layer of a primary body-building powder.

[0079] The belt 58 is cleaned with each pass by using a cleaner device 70, of a type known in the art which discharges the belt by exposing it to a an intense bright light and which removes any residual particles by brushing or scrapping means. Electrophotographic imaging devices are well-known in the art. Those interested may find useful information in the following U.S. Pat. No. 2,297,691 (Oct. 6, 1942 to C. Carlson), U.S. Pat. No. 3,969,624 (Jul. 13, 1976 to Van Biesen, et al.), U.S. Pat. No. 4,615,606 (Oct. 7, 1986 to Nishikawa) and U.S. Pat. No. 4,652,115 (Mar. 24, 1987 to Palm, et al.).

[0080] Referring to FIG. 5a-5 e, another preferred embodiment of the presently invented method and apparatus includes the operation of a programmable planar powder deposition means (82 in FIG. 5e) which includes an essentially 2-D or plate-like charging device (FIG. 5a or 80A in FIG. 5e) that is capable of providing charges to selected areas of this plate. These areas are programmable and pre-determined by a computer. These areas (the positive region of a layer) are defined by the layer data of a CAD design for the object to be built. The binder or modifier powder is attracted to this positive region only and not to other areas (negative region) of this plate. The bias voltage in each cell can be readily reversed. The charges (e.g., negative charges) produced by a cell are opposite to the charges (e.g., positive charges) provided to the binder or modifier powder when this cell is programmed to attract charges during the formation of a binder powder image. Charges of the same polarity (e.g., both being negative) are produced by this cell by simply reversing the bias charge when it is ready to release the binder powder particles attracted to this cell to a layer of a primary body-building powder material. The bias voltage provided to this plate of a matrix of capacitor cells can be manipulated so that the polarity of charges can be easily reversed once a layer of powder image is released for deposition onto a corresponding layer of a primary body-building powder material.

[0081] As shown in FIG. 5a and 5 b, the plate-like charging device comprises

160 Selected patents

basically a dot matrix of capacitors along with their charging circuits. A matrix of minute capacitor "dots" of a substantially uniform size preferably on the level of smaller than 100 µm, further preferably smaller than 10 µm, and most preferably smaller than 1 µm. Each dot can be represented by a cell, schematically shown in FIG. 5(a) and 5(b). An example of a cell circuit diagram, given in FIG. 5(c), comprises two input addresses A and B which send binary bit signals "0" or "1" through an "AND" gate G into a CK terminal of a D-trigger. The output of D is Q, which is connected to transistors TR1 and TR2 for driving a load C (a minute capacitor element). These two transistors alternately provide positive and negative charges to the cell. The gate G, load C, D-trigger, and the transistors TR1 and TR2 together constitute the essential elements of a cell. In a capacitor dot matrix, C is a capacitor that provides charges over a small area, approximately of the cell size. In this circuit, {overscore (O)} is non-Q or opposite to Q with {overscore (O)}="0" when Q="1" and {overscore (O)}="1" when Q="0". Before the start of a powder image formation operation, A and B are in the unselected status (at "0" level), while Q remains at the "0" level (C being "OFF" at the positive charge status) after a "RESET" signal is effected (a short "1" level, then "0"). Logically, the output Q will be "1" (and, hence, C is switched on to provide negative charges) once both the input addresses A and B are "1". The "1" status of the output Q will stay unchanged with C being always in "negative charge" even though either or both of A and B becomes "0". When both A and B of the same cell become "1" again or a new RESET signal comes, the output Q will be changed to "0" again with C providing positive charges. A large number of such cells or capacitor dots can be arranged in a square array as indicated in FIG. 5(b) by using a micro-electronic fabrication technique such as lithography. As further illustrated in FIG. 5(b), a planar pattern of charged areas in the shape of a capital letter H will be effected when the following pairs of input addresses are in "ON" or "1" status, in the following sequence: (A2,B1), (A2,B2), (A2,B3), (A2,B4), (A2,B5), (A3,B3), (A4,B1), (A4,B2), (A4,B3), (A4,B4), and (A4,B5). When the corresponding cells are switched on, this planar charging device (80A in FIG. 5e) can be brought to a position close to a source of a binder or modifier powder material 84, resulting in attraction of a thin layer of binder or modifier powder particles with positive charges onto the bottom surface of this planar charging plate device 80A, forming a binder or modifier powder "image" of pre-determined shapes and dimensions. In this example, this image of powder particles represents a positive region of an object cross-section designated by the letter H (FIG. 5b). After an H-shaped cross-section is formed, the above cells can be switched off by sending in a new RESET signal or re-selecting the above addresses in that sequence to release this image of binder powder to the corresponding layer of a primary body-building powder material. This implies that the coverage region of this planar image is programmable, in accordance with the CAD-defined cross-section data of a layer.

[0082]FIG. 5(d) shows another example of the logic diagram of cells in a planar charging device that can be conveniently operated. In this diagram, G1, G2, and G3 are the commonly used "NAND" gates in the field of logic circuit design. Herein, G1 is a selectable decoder while G2 and G3 serve as a R-S trigger. In the beginning, all the Cs in the planar charging plate are in the "OFF" status and the RESET terminal remains at the high or "1" level. When both input addresses are selected with "1" level, the functional element C will provide opposite charges and stay in the "ON" status until a new low level RESET signal comes again.

[0083] Referring to FIG. 5e again, the programmable planar powder deposition device 82A comprises a source of positively charged binder or modifier powder 84 inside a chamber 88 which is equipped with a piston-like member 86 that moves the binder or modifier powder up and down to supply a predetermined quantity of binder or modifier powder at a time to the bottom surface of a plate-like charging device 80A. When an image of charges are created at this bottom surface, it attracts a corresponding image of binder or modifier powder to this surface. This plate-like charging device is then moved horizontally to the right along the X-direction and precisely positioned just above a layer 90 of a primary body-building powder material previously deposited by a powder-dispensing device 22A or 22B. At this position, this plate-like device, now designated as 80B, releases the image of binder or modifier powder onto the underlying layer 90 of a body-building material by reversing the cell polarity. The plate-like charging device is then retrieved back to the position designated by 80A and, during this return trip, passes over a cleaning device 70 which removes the residual charges and powder particles on the bottom surface of this plate-like charging device. This device is now ready to prepare another image of binder powder while at the same time energy sources such as a heater and/or UV light 40 are used to consolidate the layer of body-building powder, binder and modifier materials. In the meantime, the work surface 16 is lowered vertically by one layer thickness distance and the powder-feeder 22B or 22A is activated to move from the right end of the work surface to the left end and back to deposit another thin layer of primary body-building powder material. A new cycle now begins. A multiplicity of powder feeders (e.g.,22A, 22B and more) may be utilized alternately to feed and spread up layers of different primary body-building materials. Further, a multiplicity of binder and modifier powder sources may provide alternate layers of binder and modifier powders to be electrostatically transferred by the planar charging device 80A for forming a multi-material or multi-color object.

[0084] Powder-Dispensing Devices (Powder Feeders)

[0085] A wide array of powder-dispensing devices may be used in the present freeform fabrication method and apparatus for feeding the primary body-building material powder. Powder feeders are well-known in the art (e.g., for use in conventional SLS as described in U.S. Pat. No. 4,938,816, Jul. 3, 1990 to Beaman, et al and U.S. Pat. No. 5,316,580, May 31, 1994 to Deckard and for use in 3D powder printing as described in U.S. Pat. No. 5,204,055, Apr. 20, 1993 to Sachs, et al.). We have found it satisfactory to use a device (not shown) to provide a mound of powder with a predetermined volume at a time onto one end of the work surface and move a rotatable drum (22A or 22B in FIG. 2) from this end to another end with a desired spacing between the drum and the work surface. During such a translational motion, the drum also rotates in a direction counter to the translational motion direction, leaving a powder layer thickness being approximately equal to the desired spacing. Preferably, the powder feeder works with a charging device so that the primary body-building powder material dispensed from the feeder 22A or 22B is provided with charges of the polarity opposite to the polarity of the charges in the binder powder image.

[0086] Energy Means

[0087] Several energy means can be used in the practice of the present invention, including utilizing heating sources (infrared, induction heating, dielectric heating, microwave heating, hot-air convective heating, and traditional conduction heating) and/or radiation sources (ultra violet 40, X-ray, Gamma-ray, electron beam, laser beam, ion beam, and plasma). A complete layer of a primary body-building powder material can be pre-heated by selected heat sources disposed near the object-building zone to a temperature (Tpre). For a binder powder that comprises a fusible material composition, this Tpre may be chosen to be above the melting point (Tm) of the fusible material composition so that the binder powder, once deposited onto this layer of body-building powder, is quickly melted to become a binder fluid that permeates through the gaps between powder particles. The heat is then reduced to allow the fluid to be solidified, thereby consolidating or sintering together the powder particles of the primary body-building material.

[0088] For a binder material that is a photo-curable or radiation-curable adhesive, the pre-heat temperature Tpre preferably is not sufficient to significantly initiate a cure reaction, but is sufficient to accelerate the cure reaction once initiated by a photo-initiator (included in the binder powder, e.g.) along with the UV light or other radiation source. Chemical reaction rates are known to increase normally with increasing temperature, but temperature alone may not be sufficient to start out a specific chemical reaction. The pre-heating operation would significantly reduce the light intensity requirement or exposure time that would otherwise be imposed upon the UV light or radiation source. Curing of the binder adhesive in a layer does not necessarily have to be complete before attempting to build a subsequent layer. The cure reaction in a layer may be allowed to continue while other layers are being built, provided the curing is proceeded to an extent that the layer is sufficiently rigid and strong to support its own weight and the weight of subsequent layers.

[0089] Binder Powder, Modifier Powder and Primary Body-Building Powder Materials

[0090] In this method, the photo-curable binder adhesive may consist of such adhesive compositions as a base resin, a hardening or cross-linking agent, a photo-initiator, a photo-sensitizer, and possibly with a reaction accelerator. One or more than one of these compositions (preferably those compositions in a fine solid powder form) may be included as the binder powder to be electro-photographically formed and other remaining compositions as secondary ingredients mixed with the primary body-building powder material to be dispensed one layer at a time by a powder feeder (powder-dispensing means). For instance, the photo-sensitizer (nano-scaled TiO_2 particles) along with other ingredients may be incorporated as the binder powder in the case of photo-curable acrylate materials. These TiO_2 particles, once deposited onto a layer of a mixture of a primary body-building powder material and fused acrylate prepolymer liquid (plus photo-initiators, etc.), may migrate through this layer and help to initiate/accelerate the curing reaction.

[0091] The photo-curable adhesives which can be used in the practice of the present invention are any compositions which undergo solidification under exposure to an actinic radiation. Such compositions comprise usually a photosensitive material and a photo-initiator. The word "photo" is used here to denote not only light (preferably UV light), but also any other type of actinic radiation which may transform a liquid adhesive to a solid by exposure to such radiation. A wide variety of photo-curable adhesive resin compositions are available in the art. Examples of this transformation behavior include cationic polymerization, anionic polymerization, step-growth polymerization, free radical polymerization, and combinations thereof. Cationic polymerization is preferable and free radical polymerization is further preferable. One or more monomers may be utilized in the compositions. Monomers may be mono-functional, di-functional, tri-functional or multi-functional acrylates, methacrylates, vinyl, allyl, and the like. The adhesive compositions may comprise other functional and/or photo-sensitive groups such as epoxy, vinyl, isocyanate, urethane, and the like. A large number of examples for photo-curable adhesive compositions can be found in both open literature and patents. For instance, the following U.S. patents provide a good source of these adhesive compositions: U.S. Pat. No. 6,110,987 (Aug. 29, 2000 to Kamata, et al.), U.S. Pat. No. 6,025,112 (Feb. 15, 2000 to Tsuda), and U.S. Pat. No. 5,981,616 (Nov. 9, 1999 to Yamamura, et al.).

[0092] The powder inside a powder feeder 22 may comprise a primary body-building material (fine particles), selected additives (physical or chemical property modifiers that are germane to all layers), and secondary ingredients (selected compositions of an adhesive that are germane to all layers). Those adhesive or modifier ingredients that are required to vary from point to point or layer to layer will be formed into binder or modifier powder images and transferred electrophotographically. In the presently invented method, the primary body-building powder may be composed of one or more than one type of fine particles. These fine powder particles could be of any geometric shape, but preferably spherical. The particle sizes are preferably smaller than 100 μm, further preferably smaller than 10 82 m, and most preferably smaller than 1 μm. The size distribution is preferably uniform. There are three basic types of powders that can be used in the present invention:

[0093] Type A: fine particles of a primary body-building material only. In this type, only primary body-building materials in a fine particle form are included as the ingredients in the powder; no binder or modifier composition being included. All binder or modifier compositions are present in the binder powder image. The primary body-building materials can be selected from polymers, ceramics, glass, metals and alloys, carbon, and combinations thereof. The polymers may be thermoplastic (e.g., polyvinyl chloride) or thermosetting (e.g., epoxy oligomer powder). The binder, including all selected compositions, will be deposited over a complete layer of the primary body-building material and allowed to permeate through the gaps in the powder. The binder in the positive region (corresponding to the desired cross-section) of a layer will be either solidified through cooling (of the binder fluid that contains a fusible material composition) or at least partially cured (for curable adhesive binder chemically cross-linked or otherwise hardened) to bond together the primary body building particles. The powder particles in the negative region will not be exposed to any binder material and will remain as loose or physically separable particles.

[0094] Type B: fine ceramic, metallic, glass, or polymeric particles (as primary body-building materials) each coated with a thin layer of coating comprising selected binder adhesive or modifier compositions. Once a layer of these coated solid particles is deposited, the remaining adhesive compositions of a binder powder image are then deposited, fused (if necessary) and allowed to permeate through the gaps between these particles. These other compositions are then in contact or reacted with the selected compositions in the coating to make a complete binder adhesive. The adhesive in the positive region of a layer is then at least partially cured by the energy means (to bond together body-building particles), leaving the particles in the negative region in a loose or physically/chemically separable state.

[0095] Type C: a mixture of fine particles of primary body-building materials (e.g., a silicon carbide or stainless steel powder) with at least one binder adhesive composition also in a fine powder form (e.g., powdered epoxy oligomer as an adhesive binder resin). The other remaining adhesive compositions (e.g., phot-initiator) are deposited electro-photographically onto a layer of Type C powder mixture and allowed to flow around the fine particles and react with the at least one adhesive composition. The complete adhesive formulation in the positive region of this layer is then at least partially cured to provide inter-particle bonding for those primary body-building particles in the positive region. Again, the powder particles in the negative region will remain in a separable state.

[0096] The primary body-building material can be selected from a wide variety of materials (polymers, ceramics, glass, metals and alloys, carbons, etc) provided they can be made into a powder form. Most of solid materials can be made into fine particles by using, for instance, a high-energy planetary ball-milling method.

[0097] In each of the above powder types, additional modifier ingredients may be added to impart desired physical and/or chemical properties to the object being built. These ingredients may contain a reinforcement composition selected from the group consisting of short fiber, whisker, and particulate reinforcements such as a spherical particle, ellipsoidal particle, flake, small platelet, small disc, etc. These ingredients may also contain, but not limited to, colorants, anti-oxidants, anti-corrosion agent, sintering agent, plasticizers, etc. Any of these ingredients, when intended to be used in each and every layer of the 3-D object (i.e., germane to all layers), may preferably be included in the primary body-building powder to be dispensed by a traditional powder feeder. Those ingredients that are to be deposited only at selected spots of a layer or selected layers (but not all layers) of an object may be included as a part of a modifier powder. These ingredients will then be electro-photographically formed into a modifier powder image (toner) and transferred to a corresponding cross-section of a primary body-building powder, before or after the binder powder image is transferred. Alternatively, selected ingredients may be combined with a binder powder to form a composite binder-modifier powder image.

[0098] To produce full-color layers, modifier powders may be prescribed to contain colorants. Color toners are well-known in the art. The following U.S. patents provide useful information on color toners and developers: U.S. Pat. No. 5,164,774 (Nov. 17, 1992 to Tomita, et al.), U.S. Pat. No. 5,143,809 (Sep. 1, 1992 to Keneko, et al.), U.S. Pat. No. 5,256,512 (Oct. 26, 1993 to Kobayashi, et al.), U.S. Pat. No. 5,296,325 (Mar. 22, 1994 to Ohtsuka, et al.), U.S. Pat. No. 5,660,959 (Aug. 26, 1997 to Moriyama, et al.), U.S. Pat. No. 5,756,244 (May 26, 1998 to Omatsu, et al.), U.S. Pat. No. 5,721,083 (Feb. 24, 1998 to Masuda, et al.), U.S. Pat. No. 5,919,592 (Jul. 6, 1999 to Yaguchi, et al.), and U.S. Pat. No. 6,004,711 (Dec. 21, 1999 to Bourne, et al.).

[0099] The fact that any material that is available in a powder form can be used in both the traditional selected laser sintering (SLS) and the presently invented full-area sintering technique (FAST) makes both techniques highly versatile. In the present FAST method, additional ingredients may be added by using repeated electrophotographic procedures to impart desired physical and/or chemical properties to the object being built.

[0100] Object-Supporting Work Surface and Motion Devices

[0101] Referring again to FIG. 1, the work surface 16 is located in close, working proximity to the powder-dispensing device 22 and the electrophotographic powder deposition device 19. This work surface 16 has a flat region sufficiently large to accommodate successive layers of the deposited material. The work surface 16 is supported by a build platform 64 which is equipped with mechanical drive means for moving the work surface up and down. The work surface 16 and build platform 64 are preferably contained in a chamber (chamber wall being indicated as 62 in FIG. 2) which is supported by a sturdy base member 72. This member 72 may be optionally equipped with rollers to facilitate moving of the apparatus. The powder-dispensing means 22 is provided with motion devices for moving the powder-dispensing means 22 from one end of the work surface to another end (along the X-direction, e.g.) and for depositing a thin layer of a primary body-building material powder onto the work surface or a previously deposited layer. This can be accomplished, for instance, by allowing the powder-dispensing device to be driven by at least one linear motion device to translate along the X-direction (defined in the X-Y-Z coordinate system 20 of FIG. 2), which is powered by a corresponding stepper motor, and driven to rotate in a direction counter to the translational motion to deposit a layer of powder. The work surface and the electrophotographic powder deposition device can also be moved relative to each other vertically along the Z-direction to make room for the powder-dispensing device 22. Preferably the electrophotographic powder deposition device 19 is driven by a stepper motor to move up and down in the Z-direction relative to the work surface. Motor means are preferably high resolution reversible stepper motors, although other types of drive motors may be used, including linear motors, servomotors, synchronous motors, D.C. motors, and fluid motors. Mechanical drive means including linear motion devices, motors, and gantry type positioning stages are well known in the art. The drive means, motion devices, and planar heat source are preferably subject to automated control by a computer 10, possibly through a hardware control system (14 of FIG. 1)

[0102] These movements will make it

possible for the powder feeder and the electrophotographic powder deposition device to feed successive layers of primary body-building powder, binder powder and modifier powder materials for forming multiple layers of materials of predetermined cross-sections, thicknesses and material compositions, which build up on one another sequentially.

[0103] Sensor means (e.g., optical encoder or laser scanner devices, not shown) may be attached to proper spots of the work surface or the material dispensing devices to monitor the physical dimensions of the physical layers being deposited. Dimensional sensors are well known in the art. The data obtained are fed back periodically to the computer for re-calculating new layer data. This option provides an opportunity to detect and rectify potential layer variations; such errors may otherwise cumulate during the build process, leading to some part inaccuracy. Many prior art dimension sensors may be selected for use in the present apparatus.

Selected patents 167

Three dimensional printing using imaged layers

Original title:" Apparatus for three dimensional printing using imaged layers"

Patent number	US8119053 B1
Publication type	Grant
Application number	US 11/998,151
Published	21. Febr. 2012
Application	28. Nov. 2007
Priority	18. März 2004
Inventors	Bryan Bedal, Ross D. Beers, Steven E. Schell
Original Assignee	3D Systems, Inc.

Patent citations (7), Non patent citations (1), Classifications (10),Legal Events (1)

Comment:

This invention demonstrates an exotic mix of various additive technologies. At first a 3D CAD files is sliced via software. Then layer by layer the sliced images are projected on a rotating drum, where a strong light source cures the material powder. The materialized image then gets transferred via a conveyer to the next process step, where each new layer is adhert to the previously fabricated layers to form a complete object. The process sound complicated and reminds of the laser printing technology.

Since the patent text is very long, it has been shortened for this book. See the full patent text at:

http://www.google.com/patents/US8119053

168 Selected patents

Drawings

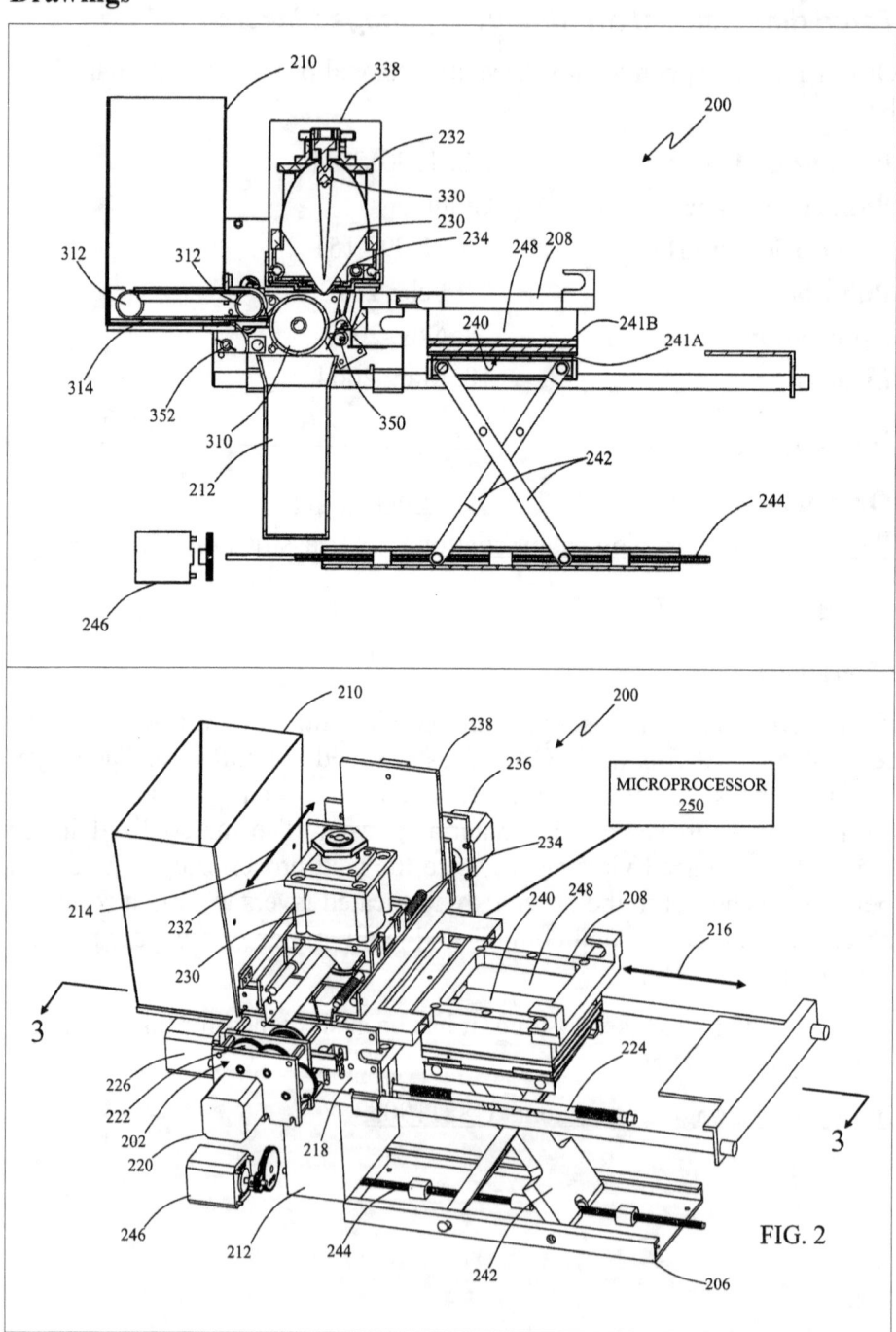

FIG. 2

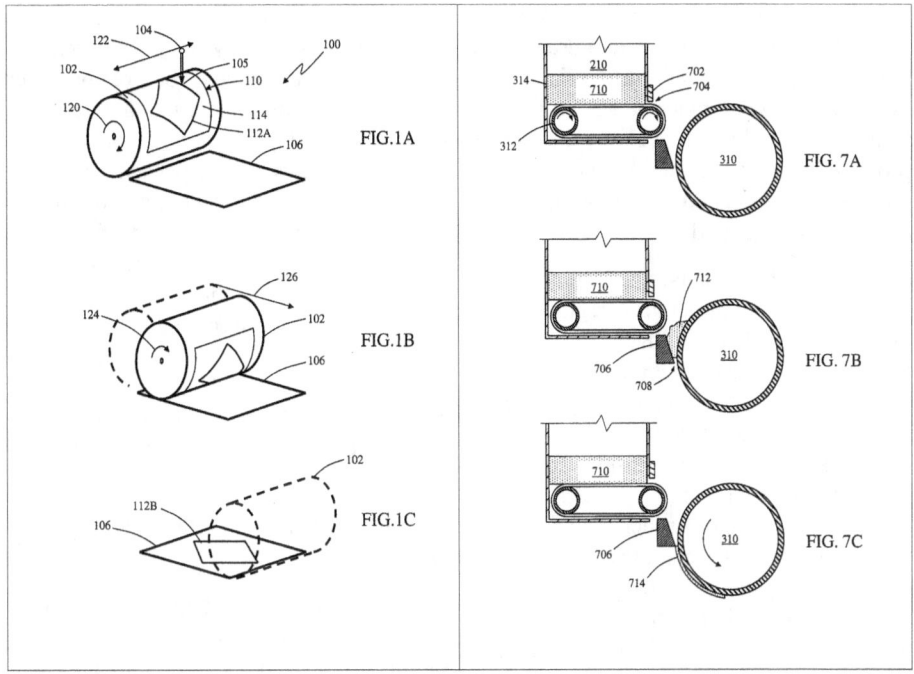

SUMMARY

The invention features a three-dimensional printer (3DP) adapted to construct three dimensional objects from cross sectional layers of the object that are formed on one surface, then subsequently adhered to the stack of previously formed and adhered layers. In the preferred embodiment, the 3DP includes a first surface adapted to receive a bulk layer of sinterable powder; a radiant energy source adapted to fuse a select portion of the layer of sinterable powder to form a sintered image; and a transfer mechanism adapted to concurrently transfer or print the sintered image from the first surface to the object being assembled while fusing the sintered image to the object being assembled. The layer of sinterable powder is preferably a polymer such as nylon that may be fused on a roller or drum, for example, with the energy provided by an incoherent heat source such as a halogen lamp. The transfer mechanism includes one or more actuators and associated controls adapted to simultaneously roll and translate the drum across the object being assembled so as to press and fuse the sintered image to the object. The transfer mechanism may further include a transfixing heater for heating the sintered image and the object immediately before the layer is applied to the object. The process of generating an image and transferring it to the object being assembled is typically repeated for each cross section until the assembled object is completed.

In some embodiments, the 3DP includes a powder applicator adapted to apply a predetermined quantity of sinterable powder to the drum for sintering. In the preferred embodiment, the applicator extracts the sinterable powder from a reservoir and permits the powder to briefly free fall, thereby separating the particles that may have compacted in the reservoir

170 Selected patents

and normalizing the density of the particles applied in layer form to the drum. The powder applicator may further include a blade which, when placed a select distance from and angle relative to the drum, produces a layer of sinterable powder with uniform thickness and density on the drum as the drum is rotated.

In some embodiments, the drum of the 3DP includes a temperature regulator and drum heating element adapted to heat the temperature of the drum at or near the fusing point of the sinterable powder to reduce the energy required by the radiant energy source to print a sintered image from the layer of bulk powder on the drum. The 3DP may further include a first heating element, a second heating element, or both to reduce the energy required to fuse the sintered image to the object being assembled. The first heating element, which is incorporated into a platform assembly on which the object is assembled, for example, is adapted to hold the object at a first predetermined temperature above the ambient temperature. The second heating element is preferably a hot pad adapted to contact and maintain the temperature of the upper surface of the object being assembled at a second determined temperature until the next sintered image is applied to the upper surface. The second determined temperature is less than the melting temperature of the sinterable powder.

The 3DP in some embodiments further includes a layer thickness control processor adapted to regulate the thickness of a sintered image fused to the object being assembled. The layer thickness control processor may vary the thickness of the sintered image before or after transferring to the object being assembled by, for example, varying the quantity of sinterable powder dispensed by the applicator, regulating the position of an applicator blade with respect to the drum, regulating the time and pressure applied by the drum to transfer the sintered image to the object being assembled, compressing the sintered image after it is fused to the object being assembled, and removing excess material from the object being assembled by means of a material removal mechanism.

BRIEF DESCRIPTION OF THE DRAWINGS

The present invention is illustrated by way of example and not limitation in the figures of the accompanying drawings, and in which:

FIGS. 1A-1C are schematic diagrams demonstrating the operation of the three dimensional printer of the first preferred embodiment of the present invention;

FIG. 2 is an isometric view of the three dimensional printer in accordance with the second preferred embodiment of the present invention;

(..)

FIGS. 7A-7C are schematic diagrams demonstrating the operation of the powder applicator in accordance with the second preferred embodiment of the present invention;

Selected patents 171

Hexapod

Patent number	US5401128 A
Publication type	Grant
Application number	US 07/947,819
Published	28. März 1995
Application	18. Sept. 1992
Priority	26. Aug. 1991
Fee status	Expired
Also published as	DE69308708D1, 4 et al»
Inventors	Paul A. S. Charles, Thomas J. Lindem
Original Assignee	Ingersoll Milling Machine Company

Patent citations (25), Non patent citations (8), Referenced by (69), Classifications (15), Legal Events (11)

External links: USPTO, USPTO assignment, Espacenet

Comment:

This patent shows an expired design for a steward plattform. It is quite interesting, since so called **deltabots** (who use similar kinematics like the steward platformhave become very popular among DIY activists.

172 Selected patents

U.S. Patent Mar. 28, 1995 Sheet 1 of 5 5,401,128

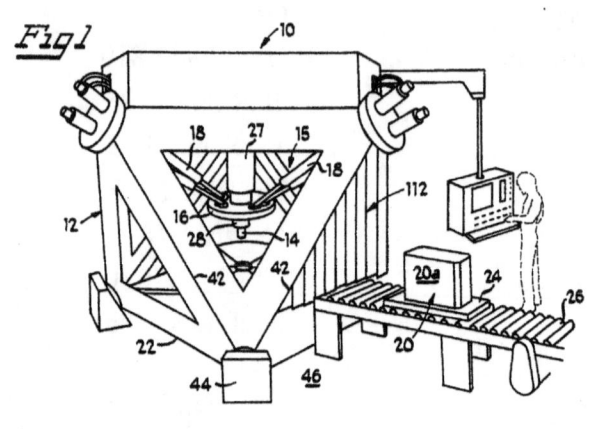

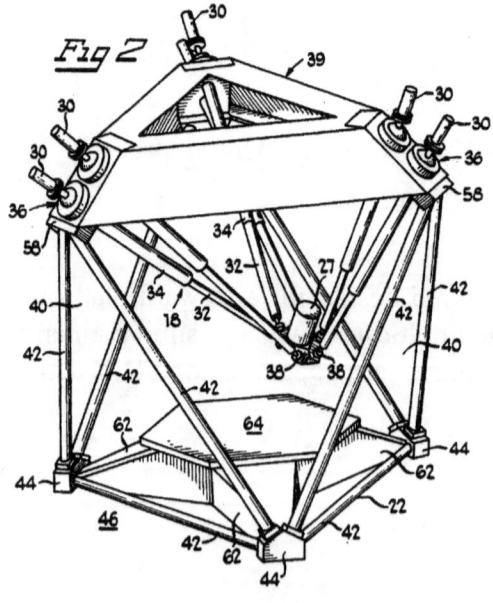

3D Scanner

174 Selected patents

Scanner system and method for scanning

Patent number	US8294958 B2
Publication type	Grant
Application number	US 12/299,349
PCT Number	PCT/GB2007/001610
Published	23. Oct. 2012
Application	3. May 2007
Priority	4. May 2006
Also published as	EP2024707A1, EP2024707B1, US20090080036, WO2007129047A1
Inventors	James Paterson, Ronald William Daniel, David Claus, Andrew Fitzgibbon
Original Assignee	Isis Innovation Limited

Patent citations (34), Non patent citations (19), Referenced by (1), Classifications (15), Legal Events (1)

External links: USPTO, USPTO assignment, Espacenet

Comment:

One of the most detailed patent on scanning three dimensional objects, including formulars and very precise instructions as well as examples of the results to be expected.

Selected patents 175

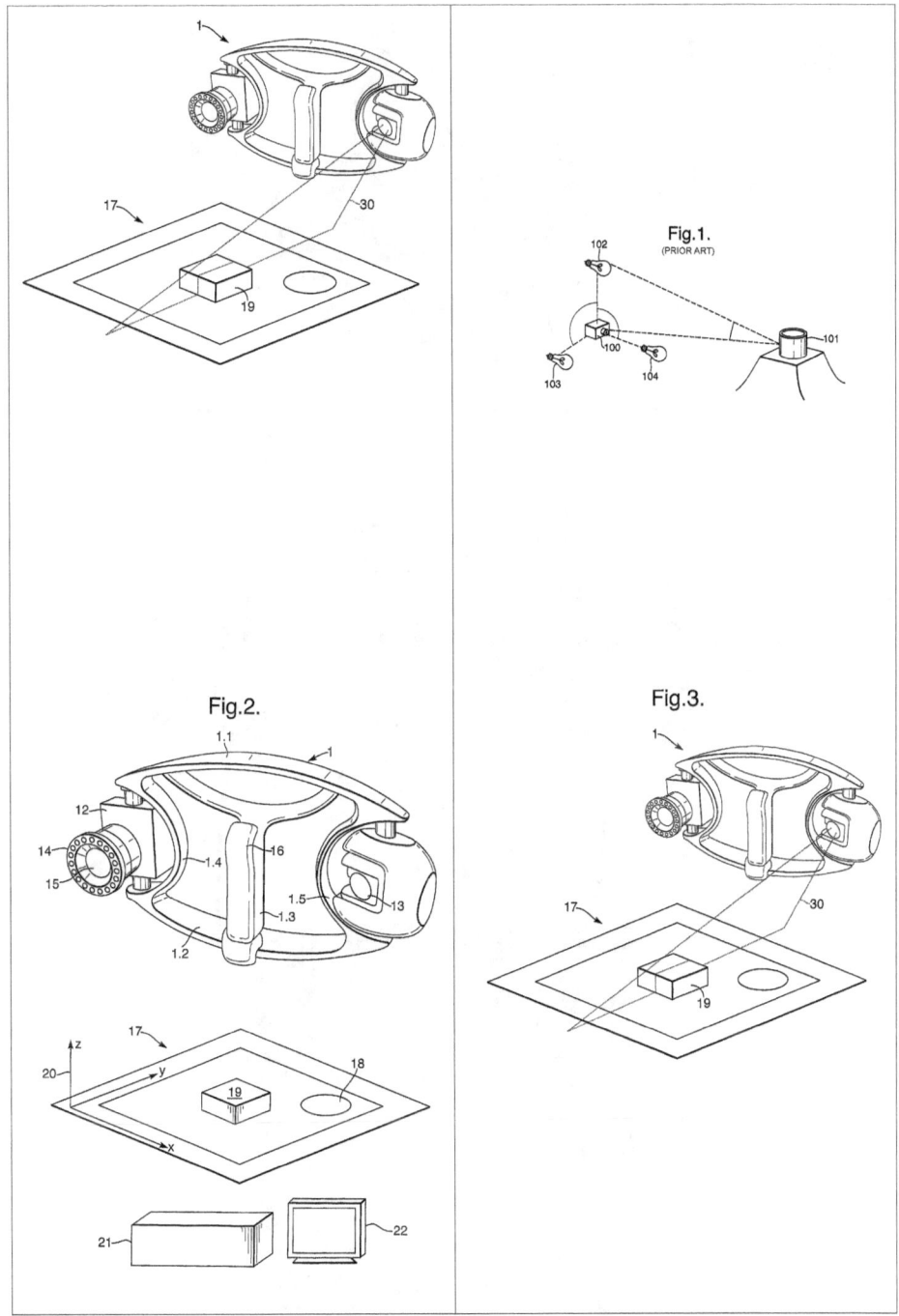

176 Selected patents

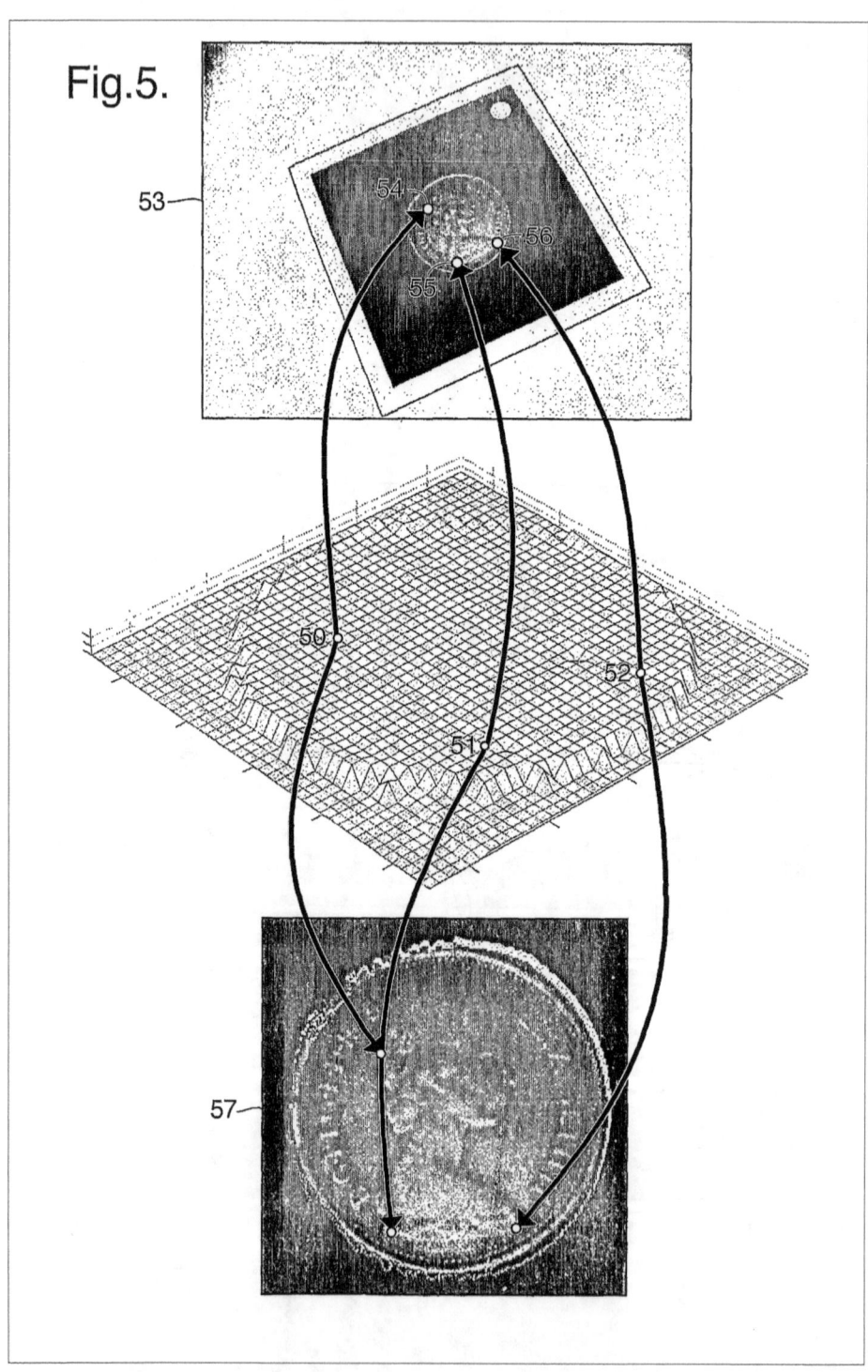

Fig.5.

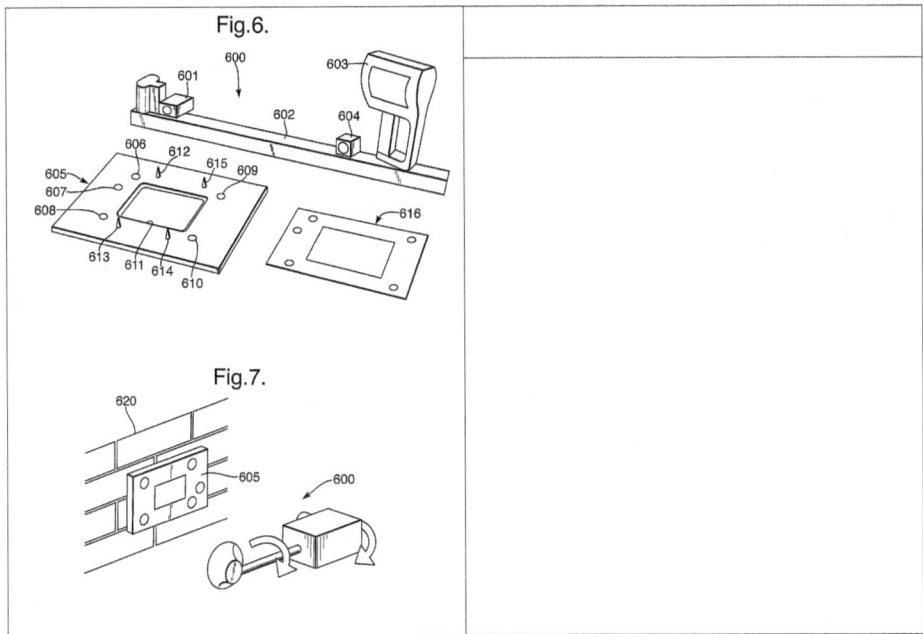

Fig.6.

Fig.7.

Summary

A scanner system and corresponding method, the system comprising: a scanner device (**1**); a target **17**) and a processor (**21**). The scanner device (**1**) comprises: an emitter (**13**) for projecting patterned light and a sensor (**12**) for capturing images of the object (**19**). The target (**17**) has predetermined features visible to the sensor simultaneously with the object for enabling the processor to determine the location of the sensor with respect to the object. The generates a three-dimensional model of the object on the basis of images of the object with the patterned light projected thereon. The scanner device further comprises a light source (**14**) for directionally illuminating the object (**19**), and the sensor (**12**) is arranged to capture images of the illuminated object. The processor generates sets of photometric data for the object when illuminated from different directions. The processor combines the geometric data and photometric data to output a model comprising geometric information on the object together with photometric information spatially registered with the geometric information.

Description

The present invention concerns a system, and corresponding method, for scanning a real object. The object of the scanning may be an entire article, or a portion thereof, or the surface or portion of the surface of an article. The system and method of the invention is capable of the acquisition of geometry and material surface reflectance properties of the object of the scanning. Examples of such material surface reflectance properties include the surface colour and specularity, which may also be referred to as reflectance properties.

Systems are known for 3D geometric

178 Selected patents

acquisition of the shape of an object, for example as disclosed in WO 2005/040850. However, geometric information alone is not always sufficient for particular scanning applications, such as full colour model acquisition for example for video games and animated films (e.g. scanning and reconstructing a figure for subsequent animation), interactive visualization (e.g. for medical uses or for academic use such as scanning antiquities for subsequent study), and quality control (e.g. inspecting the surface finish of an object for desired gloss or satin finish, inspecting completeness of paintwork on a painted object).

Other systems are known for acquiring information on an object via "photometric stereo" (PS), i.e. obtaining spatial information on the properties of the interaction of the surface of an object with light. FIG. 1 shows an example of a traditional hardware setup for object acquisition via photometric stereo. A single camera **100** is positioned to capture images of an object **101** illuminated individually and sequentially by a number of light sources **102**, **103**, **104**, the geometrical positions of the light sources with respect to the object having been obtained via prior calibration. In FIG. 1 three light sources are shown, which represents a typical minimum setup. However, there are problems and limitations with such a system: for example, depending on the material reflectance model used, the determination of the PS information for the object can be intractable or require an extremely large amount of processing power or time. The range of applicable materials may be very limited, for example objects which exhibit specular reflection cannot be correctly acquired. The use of additional light sources and more advanced reflection models can assist, but this increases the hardware requirements and the difficulty of calibration. Furthermore, a PS system as described above is inconvenient to operate and to set up, in particular multiple geometrically and radiometrically calibrated light sources are required. It does not lend itself to enabling convenient, moveable (such as hand-held) scanners to be achieved. PS data in which the geometry is recovered by integration also suffers from the problem of being "non-metric" in the sense that it does not provide absolute height, width and breadth information, and can be subject to low-frequency drift due to the integration, implying a possible curvature in space.

A further problem is to register and combine, i.e. reconcile, geometric data and photometric data for an object acquired with different techniques.

The present invention aims to alleviate, at least partially, one or more of the above problems.

Accordingly, the present invention provides a scanner system for scanning an object, the system comprising:

a scanner device; a target; and a processor,

wherein the scanner device comprises: an emitter for projecting patterned light on the object; and a sensor for capturing images of the object,

wherein the target has predetermined

features visible to the sensor simultaneously with the object for enabling the processor to determine the location of the sensor with respect to the object,

wherein the processor is arranged, in use, to generate geometric data, comprising a three-dimensional model of the object, on the basis of images of the object with the patterned light projected thereon by the emitter,

wherein the scanner device further comprises a light source for directionally illuminating the object, and the sensor is arranged to capture images of the object illuminated by the light source,

wherein the processor is arranged, in use, to generate sets of photometric data for the object when illuminated from different directions by the light source, and

wherein the processor is arranged, in use, to combine the geometric data and photometric data to output a model comprising geometric information on the object together with photometric information spatially registered with the geometric information.

The present invention also provides a method for scanning an object comprising steps of:

providing a target that has predetermined features, and capturing images of the object and target features simultaneously using a sensor; determining the location of the sensor with respect to the object on the basis of the captured images; projecting patterned light on the object; generating geometric data, comprising a three-dimensional model of the object, on the basis of images of the object with the patterned light projected thereon; directionally illuminating the object using a light source; generating sets of photometric data for the object when illuminated from different directions by the light source; and combining the geometric data and photometric data to output a model comprising geometric information on the object together with photometric information spatially registered with the geometric information.

A system embodying the invention is able to offer advantages including improved accuracy, reduced cost and increased usability over conventional technologies, and may be produced in a portable hand-held package. As well as the standard applications for 3D geometric acquisition (such as e.g. reverse engineering, quality control), the system's ability to capture material surface reflectance properties such as inhomogenous colour and specularity make it applicable for a wide range of other fields, such as full colour model acquisition, interactive visualization, and material analysis for example quality inspection of paint work or surface finish.

A system or method embodying the invention advantageously only requires a single sensor (e.g. camera) for capturing images of the object. Furthermore, a system embodying the invention advantageously only requires a single light source, which may be a composite light source, but the light source can be compact with a maximum

180 Selected patents

dimension of say 150 mm or smaller. Also, additional backlighting sources are not required. All of these features enable the scanner device of the invention to be made portable, and preferably hand-held. Of course, multiple light sources may optionally be used if the application requires it, but the scanner device itself can still be a single, portable, preferably hand-held unit,

Embodiments of the invention will now be described, by way of example only, with reference to the accompanying drawings in which:

FIG. 1 depicts a previous system for acquiring photometric stereo information on an object;

FIG. 2 depicts a system comprising a scanner, optical target, object and processor according to a first embodiment of the invention;

FIG. 3 depicts the system of the first embodiment acquiring geometric information;

FIG. 4 a shows a set of photometric images of an object acquired by the system of FIG. 2 from different viewpoints;

FIG. 4 b shows the photometric information from FIG. 4 a after processing to give a set of reconstructed images from the same viewpoint, but effectively illuminated by a light source from different directions;

FIG. 5 depicts schematically the processing to transform one of the images from FIG. 4 a to the corresponding image in FIG. 4 b;

FIG. 6 illustrates a system according to a second embodiment of the invention; and

FIG. 7 depicts the system of FIG. 6 in use.

A system according to a first embodiment of the invention will now be described. FIG. 2 shows the hardware component of the system, which in this embodiment consists of a hand-held scanning device 1, optical target 17, and processor 21. Components of the hand-held scanner 1 include: the main body of the scanner 1, upon which the remaining components are attached; a camera 12; a laser stripe projector 13 or other suitable source for projecting one or more planes of light onto the target 17 and object thereon to produce a line or stripe of light visible to the camera 12; and at least one photometric light source 14. Components 1, 12 and 13, together with the optical target 17, are described in the publication WO 2005/040850; the photometric light source 14 is an addition to form the system that is the focus of the present invention.

FIG. 2 the photometric light source 14 is a bright light composed of multiple LEDs arranged in a ring around the camera lens 15, although this is by no means the only configuration, and additional lights such as e.g. a clustered LED source placed next to the laser stripe projector 13 may be advantageous. In the depicted embodiment, the photometric light source is arranged to be substantially co-linear with the camera lens 15; in this context, "co-linear" simply means that the object is illuminated from substantially the same direction as that from which it is viewed, although this is not an essential feature of the invention.

The LEDs referred to here emit blue light that interacts with one or more phosphors in their package to generate approximately white light. Other sources can, of course, be used, such as a camera flash bulb.

The main body of the scanner in the embodiment depicted in FIG. 2 consists of a frame comprising two spaced-apart lateral members **1.1**, **1.2**, joined by three bars **1.3**, **1.4** and **1.5**, approximately perpendicular to the lateral members. The middle bar **1.3** constitutes a hand grip and is provided with a trigger **16**, the trigger being used to switch laser generation on or off. Additional controls may also be provided on the scanner **1** e.g. for switching the photometric light source(s) on or off. The camera **12** and laser stripe projector **13** are provided adjacent to respective end bars **1.4** and **1.5** of the scanner. A further feature of this particular embodiment is that the camera **12** and laser stripe projector **13** are adjustable with respect to the scanner body about the vertical axis. This is achieved by attaching these two components to the main scanner body **1** via a rod and socket, and allows the hand-held scanner **1** to have adjustable baseline between camera **12** and laser source **13** to accommodate differently sized objects.

The camera **12** is any suitable electronic image sensor, for example using a CCD or CMOS light sensor element, and a lens or lens system **15** for focusing an image of the object **19** and target **17** onto the sensor element.

The optical target **17** consists of a planar target with pattern of known dimensions, in this instance a black square with surrounding line. An orientation marker, in this case a white circle **18**, is placed in the upper left of the black square. It should be understood that the optical target can take other forms, such as a three dimensional shape, however its metric dimensions must be known in advance up to a specified accuracy (the metric properties of the target are discussed in WO 2005/040850). An additional property of the optical target is that it is of known reflectivity, for example in the case of using white card with laser printing, the card is known to be matte and substantially equally reflective across the spectral range of visible light (an additional calibrating property available in the new technology being described in this document). Target geometry and reflectance properties can be calibrated in advance as required. During operation the object to be acquired **19** is placed on the target **17**, which may vary in overall scale depending on the size of the object being acquired. In the embodiment described below during operation the hand-held scanner is moved with respect to the stationary target, however in other embodiments the scanner may remain fixed, with the target moving relative to it, for example in the case of examining parts moving on a conveyor belt with multiple affixed targets.

The processor **21** may be a standard desktop or laptop computer, and is required to perform the image and data processing necessary for the various functions of the system, as well as storage of intermediate and final data describing the acquired object. An

182 Selected patents

attached CRT or LCD monitor **22** allows display of intermediate and final data to the user, along with controls for interaction. The scanner **1**, processor **21** and monitor **22** may be connected by cables for communication of data. Alternatively, communication between the components may be wireless. It is also not essential for the processor **21** to be external to the scanner; with appropriate miniaturization, the necessary dedicated processor hardware and display may be provided integrally in the hand-held scanner.

A method of operation of the scanner system, according to an embodiment of the invention, will now be described in terms of the following functions performed, namely: camera localization; metric recovery of geometric shape data of the object; acquisition of photometric data of the object; and combination of the geometric data and photometric data to produce a refined model of the object's geometry and surface reflectance properties.

As described in WO 2005/040850, the first function of the system is to perform optical camera localization, i.e. determining the position of the camera in space (specifically camera roll, tilt, and yaw angles and effective camera centre coordinates X,Y,Z) with respect to a chosen absolute coordinate frame on the target, shown in FIG. 2 as a set of axes **20**. As the target is of a known metric size the relative position of the camera can be determined metrically given knowledge of certain camera imaging properties such as e.g. focal length. Geometric calibration of a camera is a known technique and can be performed in an image-driven approach. In one example of this, multiple images of a 2D camera calibration target of known feature dimensions are acquired, the calibration target not necessarily being the same one as used during object scanning. Image processing operations are then performed to extract the locations of features on the target in the calibration images, then a series of operations based on projective geometry used to obtain parameters determining the camera's imaging properties.

With knowledge of the camera's imaging characteristics (or intrinsic parameters) metric localization of the camera with respect to the optical target **17** can be performed from a single image of the target. This is achieved by finding certain specific features of the target in the image (for example the sides of the line surrounding the centre black square of the target), then applying projective geometry to determine a homography from the coordinate frame of the target to the camera. WO 2005/040850 gives further details of camera localization via imaging an optical target.

As described in WO 2005/040850, the second function of the system is to perform metric recovery of geometric shape information from the object. FIG. 3 demonstrates this process. A plane, or multiple planes, of light **30** is projected onto the target **17** and the object thereon **19**, from the scanner **1**. A calibration phase (not shown) determines the relative distance and orientation of the plane or planes of light with respect to the effective camera centre, which remains fixed during the scanning process. The output from the localization function provides the position and orientation of the camera with respect to the optical target, and hence the angle and relative position of the light plane with respect to the target. Image processing routines are applied to detect the position of the light stripe in the image, both on the object and on the target, which is straightforward as the stripe is very intense compared to ambient light from e.g. standard room lighting. Knowledge of the position and orientation of the target plane in the image thus allows the intersection of the or each light plane with the target plane to be determined. Information on the geometric shape of the object placed on the target can then be determined from the distortion observed in the light line in the camera image. Detection of the stripe on the target is used to improve the accuracy of the geometric recovery using disparity. The result is to acquire a single "strip" of metric geometric samples (i.e. 3D points) across the object. The light line is preferably "swept" over the object in order to acquire a set of samples of the surface of the object.

Particular advantages of the target based approach to geometry acquisition include the removal of costly precision camera localization equipment (equivalently the removal of accurate object moving equipment such as e.g. precision turntables), and that geometric recovery is now performed with respect to a known metric object in view, reducing errors to second order. Acquisition of 3D data with respect to an absolute coordinate frame also allows statistical modelling to be applied to further reduce overall error. WO 2005/040850 gives further details. It should be noted that the geometry recovered here is metric, however it will be subject to a level of unbiased measurement noise depending on e.g. accuracy of camera localization, geometric calibration and laser stripe localization in the image. It is important to note that the use of the reference metric optical target generates unbiased measurements that are subject to spatial high frequency noise. Other systems admit bias through their reliance on measurement arms and other features that must be separately calibrated and registered to the object coordinate system.

The third function of the scanning system is to perform photometric acquisition of the object. The fundamental principle applied is that of photometric stereo (PS). The underlying concept is to acquire a series of photometric images of the object via the camera, with the images consisting of the object remaining in a fixed position relative to the camera but with geometrical variation in the lighting conditions.

Photometric stereo requires an approximating model of the object's (possibly inhomogeneous) material reflectivity properties, which in the general case is modelled via the Bidirectional Reflectance Distribution Function (BRDF). To render the problem tractable, typically a very simplified model of the BRDF is used, for example the Lambertian Cosine Law model. Here material reflectivity is expressed as uniform across all variation of direction of incoming irradiance and exitant radiant energies. In this simple model variation in intensity across the object as observed by the camera is dependent only on the quantity of incoming irradiant energy from the light source and foreshortening effects due to the geometry of the object. In particular

$I = P\rho L \cdot N$ (Eqn 1)

Where I represents the intensity observed at a single point on the object by the camera, P the incoming irradiant light energy, N the object-relative surface normal, L the normalized object-relative incoming light direction, and ρ the Lambertian reflectivity of the object at that point.

In a standard implementation of PS, variation in P across the object is typically determined approximately in a prior calibration step, and hence can be compensated. In the case of the conventional example of FIG. 1 the relative orientation of the camera and object remains fixed during each change in lighting direction. The intensity observed by the camera at a specific location (i.e. pixel) in the set of photometric images must always correspond to the same area on the surface of the object. The intensities at a particular pixel location in the image can therefore be considered as a set of photometric samples from the surface of the object visible at that pixel location in the camera view. Let the N intensities and corresponding light directions for a particular set of photometric samples be denoted by superscript, then $I^N = \rho L^N \cdot N$ (where • denotes vector dot product).

Note that L^N has been determined via prior calibration (this can be achieved via e.g. a so-called "sundial" approach, see for example: Rushmeier et al. *Design and use of an in-museum system for artefact capture*, IEEE/CVPR Workshop on Applications of Computer Vision in Archaeology 2003, and as described herein in the context of the second embodiment of the invention). Then stacking the vectors N (Eqn 1) from the N photometric samples gives:

[I 1 I 2 ⋮ I N] = ρ 嬡 [L X 1 L Y 1 L Z 1 L X 2 L Y 2 L Z 2 ⋮ ⋮ ⋮ L X N L Y 1 鎖 N L Z N] · [N X N Y N Z] (Eqn 鎖鎖 2)

Which can be solved in a least squares sense via e.g. psuedoinverse. The surface normal is of unit length, hence the derived surface normal N is normalized, with ρ taken as norm (N).

It should be clear from this description that PS can, given an appropriate and tractable model of material reflectivity, be used to derive object geometry in the form of a set of surface normals, and material properties (in the example above possibly inhomogeneous Lambertian reflectivity coefficients). This is a known standard technique. It is also possible to perform a similar operation with colour photometric images (such as the R,G,B channel images common in model digital imaging), recovering knowledge of e.g. the object's diffuse albedo.

The scanning system of this embodiment of the invention improves on the prior arrangement of FIG. 1 by attaching at least one photometric light source to the scanner, which is itself freely moveable with respect to the object. This allows the acquisition of a potentially unlimited number of photometric images in that any light sources can now be arbitrarily positioned, as long as the object remains in view of the camera and in the illumination path of the light source. In the example of the hand-held scanner of FIG. 2, a single camera co-linear light source **14** is shown. The issue now is that moving the light source (and hence camera) results in the position, orientation, and potentially the visibility of the object (due to self-occlusion) changing in the image. This results in the position of the photometric sample corresponding to a particular region of surface geometry varying between photometric images; in addition object self-occlusion with respect to the camera or light may result in photometric samples for a particular region being unavailable in some or all of the photometric images. FIG. 4(*a*) illustrates this, showing a set of photometric images of an object (a coin) acquired by moving the camera-light system i.e. scanner **1**. Clearly the geometry observed under the pixels of the images varies across the set. A major component, therefore, of the scanning system is to process the captured photometric images such as to obtain a set of geometrically aligned photometric samples.

In this described embodiment the approach taken will be to rectify the captured photometric images to a common orientation, in doing so determining surface visibility. This requires prior knowledge of the object's metric geometry, as provided by the laser scanning component of the system. Thus the photometric component of the system is dependent on data from the laser component, and as the rectification improves with the quality of the metric data the photometric component is clearly enhanced by improved performance in the geometric acquisition stage. Rectification of a photometric image is performed by projecting previously acquired metric geometry into the image. This requires knowledge of the camera position and orientation used to acquire the image (obtained from the optical localization stage of the system) and camera imaging parameters such as e.g. focal length (acquired during camera geometric calibration). Other parameters such those defining a model of camera radial distortion can optionally be applied to improve the accuracy of the projection of the model. The result of projection is to obtain the 2D locations of the points comprising the 3D surface geometry in each photometric image. A re-projection of the object at an arbitrary viewpoint is then achieved by rendering the object, assigning colour value to the vertices as provided by sampling the original image. FIG. 5 shows an example of model projection—the 3D data of the model **50,51,52** is projected into the image **53** to provide 2D locations of the geometry in the photometric image **54,55,56**. The photometric image is then sampled at these locations and the model rendered with these colour values to construct a rectified view at a chosen canonical viewpoint **57**, in this case fronto-parallel to the major plane of the coin.

The metric 3D data itself provides only

a set of 2D sample locations in the photometric images. To determine visibility the surface of the object must be defined in some form. One example of this is to define triangle-based connectivity between the points. This is trivial if the points are e.g. defined as height samples on a regular sampling grid (as is easily performed given the metric data is acquired with respect to a metric planar optical target in our system). In the case of an arbitrary cloud of points defining a convex object e.g. the 3D Delaunay triangulation can be applied. Other schemes and representations exist, such as Radial Basis Function methods for defining implicit surfaces. Having obtained a surface representation, visibility with respect to the camera can be determined by e.g. ray casting from the camera centre through the object, or by projecting the surface into the image as a set of e.g. raster filled triangles, using standard depth buffer techniques to obtain the closest point to the camera at each pixel in the image. Occlusion with respect to the light (i.e. self-shadowing) can be determined in a similar manner, in this case casting rays from the effective centre of the light, or rendering a depth buffer from the perspective of the light source (a component of the shadow buffering technique known in computer graphics).

The result is to determine the 2D location and visibility of each 3D point representing the object geometry in each image. In this description of the system the photometric images are then sampled at these locations to reconstruct the photometric images from a single canonical viewpoint, thus performing rectification. FIG. 4(*b*) shows an example of this; the input photometric images (FIG. 4 *a*) show the object under varying camera-relative pose and orientation. After projecting the model into the images a set of corresponding rectified views are obtained, with the major plane of the coin fronto-parallel to the reconstruction viewpoint (FIG. 4 *b*). Note that in some of the photometric images the object geometry is determined to be occluded with respect to the camera, and thus cannot be recovered in the rectified view; these samples are shown as pale grey pixels in FIG. 4 *b*. Thus there may be a varying number of photometric samples across the locations in the rectified images.

Having obtained a number of sets of geometrically aligned photometric samples (i.e. FIG. 4 *b*), it remains to determine the incident light direction (denoted L above) under which each sample was taken. It has already been commented that the camera location can be determined with respect to the optical target and hence any point on the object via the localization function of the system. Consider now that the light source rigidly attached to the camera during acquisition; then if the camera-relative position of the light is obtained via a pre-calibration step (this again can be achieved via e.g. a sundial type approach) the light position can be derived for each photometric image. In particular, given camera relative light position L_C, camera rotation and translation with respect to the target as matrix R and vector t, then:

$$L_T = R^T(L_C - t) \quad \text{(Eqn 3)}$$

Where L_T gives the target relative position of the light, and R^T denotes the transpose of matrix R. The photometric samples may now be processed to recover geometry with respect to the target coordinate frame and material reflectance properties as described in e.g. Eqn 2.

In the disposition above, the example of rectifying the images to a single canonical viewpoint has been given to aid understanding, however in a more advanced implementation multiple viewpoints may be used, and indeed are required to recover objects of more complex geometry than the coin. Extending to the general case, it is possible to recover photometric samples in a viewpoint-free manner, extracting sets of photometric samples for individual surface locations on any arbitrary 3D geometry.

The final function of the systems is to combine the acquired geometric and photometric data to produce a final model of the object's geometry. Material properties such as colour may be expressed as e.g. standard texture maps and are independent of this process. The geometric data provides an unbiased but noisy metric estimate of model geometry, typically at a relatively lower spatial resolution than the photometric sampling. The photometric data provides a relatively high resolution but biased estimate of the differential of the object geometry as a set of surface normals. Integrating the surface normals can produce an estimate of underlying model geometry, however this is subject to low frequency distortion and hence is not metric. The combination of the two modalities of data is therefore very powerful as it potentially offers metric accuracy and high acquisition resolution.

Various different techniques can be applied to combine the two sets of data to produce a final model. A simple example is when the metric height data is represented as a 2D grid of distances off the target plane (also known as a height or distance map), and the surface normals are represented by a similarly sampled 2D array. Note that in the case of higher normal resolution the height map may be interpolated via e.g. linear or cubic interpolation to obtain an estimate of metric geometry at the same sampling rate. The two data sets can then be combined using a filter.

The two sets of data, i.e. laser-scanned geometric and PS, have very different noise characteristics. The laser data is metric, with low bias, but is subject to high frequency spatial noise. The laser data can be thought of as a low frequency mean field measurement of points on the scanned object's surface. The PS data, on the other hand, is non-metric and provides information on the normal to the object's surface on a very high density sample grid. The system thus offers two sensor modalities, one generating noise corrupted estimates of the surface locations in 3D, the other providing the spatial derivatives of the object's surface. The two sensor modalities are combined to optimise their individual noise characteristics, the laser scanner providing low frequency information and the PS the high frequency information.

The mathematical description of the

operation of integration of the two sensor modalities can be illustrated by considering the discrete models

$$z = \hat{z} + n_1$$

$$(\delta z)_x = (\delta \hat{z})_x + n_2$$

$$(\delta z)_y = (\delta \hat{z})_y + n_3 \quad \text{(Eqn 4)}$$

where z denotes a measurement of a surface position; n_1, n_2 and n_3 are three independent noise sources corrupting the true measurements denoted by the 'hat' sign ˆ; (δz) denotes spatial derivative of the surface location with respect to 'x' and 'y' as indicated by the following subscript. The laser scanner data is modelled by the upper equation and the PS data is modelled by the lower equations.

There are many ways of combining the two measurements modelled by Equation 4. One particular apposite method is to use a Wiener filter. A Wiener filter is the steady-state solution for the optimal state estimation problem as solved using a Kalman filter. A Wiener filter is of particular value when there are measurements of a derivative of a signal, such as in the case of the combination of laser scanned geometry and PS data. The Wiener filter is the result of finding the minimum variance estimate of the steady state reconstructed height. The Wiener filter is obtained by finding the Fourier transforms of the measurement signals and assuming that these signals were generated by white noise processes and are corrupted by measurement noise of known frequency spectrum. In this embodiment we assume that, by way of example, the noise processes are themselves white.

If the estimated value of the object's surface position is denoted as z then the Wiener filter minimises

$$E[\iint (z-\hat{z})^2 dx dy] \quad \text{(Eqn 5)}$$

where E[] denotes the expected value.

An alternative is to approach the integration in a deterministic manner in which a measurement 'd' is obtained from the three measurements in equation 4 by using the equation

$$d = \iint |z_x - \hat{z}_x|^2 + |z_y - \hat{z}_y|^2 + \lambda |z - \hat{z}|^2 \, dx dy \quad \text{(Eqn 6)}$$

Here lambda specifies an overall relative weighting on the original height data. Increasing lambda restricts the output to be closer to the original metric data. In practice this may be achieved very quickly in the frequency domain via use of standard techniques such as the Fast Fourier Transform (FFT). The use of frequency domain transforms in integrating normal data is also demonstrated in the published literature, however there is no attempt to combine with metric data. Note that the use of the FFT here is to achieve speed rather than solving a least-squares problem, as in the Wiener filter. Other techniques may also be employed, for example using the Fast Wavelet Transform.

The result of this process is to output high resolution, high-accuracy geometrical information on the object (such as a height map), together with reflectance information (i.e. material properties of the object, such as surface finish) spatially registered with the geometric information. This information has been obtained from noisy, medium resolution geometric data and biased, low accuracy photometric data. The output information can be further processed for provision to a modelling application, such as a conventional CAD or animation application or the like.

It should be noted that there is no inherent need to acquire the photometric and geometric data in distinct phases, and indeed there may be inherent benefits in not doing so. It has been shown above that prior knowledge on **metric** shape is essential in order to achieve photometric recovery with a moveable camera. It is also noted that prior knowledge on the surface geometry can aid the laser scanning process by e.g. allowing the prediction of where specular highlights might occur in the camera image (potentially leading to false laser line detections). High resolution estimates of surface normals can also be used to quantify varying surface roughness to detect areas with a high likelihood of laser "speckle", again leading to false line detections.

Multiple interacting passes of photometric and geometric acquisition may therefore increase the accuracy and overall quality of the data characterizing the object. Photometric characterization of objects of complex geometry may require many images with a wide variety of camera locations. The combined photometric-geometric system is well suited to provide this and may, for instance, provide an on-line display to an operator as to the quality (e.g. number of samples and variability of camera/light location) of the photometric data acquired across the object geometry, and/or may indicate to the operator the directions from which more photometric data should be obtained. These benefits are of course made possible by the target based system as it greatly facilitates and extends the usability of the photometric acquisition, and is in contrast to previous photometric/geometric systems which typically have distinct hardware and acquisition phases, having fixed variation in photometric geometry.

A second embodiment of the invention will now be described which comprises a system capable of acquisition of geometry and material properties such as colour from a real object. In this embodiment the focus is on acquisition of geometry and material properties from a surface such as a wall or floor rather than an entire object. Applications for this particular embodiment are more specialized than the general object scanner described previously in FIG. 1, however they include acquisition of surfaces for synthetic environments such as film or video games, capture of carvings or hieroglyphics, and high detail capture of wrinkles, scars or other body features for quantitative analysis of cosmetic surgery.

FIG. 6 shows some hardware components of this embodiment. The first part **600** of the system comprises a digital stills camera **601** attached on a rigid boom **602** to at least one photometric light source **603**. In this example the light source **603** is a high-power photographic flash gun, however

190 Selected patents

other light sources such as a LED or standard bulb source may be used. It may also be of benefit to attach additional photometric lights, such as a ring-flash to the camera **601**. In addition to the photometric light source **603** or sources at least one laser stripe source **604** is also attached to the boom, and may be triggered synchronously or asynchronously with the photometric light source(s) **603**. The second hardware component is an optical target **605**, similar in essence to the optical target **17** of FIG. 2. Primary differences are in the geometric pattern applied on the target (in this case a pattern of five dot fiducials **606-610**), the hole **611** in the centre of the target **605** and the four cones **612-615** used for light source calibration. A third optional hardware component is a lightweight printed target **616** consisting of a cardboard sheet with an identical geometric pattern of dots (fiducials) to those of the target **605**.

The use of this system is similar to that of the previous embodiment, however, rather than placing an object on the target **605**, instead the target **605** itself is attached to the surface under inspection, such as the wall **620** in FIG. 7. The objective is to perform a largely photometric driven reconstruction of this surface using minimal metric data from the laser striper. This is performed by taking a series of still images of the target **605** (with the surface visible through the aforementioned hole **611**) then processing the images off-line. The arrows in FIG. 7 depict moving and rotating the boom of the system **600** between acquiring successive images in order to obtain images from different view points illuminated from different directions. The flash **603** and laser striper **604** are fired with each image acquisition of the camera **601**, respectively providing photometric and metric information about the target **605**. As with the disclosure earlier, reconstruction of the surface requires knowledge of:

1) the physical parameters of the optical target **605** (known by design);

2) the intrinsic parameters of the camera **601**, such as focal length (camera calibration can be carried out by well known image-based methods);

3) the location of the camera **601** with respect to the target **605** in each image (computable from the observed orientation of the target fiducials **606-610** in a manner similar to the previous embodiment);

4) the location of the light source **603** with respect to the target **605** in each image; and

5) the location and orientation of the laser striper **604** with respect to the target **605** in each image.

Requirements 4) and 5) can be reduced to finding the location of the light source **603** and striper **604** with respect to the camera **601**, as these components are rigidly affixed on the boom **602**. In this case knowledge of 3) allows the transformation of camera-relative locations into target relative location for each captured image.

Camera-relative stripe position may be found using standard techniques as disclosed in e.g. WO 2005/040850. In the embodiment of FIG. 6, camera-relative light position is found by observing the triangular shadows cast by the cones **612-615** onto the target **605**, in a manner similar to the traditional sundial. The height of the cones **612-615** is known in advance and thus the position of the light **603** can be found by intersecting rays from the tips of the cast shadows through the known geometric tips of the cones **612-615** on the target as known in the art.

In practice, a calibration phase is performed in advance using the target **605**, which may be made of metal. Then a capture phase is performed using the lightweight target **616** attached to the actual surface that is the object being scanned. This has the advantage that only the lightweight target **616** needs to be carried around, which is more convenient, and is easier to attach onto surfaces. Alternatively, in principle, both calibration and capture could be performed using a single target **605**, and the lightweight target **616** would be unnecessary. With both this embodiment and the previous embodiment, the scanner may be supplied pre-calibrated if the position and orientation of the camera relative to the light source and striper are fixed.

Photometric recovery is then performed by rectifying the input views to a canonical fronto-parallel viewpoint (as described above and illustrated in FIG. 4 *a* and **4** *b*), and performing photometric stereo. According to a previous technique this rectification is performed without prior metric knowledge of the surface. This is done by performing multiple passes of reconstruction. In the first a planar surface is assumed, and rectification performed. Typically a large number of artefacts will be seen in the rectified views due to e.g. parallax effects in the input images. This leads to a limited accuracy geometric recovery. In the second pass the approximate recovery from the first is used to perform fully 3D rectification, allowing for improved rectification of the original images set and leading to a much improved subsequent geometric recovery.

This previous approach is quite limited in nature and in particular to perform integration of the acquired photometric data (i.e. the solution of Eqn 5) requires hand marking a number of sparse correspondences in the input images to acquire a small set of truly metric data via triangulation. This is time consuming for the user and often inaccurate. With the system according to this embodiment of the invention, the laser striper is applied to acquire a "stripe" of truly geometric data from the surface in each input image. Combining information across multiple images allows a relatively large number of metric samples to be taken simultaneously with the photometric data. This is insufficient for detailed surface recovery but provides enough information for the integration of the photometric data in an automated manner. In doing so it removes the need for hand marking points across input images and allows much more accurate and timely processing.

More relevant patents

More relevant patents

Some often cited relevant patents in short form:

Patent number	Date	Applicant	Title
US3016451	04.06.57	The Auto Arc-Weld Mfg. Co.	Electrode feed roll means
US3841000	26.03.73	W Us Simon	Reel closure
US3917090	02.11.73	Pitney-Bowes, Inc.	Postage meter tape recepticle system
US4152367	25.07.78	Bayer Aktiengesellschaft	Branched polyaryl-sulphone/polycarbonate mixtures and their use for the production of extruded films
US4575330	08.08.84	Uvp, Inc.	Apparatus for production of three-dimensional objects by stereolithography
US4665492	02.07.84	Masters; William E.	Computer automated manufacturing process and system
US4749347	21.10.86	Valavaara; Viljo	Topology fabrication apparatus
US4844373	18.12.87	Fike, Sr.; Richard A.	Line storage and dispensing device
US4898314	20.10.88	International Business Machines Corporation	Method and apparatus for stitcher wire loading
US4928897	18.01.89	Fuji Photo Film Co., Ltd.	Feeder for feeding photosensitive material
US4961154	02.06.87	Scitex Corporation Ltd.	Three dimensional modelling apparatus
US5031120	22.12.88	Barequet; Gill	Three dimensional modelling apparatus

194 More relevant patents

US5059266	23.05.90	Brother Kogyo Kabushiki Kaisha	Apparatus and method for forming three-dimensional article
US5121329	30.10.89	Stratasys, Inc.	Apparatus and method for creating three-dimensional objects
US5134569	26.06.89	Masters; William E.	System and method for computer automated manufacturing using fluent material
US5136515	07.11.89	Helinski; Richard	Method and means for constructing three-dimensional articles by particle deposition
US5140937	23.05.90	Brother Kogyo Kabushiki Kaisha	Apparatus for forming three-dimensional article
US5149548	18.06.90	Brother Kogyo Kabushiki Kaisha	Apparatus for forming three-dimension article
US5169081	06.01.92	Draftex Industries Limited	Strip handling apparatus and method
US5204055	08.12.89	Massachusetts Institute Of Technology	Three-dimensional printing techniques
US5216616	01.12.89	Masters; William E.	System and method for computer automated manufacture with reduced object shape distortion
US5257657	08.07.92	Incre, Inc.	Method for producing a free-form solid-phase object from a material in the liquid phase
US5263585	07.05.92	Microbiomed Corporation	Package for an elongated flexible fiber

More relevant patents

US5303141	22.03.93	International Business Machines Corporation	Model generation system having closed-loop extrusion nozzle positioning
US5312224	12.03.93	International Business Machines Corporation	Conical logarithmic spiral viscosity pump
US5340433	08.06.92	Stratasys, Inc.	Modeling apparatus for three-dimensional objects
US5402351	18.01.94	International Business Machines Corporation	Model generation system having closed-loop extrusion nozzle positioning
US5418112	10.11.93	W. R. Grace & Co.-Conn.	Photosensitive compositions useful in three-dimensional part-building and having improved photospeed
US5434196	01.07.94	Asahi Denka Kogyo K.K.	Resin composition for optical molding
US5474719	14. Febr. 1991	E. I. Du Pont De Nemours And Company	Method for forming solid objects utilizing viscosity reducible compositions
US5503785	02.06.94	Stratasys, Inc.	Process of support removal for fused deposition modeling
US5587913	12.10.94	Stratasys, Inc.	Method employing sequential two-dimensional geometry for producing shells for fabrication by a rapid prototyping system
US5594652	07.06.95	Texas Instruments Incorporated	Method and apparatus for the computer-controlled manufacture of three-dimensional objects from computer data

196 More relevant patents

US5690865	31.03.95	Johnson & Johnson Vision Products, Inc.	Mold material with additives
US5695707	15.05.95	3D Systems, Inc.	Thermal stereolithography
US5714541 *	16. Sept. 1996	Bayer Aktiengesellschaft	Thermoplastics having a high heat deflection temperature and improved heat stability
US5738817	8. Febr. 1996	Rutgers, The State University	Solid freeform fabrication methods
US5764521	13.11.95	Stratasys Inc.	Method and apparatus for solid prototyping
US5765740	30.06.95	Ferguson; Patrick J.	Suture-material-dispenser system for suture material
US5807437	5. Febr. 1996	Massachusetts Institute Of Technology	Three dimensional printing system
US5866058	29.05.97	Stratasys Inc.	Method for rapid prototyping of solid models
US5893404	20. Sept. 1996	Semi Solid Technologies Inc.	Method and apparatus for metal solid freeform fabrication utilizing partially solidified metal slurry
US5900207	20.05.97	Rutgers, The State University Old Queens	Solid freeform fabrication methods
US5932055	11.11.97	Rockwell Science Center Llc	Direct metal fabrication (DMF) using a carbon precursor to bind the "green form" part and catalyze a eutectic reducing element in a supersolidus liquid phase sintering (SLPS) process
US5939008	26.01.98	Stratasys, Inc.	Rapid prototyping apparatus

More relevant patents 197

Patent	Date	Assignee	Title
US5943235	27. Sept. 1996	3D Systems, Inc.	Rapid prototyping system and method with support region data processing
US5968561	26.01.98	Stratasys, Inc.	High performance rapid prototyping system
US6004124	26.01.98	Stratasys, Inc.	Thin-wall tube liquifier
US6022207	26.01.98	Stratasys, Inc.	Rapid prototyping system with filament supply spool monitoring
US6027068	19.03.98	New Millennium Products, Inc.	Dispenser for solder and other ductile strand materials
US6043322 *	23.12.97	Eastman Chemical Company	Clear polycarbonate and polyester blends
US6054077	11.01.99	Stratasys, Inc.	Velocity profiling in an extrusion apparatus
US6067480	02.04.97	Stratasys, Inc.	Method and apparatus for in-situ formation of three-dimensional solid objects by extrusion of polymeric materials
US6070107	20.05.98	Stratasys, Inc.	Water soluble rapid prototyping support and mold material
US6085957	08.04.96	Stratasys, Inc.	Volumetric feed control for flexible filament
US6095323	12.06.98	Ferguson; Patrick J.	Suture-material-dispenser system for suture material
US6119567	10.07.97	Ktm Industries, Inc.	Method and apparatus for producing a shaped article
US6127492	11.05.99	Sumitomo Chemical Company, Limited	Thermoplastic resin composition and heat-resistant tray for IC
US6129872	29.08.98	Jang; Justin	Process and apparatus for creating a colorful three-dimensional object

198 More relevant patents

US6133355	12.06.97	3D Systems, Inc.	Selective deposition modeling materials and method
US6162378	25. Febr. 1999	3D Systems, Inc.	Method and apparatus for variably controlling the temperature in a selective deposition modeling environment
US6165406	27.05.99	Nanotek Instruments, Inc.	3-D color model making apparatus and process
US6166137 *	10.12.98	General Electric Company	Poly(arylene ether)/polyetherimide blends and methods of making the same
US6175422	31.07.92	Texas Instruments Incorporated	Method and apparatus for the computer-controlled manufacture of three-dimensional objects from computer data
US6193923	14.07.99	3D Systems, Inc.	Selective deposition modeling method and apparatus for forming three-dimensional objects and supports
US6214279	02.10.99	Nanotek Instruments, Inc.	Apparatus and process for freeform fabrication of composite reinforcement preforms
US6228923	11.06.98	Stratasys, Inc.	Water soluble rapid prototyping support and mold material
US6242520 *	13.03.97	General Electric Company	Flame retardant polymer compositions with coated boron phosphate
US6252011 *	31.05.94	Eastman Chemical Company	Blends of polyetherimides with polyesters of 2,6-naphthalenedicarboxylic acid
US6257517	10.08.99	Sandvik Steel Co.	Method and apparatus for feeding welding wire

More relevant patents

US6261077	8. Febr. 1999	3D Systems, Inc.	Rapid prototyping apparatus with enhanced thermal and/or vibrational stability for production of three dimensional objects
US6322728	09.07.99	Jeneric/Pentron, Inc.	Mass production of dental restorations by solid free-form fabrication methods
US6376571	06.03.98	Dsm N.V.	Radiation-curable composition having high cure speed
US6407163 *	07.12.99	Bayer Aktiengesellschaft	Highly impact-resistant ABS moulding materials
US6572228	31.05.01	Konica Corporation	Image forming method
US6645412	11.05.01	Stratasys, Inc.	Process of making a three-dimensional object
US6685866	09.07.01	Stratasys, Inc.	Method and apparatus for three-dimensional modeling
US6722872	23.06.00	Stratasys, Inc.	High temperature modeling apparatus
US6730252	20. Sept. 2001	Dietmar Werner Hutmacher	Methods for fabricating a filament for use in tissue engineering
US6790403	19.04.00	Stratasys, Inc.	Soluble material and process for three-dimensional modeling
US6869559	05.05.03	Stratasys, Inc.	Material and method for three-dimensional modeling
US20020013416 *	14.06.01	Noel Oscar French	High flexural modulus and/or high heat deflection temperature thermoplastic elastomers and methods for producing the same
US20020033563 *	28. Sept. 2001	Certainteed Corporation.	Apparatus for continuous forming shaped polymeric articles

200 More relevant patents

US20020055563 *	13. Sept. 2001	Takayuki Asano	Flame retardant resin composition
US20030090034	01.12.00	John Hendrik	Device and method for the production of three-dimensional objects
US20040245663	10. Sept. 2003	Macdougald Joseph A.	Method for manufacturing dental restorations

Links and faires

Links

http://patents.com

Easy To Use Patents Search & Patent Lawyer Directory

http://www.patentlens.net

A free public resource for patent system navigation worldwide.

http://www.rapidtoday.com

English website with lots of up-to-date information on Rapid prototyping.

http://reprapmagazine.com/

Official RepRap project news magazine.

http://3druck.com

German 3D Printing online magazine

http://reprap.org

Largest Open Source 3D printer project

http://www.fabathome.org

Another Open Source 3D printer project (ended in 2012)

http://www.simple3d.com/

Helpful website around 3D scanning

Fairs

Euromold Frankfurt

Largest european fair for plastic extrusion machines and tools. Also largest german fair on 3D printing and rapid prototyping.

http://www.euromold.com

202 Links and faires

Maker Faires

London Mini Maker Faire
http://makerfaireelephantandcastle.com/

World Maker Faire New York
http://makerfaire.com

Largest Maker faire in the world.

Maker Faire Hannover
Hannover Congress Centrum
Glashalle & Stadtpark
Theodor-Heuss-Platz 1-3
30175 Hannover

Largest German maker faire

Index

Index

3D Systems..47, 167
ABS...39, 103, 199
ABS-like...50
Afinia...20
Binder..................................34, 90f., 141, 143ff., 147ff., 166
Closed-loop..125, 195
Dispenser..135, 196f.
Epoxy....................................47ff., 145, 148, 156, 163f.
Extrusion.....................69, 100f., 104, 106, 125ff., 195, 197
FDM...20f., 68, 117, 132f., 144
Filament.6, 69, 77f., 83ff., 101, 105ff., 109ff., 119, 123, 126, 131ff., 197, 199
Formlabs...18f.
Hexapod..171
Infringement...............................10ff., 17f., 20, 22
Inkjet...33, 39, 144, 150
Maker..202
Makerbot..30, 85
Nozzle...100, 104, 144f., 195
Open Hardware..30
Open Source...14, 18, 23, 201
Paste..49
Patent 6ff., 17ff., 28ff., 34f., 45, 47, 50, 52ff., 56f., 59, 61, 67, 69, 77, 85, 89, 93, 97, 99, 107, 109, 115, 117, 123, 129, 136, 141, 146f., 163, 165, 167, 171, 174, 192f., 201
Patent citations..34, 47, 93, 167, 171
Patent pending...13
Patent Research...25
Photocurable..47ff.
Powder..34, 39ff., 49, 143ff., 169f.
Powder printing...33
Print head...39
Prior art........................8f., 13f., 54f., 78, 109, 125, 147, 149, 166
Rapid prototyping.......................................125, 195ff., 201
Reprap..18, 22, 30, 201
Resin 6, 18, 45, 47, 50, 52ff., 61ff., 90f., 101ff., 119, 122, 134, 145, 148f., 151, 156f., 162ff., 195, 197, 200
Sand..33

Index

Servo..169
Step..48f.
Stereolithography..44, 193, 196
Stratasys..69, 77, 89, 99, 123, 194ff.
Support material..102
....34, 47, 167, 171

www.ingramcontent.com/pod-product-compliance
Lightning Source LLC
Chambersburg PA
CBHW051803170526
45167CB00005B/1863